DISCOVERING COGGESHALL 2

The 1575 rental survey and the dated buildings

edited by

David Andrews

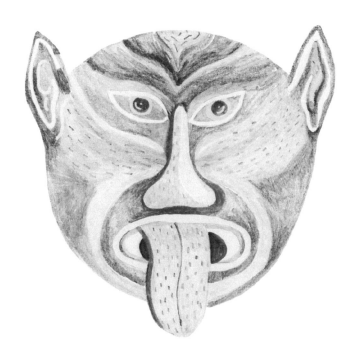

John Lewis
Coggeshall
2013

Published by
John Lewis of Coggeshall, England

www.discoveringcoggeshall.co.uk

© Coggeshall Heritage Society

ISBN 978-0-9539165-2-8

Printed by Gipping Press Ltd.
www.gippingpress.co.uk

Previous page: carving from Cavendish House, Market End (Ellie Andrews)

CONTENTS

ACKNOWLEDGEMENTS

The Discovering Coggeshall project was made possible by the generosity of the funding bodies, the patience and interest of the residents of Coggeshall who live in timber-framed buildings, and the perseverance and dedication of the organising committee, the surveyors and authors. The project was organised by the Coggeshall Heritage Society. Finance was made available primarily by the Heritage Lottery Fund, with further grants from the Council for British Archaeology, the Vernacular Architecture Group, the Essex Heritage Trust, the Coggeshall Heritage Society, Coggeshall Parish Council, and the Essex Historic Buildings Group. The organising committee was led first by the late Alan Willis, and then by John Lewis. Its members included Dennis Gray, Robin Powell (treasurer), Jayne Seymour, Sarah Glossop, Stanley Haines, Natalie Butler, Brenda Watkin, John Walker, Michael Horne, Mike Meadows, Dave Stenning, Richard Shackle, Michael Bowes and David Andrews. In its approach to the project, the committee benefited from the professional advice of David Martin. Documentary research was carried out by Michael Horne, and his transcription of the 1575 rental enabled Mike Meadows to reconstruct the map of the town at that time. Sally Gale of Essex County Council Historic Environment Record created the digitised maps of the 1575 rental survey. The building surveyors included Richard Shackle, Ann Smith, John Walker, Brenda Watkin, Elphin Watkin, David Stenning and David Andrews. The tree-ring dating was carried out by Ian Tyers. Photographs of the buildings in Appendix 2 were taken by Keith Cullum; other photographs are by the authors. The axonometric drawings are by Dave Stenning. The project website was set up by Peter Kemp and maintained by Michael Bowes.

For Alan Willis, who organized the funding and
launched the Discovering Coggeshall project

INTRODUCTION

Coggeshall is one of about thirty small market towns in Essex. It is situated in the north of the county to the east of Braintree on the main east-west Roman road, Stane Street, now the A120, at junctions with roads to Kelvedon to the south and Earls Colne (and formerly also Halstead) to the north. It differs from other such towns in owing its origins, at least in part, to a Cistercian abbey, the remains of which stand to the south of it, and in having a historic centre which is one of the better preserved in the county, with almost 300 listed buildings. The former Grange Barn of the abbey, and an outstanding timber-framed building, Paycocke's House, are both National Trust properties. Paycocke's House, built in 1509 by a wealthy clothier of that name, is the most striking memorial to the local cloth industry for which Coggeshall was famous in the 15th to 17th centuries. The prosperity brought by that industry has left it today with a remarkable heritage of timber-framed buildings which makes for an attractive historic town centre. The relative decline of the industry from the 17th century accounts for why these buildings have escaped significant redevelopment, apart from often being given plain plastered Georgian facades with sliding sash windows beneath roofs parallel to the street.

Because documentary sources are very incomplete before the 16th century, and the scope for archaeological excavation is constrained by the listed buildings and town centre conservation area, the fabric of the buildings themselves constitutes a valuable source for the investigation of the town's past. There has long been an awareness of their importance, arising partly from active conservation policies promoted by Essex County Council and Braintree District Council. The last 50 years have seen great progress in the study of timber-framed buildings. Much of the groundwork was done by Cecil Hewett originally of Laindon and later resident in Coggeshall and Kelvedon, who traced the development of carpentry joints and revealed their value for dating buildings. His work, and that of others, has been confirmed by and supported by the refinement of tree-ring dating or dendrochronology from the 1970s onwards. The work to establish a reference 'curve' for tree-ring dating Essex buildings was largely achieved through sampling the buildings at Cressing Temple in the late 1980s and early 1990s.

Once dendrochronology had been developed to the point where reliable results could be obtained, it was a logical step to apply it to the study of not just buildings but settlements. The main obstacles to this are the cost and scale of the enterprise involved, but with community involvement and financial support from the Heritage Lottery Fund, projects of this sort have now been carried out at places such as New Buckenham and Talconeston in Norfolk and Pembridge in Herefordshire.

Coggeshall lent itself to such a project not simply because of its many old buildings, but also because, as is explained below, their timbers were assessed as having unusually good potential for successful dating. This led to the proposal that the Coggeshall Heritage Society undertake a project to study and date a group of houses in the centre of the town, an ambition realised by generous grant support obtained from the Heritage Lottery Fund and other funding bodies.

The size of the town meant that only a sample area could be analysed. The 'triangle' of land between the East Street and Church Street junction and Swan Yard to the east was chosen for the study, with a view amongst other things of tracing the process of market infill which had clearly taken place where the streets meet in what had once been an extensive marketplace. Tree-ring dating of timber buildings is most suitable for those earlier than *c*.1650, giving the project an end date. A project design was put together, a successful application was made to the Heritage Lottery Fund and work began at the end of 2009.

Because it was unsatisfactory to view a small part of the town in isolation, the study expanded to encompass most of the town and its layout and topographical development. It did not, however, include Little Coggeshall to the south of the river Blackwater where the abbey is situated. A companion publication, containing axonometric drawings of most if not all the surviving timber framed buildings in the town centre, was published in 2013.[1] The study of the buildings has been assisted by archival research and a transcription of a manorial rental of 1575 which lists the property holders and, exceptionally, gives the dimensions of the plots, making it possible to reconstruct a map of the town in that year showing the landowners.

As the work has grown in scope, so it has become more protracted. It is also true that the complexity of analysing much altered and densely built up houses now in multiple occupation was underestimated. We are grateful to the Heritage Lottery Fund and our other supporters, as well as to the owners of the houses, for their patience and indulgence. Interim results and detailed building reports and other material have been made available since 2012 on the project's website (*www.discoveringcoggeshall.co.uk*).

This account of Coggeshall and its buildings sets out the results of the tree-ring dating and what has been learnt about the development of the town, and its urban buildings and their carpentry. With the companion volume, it is the first attempt at a study of the late medieval fabric of an Essex town, and despite its many limitations is a step forward in understanding our towns of that period. What has emerged is a remarkable picture of a town which long before the Industrial Revolution was organised around the production and the marketing of cloth, and how that trade affected the town's buildings and layout.

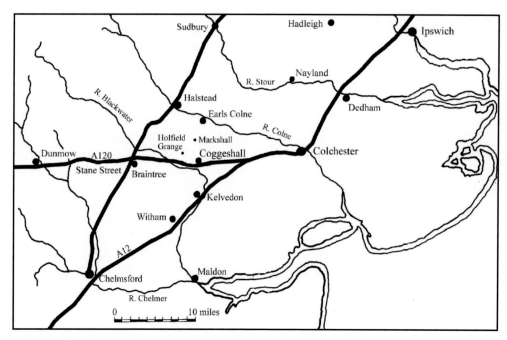

Map to illustrate places mentioned in the text

1   D. F. Stenning, *Discovering Coggeshall. Timber-framed buildings in the town centre*, 2013.

COGGESHALL. ITS TOPOGRAPHY, ORIGINS, AND EARLY HISTORY

Topography

Coggeshall owes its location and significance to water and to roads, the river valleys and the road being key features in the development of the settlement. In the Boulder Clay plateau lands of central Essex, prehistoric settlement initially followed the river valleys which offered not just sources of water but also a variety of soil types. Coggeshall lies in the valley of the river Blackwater which runs eastwards from Braintree, first to the north and then to the south of the Roman road which it crosses at Bradwell. The river and the streams that flow into it from the higher ground to the north provided the town with an abundance of water and power for mills. They constituted the framework within which the town developed, one that was not fixed but which has changed over time.[1]

Flowing to the south of West Street, the river Blackwater would have originally turned north, not south as now, and joined the ox bow lake behind Sunnedon and Paycockes House, continuing thence into the Back Ditch and under Short Bridge. The river would not have turned south towards the Abbey where it does today, but would have flowed almost due east and along what is now the parish boundary, then south towards the water pumping station, finally rejoining the present river course south east of the Abbey Mill.

The streams of significance in the area of the town centre are the Pissing Gutter, the larger Robins Brook, and Church Pond Stream. The source of Pissing Gutter is just to the north of the old isinglass factory. Now in a culvert for much of its course it flows beneath the former factory buildings and the road, and across the site of the Dutch Nursery to the river. Robins Brook rises in the Markshall Park to the north, and would have crossed West Street to the east of Hares Bridge, and run along the Gravel and into the river east of Short Bridge. The brook was a significant obstacle in the line of Stane Street and would have formed a natural western boundary to the initial development of the town. Church Pond Stream rises near the church just west of Vane Lane. It was channelled to run down Church Street and it now runs in a conduit so that it is invisible today. Originally it would have joined Robins Brook north of Hares Bridge.

The contours reveal the Blackwater flood plain to have been extensive, especially where Robins Brook joins it. This area must have been at risk of being water logged. Excavation in West Street in 1988 showed that its surface was built up on timber piles datable to the 18th century which were well preserved because of damp ground conditions.[2] The valley of Robins Brook in contrast is V-shaped, steep by Essex standards. The dry valley indicated by the contours suggests that the source of the Church Pond stream may have been to the north of the church. The contours in that area can be compared with those for the Pissing Gutter valley. Contours also show a dry valley along the alignment of Windmill Lane/Highfields Farm drive which may be a dried up water lane or else a man made hollow lane or earthwork.

Along the north side of the river Blackwater valley there are a number of river terraces. Too shallow to be revealed by the contour line spacing, they have been marked on the map of the early topography with a dashed line.

---

1   The observations which follow on the rivers and historic landscape are based on close familiarity with the local topography acquired over many years.
2   Godbold and Andrews 1992.

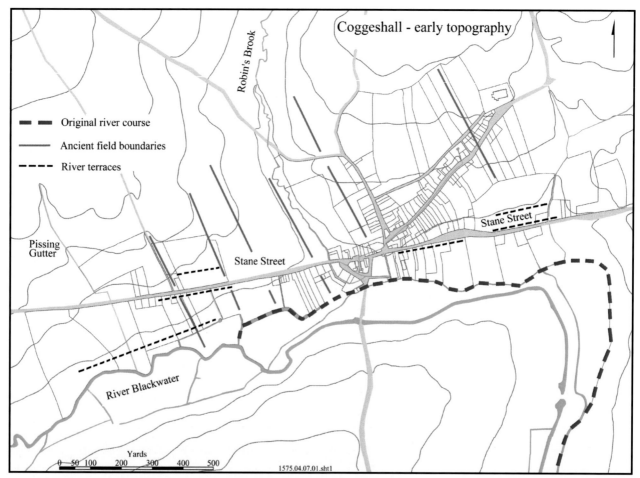

Coggeshall – the 1575 map related to the early topography of the town

Prehistory and the Iron Age

Scope for archaeological investigation in the historic town centre is limited by the restrictions on development, but excavations at the St. Peter's Primary School site and the former Lawns residential home in Church Street in the 1980s, and minor interventions elsewhere, add detail to the picture of ancient settlement in the area of the town, without however leaving it much better defined. Worked flints testify to occupation from the Neolithic to the Bronze Age. Two early Iron Age structures were found on the St. Peter's School site, but later Iron Age occupation seems to have been absent.[3]

With 450 years of later development stripped out, the map of the 1575 rental clearly shows a number of parallel boundary features 25 degrees west of grid north. Clear examples are the Windmill Lane/Highfields Farm drive, the field boundaries north of West Street, the Paycockes House plot, the rear garden boundaries of the houses on the west side of Stoneham Street, and the Butt Field/allotment boundary west, running south of Church Street and across East Street and further south. The local historian Beaumont was aware of these boundaries, particularly in the Highfields area. It is noteworthy that these boundaries are not at right

---

3   Clarke 1988; Isserlin 1995.

angles to Stane Street which seems to cut through them, suggesting they are pre-Roman and possibly older still. Connecting the Iron Age Trinovantian and Catuvellaunian strongholds of Colchester and St. Albans respectively, any pre-Roman equivalent of the Stane Street route would probably have bypassed the water-logged Gravel area and crossed Robins Brook north of Hares Bridge in the easily fordable V-shaped valley close to the alignment of the footpath across Vicarage Field.

The Roman period

Much evidence for Roman occupation has been found in and around Coggeshall. Beaumont records the discovery of a cremation cemetery found in Crow Barn Field, west of the town centre and north of the Roman road near the former isinglass factory, and speculated that the north-south bank flanking the path up to Highfields Farm was associated with a Roman camp.[4] In the town itself, Roman finds have been recovered from the churchyard and around the Woolpack, with building debris and foundations extending beneath Church Street and into the garden of the Lawns.

A possible Roman timber building was found in the 1980s excavations to the south of the Lawns in Church Street, whilst the St. Peter's School site revealed north-south aligned ditches dating from the 1st to 2nd centuries AD, their alignment comparable to those identified in the analysis of boundary lines presented above. These ditches were filled in, but occupation continued into the 4th century. The ditches were interpreted as a large enclosure surrounding a Roman villa, but an alternative view is that they represent paddocks and a drove way, with a roadside ditch to Stane Street.[5] Whatever the case, the presence of flue tile (indicating a hypocaust heating system) and tesserae for mosaics are generally interpreted as pointing to the existence of a significant building such as a farmstead or villa. It is arguable that, like a number of churches elsewhere, St. Peter's stands on or close to a Roman building. Finds of high status building material also suggest the existence of villas or farmsteads at Scrips Farm and Farm Hill to the south of the town and to the west of the Blackwater valley where it runs between Coggeshall and Kelvedon.

In origin Stane Street is probably an Iron Age track way effectively linking tribal capitals at St. Albans and Colchester, and up graded during the Roman occupation by straightening sections connected by very visible kinks, though never rebuilt to the high military standards of the Colchester to London road (A12) to the south. Combining the evidence of the 1575 rental map, modern satellite technology and a close reading of the landscape on the ground, there are clues for identifying the exact location of the road within Coggeshall. Stane Street runs along the alignment of East and West Street but in Roman times would have been wider, overlapping the present road to the north. The road runs between two river terraces and well above the flood plain. In the town centre the rear garden boundaries north of East and West Street seem to be on the alignment of the north roadside ditch. Church Pond Stream would have flowed into this ditch, and both the Pissing Gutter and Robins Brook would have been realigned at this time so as to cross the road at right angles.

If the alignment of the Kelvedon to Coggeshall road is extended from the top of Grange Hill north towards the town, it picks up the rear garden boundary of 19 Bridge Street and the confluence of Robins Brook and the Back Ditch. This point is identifiable with Tye Mill Lane on the 1575 rental. This may have been the original route of the Roman road to Kelvedon, avoiding the Robins Brook and only having to cross the river Blackwater.

---

4   Beaumont 1890, 7-8.
5   Clarke 1988; Flook 1988; Isserlin 1995.

Coggeshall in the early Middle Ages

The Anglo-Saxon period generally appears as a gap in the archaeological record in Essex, timber buildings disappearing with little trace and pottery possibly not having been made for long periods. However, a very few potsherds with an estimated date range of 400-600AD were found in the excavations at the Lawns site south of Church Street. It is probable that there was some degree of continuity of settlement in the area of the church until medieval times.

Coggeshall is first recorded in the years before the Norman Conquest when Godwin and his wife Wulfgyth gave part of their lands there and in Stisted to Christ Church, Canterbury. Christ Church had a small landholding at the time of Domesday Book (1086), when the manor belonged to Eustace of Boulogne, a powerful Norman lord and a great landowner. There were later three manors in Coggeshall: Great Coggeshall, Little Coggeshall and Coggeshall Hall. Although separated by the river Blackwater and at times jurisdictionally distinct, Great and Little Coggeshall were to all intents and purposes treated as one manor most of the time.

Coggeshall Hall is usually identified with the Canterbury landholding. The site of the manor house of Coggeshall Hall is in the south of the parish, on the boundary with Kelvedon and Feering. Its property was not confined to that area but included tenements in the town, as the 1575 rental shows. In the later Middle Ages, it belonged to the influential de Coggeshall family.

Beaumont identified the manor of Great Coggeshall with Hovells or Holville or Old Field, a house to the north of Holfield Grange north of Stane Street. This location is where one might expect a manor to be in relation to the Roman road, that is set back from it. However, unlike many Essex manor houses, which are close to the church, Hovells if indeed the manor is distant from St. Peter's church. It is assumed that there was a church in the present position before the Norman Conquest. Coggeshall is one of the few places in Essex which Domesday Book (1086) records as having had a priest, and hence presumably a church. The area round the church was Church Green, an open space which may once have been more extensive.

The monastic town

King Stephen, and his queen Matilda, who was the daughter of Eustace of Boulogne, are believed to have founded the abbey in about 1140. They endowed it with the manor of Great Coggeshall. The abbey site is enclosed by the bend in the river Blackwater as it turns south to Kelvedon, a site which brought ready access to water for drinking, washing, cleansing latrines, supplying fishponds and powering mills. To manage the water supply more effectively, and doubtless also to control flooding and feed a system of water meadows, the Cistercians moved the course of the Blackwater to the south and west. The former river course, known as the Old River, or Back Ditch, is now an insignificant stream crossed by the Short Bridge, whilst the much wider new river is spanned by the Long Bridge.

The Cistercians also actively intervened in the town's economy. They obtained royal grants of a fair (1250) and a market (1256), though these might be confirmations of earlier charters. These would have brought them financial advantage, in that they could levy tolls on those attending and buying and selling. This was a normal strategy for proactive manorial lords, and is well illustrated at nearby Witham, where the Knights Templar effectively set up a new town around their market on the old Roman road (the former A12) which became known as Newland Street, separate from the old village centre and original market at Chipping Hill.

At Coggeshall, a marketplace would have been established, and it is also possible that house plots were laid out, as at Witham.

In some towns, manorial lords offered advantageous terms to their tenants, what was known as burgage tenure, which enjoyed a high degree of freedom from the burdens of labour and customary services and financial dues imposed on other tenants. This was one way to bring people to the town and to ensure the success of its market. There is however no record of burgage tenure at Coggeshall.

Instead, this was very much a manorial town, run through the manorial courts which policed society to ensure good order, and managed the occupation and transfer of property held from the lord. Originally the majority of the inhabitants were probably 'copyholders', holding their properties by 'copy' of entry in the court roll of a record of their having been admitted to it, a fine or fee being paid to the lord when that happened. In origin, the copyholders would have been unfree tenants subject to labour services and working the lord's land, but these were later changed to money rents. Their properties, although held of the lord, were effectively owned by the family and were passed from generation to generation. Although transfers of property were closely monitored by the manorial courts, manorial control was more theoretical than real, and by the end of the Middle Ages there was an active land market which allowed property to be bought and sold with relative freedom.

Roman settlements were set back from the main roads, which were similarly avoided by medieval churches. Church Street has the appearance of a short cut on the diagonal between the church and the market and the river crossing. The archaeological evidence helps confirm this since the road cuts across the alignment of the Roman ditches found in the excavations, and also apparently overlies Roman foundations. Since the Cistercians established the marketplace and also the existing bridgehead, which it has been argued may have been to the east of the present position, the alignment of Church Street ought to date from the time of their arrival in the 12th century, though it cannot be excluded that it was earlier. The oldest house types found in the course of this project are in Church Street, and this fits with this picture of it being the oldest street in the town.

The building up of Church Street may have superseded a settlement in the area of Church Green, where initially the market may have been situated. Around this early settlement were the open fields, which included Over Church Field to the north of Church Street, and Nether Church Field to the south. The long house plots on the south side of Church Street look as if they were laid out in the strips in Nether Church Field, something which is explored further in the analysis of the 1575 rental in chapter 4.

A late 13th-century deed, probably of the 1270s, reveals the centre of Coggeshall to have a layout already recognisable with its appearance today .[6] The property referred to in the document is thought to have been located at Doubleday Corner. It is described as having had the king's highway from Colchester to Braintree to the south, a stream running from Church Pond to the north, the property of Richard le Carpenter on the west, and the road leading from the market to the church to the east. All this seems very familiar, and implies the basic town plan had been established by the late 12th or early 13th century.

---

6   Essex Record Office D/DU 564/2.

Reconstructed view looking north up the east side of Stoneham Street (Dave Stenning)

THE 1575 RENTAL MAPPED AND ANALYSED FOR GREAT COGGESHALL

Introduction

The 1575 rental survey of Great and Little Coggeshall was drawn up for the Duchy of Lancaster which then held the manor, and is stored in the National Archives at Kew.[1] This was an account of the rental income derived from properties held of the manor. The Survey occupies pages 93 to 132 of a large volume of 144 pages, entitled 'Coggeshall in Essex', in which various documents connected with the manors of Great and Little Coggeshall are recorded. The handwriting of the rental is difficult to read, and the first task was to transcribe it and word process the text.

The survey is remarkable in that it not only gives the names of the occupants and a description of their properties, but includes the position of each house within its street and the size of each plot, usually in perches. Normally the information in a rental is much more limited, and indeed there are sections in this volume which provide much simpler, and therefore unsatisfactory, lists. There are also several other lengthy surveys of Coggeshall dating from the 16th century, but none of these provides anything like the details of the 1575 rental.

This objective dimensional information enabled a map to be drawn for Great Coggeshall. Tudor rentals were usually accompanied by a map, such as those made by the Walkers of Hanningfield for Chelmsford and other manors.[2] This new map may in effect replace one which has been lost. The mapping exercise has been complementary to the building research; it has identified areas of encroachment, and specific buildings and lanes not known about previously. As such, it has added greatly to the understanding of the development of Coggeshall from the late 16th century. In addition it has given information on patterns of property ownership and tenure in the town.

How the 1575 rental survey was compiled

At least two or three surveyors were deployed in drawing up the rental. Their writing styles and how they describe property boundaries differ. The spelling of owner names also varies. For example Paycocke is sometimes spelt with an 'e' and sometimes without. Other entries are spelt as 'Peacock'.

The survey is broken down by street and by property. For almost every property the name of the owner is recorded, sometimes the property name and a description such as tenement, garden, orchard etc. But most importantly the north, south, east and west linear boundary lengths are recorded. Details of the owners of adjacent properties are also given.

Invariably the surveyor would proceed up one side of a street and down the other, often starting at the market chapel, a building which stood in Stoneham at the junction with Church Street. That is with the exception of West Street. Here the surveyor started at Hares Bridge over Robin's Brook and walked in a westerly direction, listing plots on either side of the road. Additionally for this street the surveyors recorded only the area for each property or field, omitting the linear dimensions. This made the mapping of this area much more difficult but still achievable, though the results are more subjective than elsewhere.

---

1   National Archives DL 43/2/11. The rental was transcribed by Michael Horne.
2   Edwards and Newton 1984.

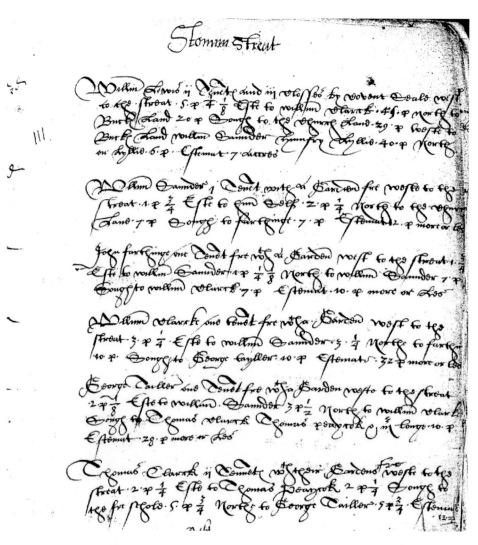

Page from the rental for Stoneham Street

Coggeshall Hall manorial land is referred to under the name of Mr. Longe, the lord of that manor, and no specific boundary dimensions are recorded. We only know of Mr. Longe's land holdings from adjacent plot information. The same applies to church land.

A typical survey entry

The entry for a well known property on the east side of Stoneham Street, nos 4-6, currently Baumann's Brasserie restaurant, is as follows:

> '2s 3d, The Free School, house with a garden, west to the street 3 perches, east to Thomas Paycock 2 perches ¾ $^1/_8$, north to Thomas Clark 5 perches ¾ , south to Thomas Peaycok 5 perches ¾ , estimate 17 perches more or less.'

The plot was almost rectangular but it could have been trapezoid. The exact shape can only be found out at the mapping stage.

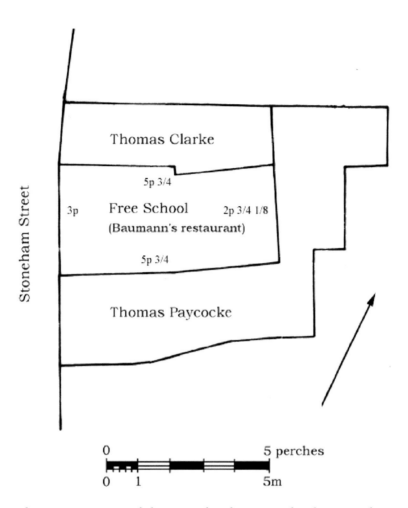

Diagram to illustrate the interpretation of the entry for the Free School site on the east side of Stoneham Street

Units of measurement used

The basic unit of measurement used is the perch. The length of a perch can vary from one region to another but it is usually accepted to be 16½ feet, or 5½ yards, or 5.03 metres. By reference to a building in the rental which still exists today, the unit of length used was verified at 16½ feet. The perch was the unit of measurement commonly used by medieval carpenters, and it can often be recognised as having been used when timber-framed buildings are surveyed today. The area measurements in the rental are given in perches, roods, and acres, which are explained in the table below.

		Metric equivalent
272 ¼ square feet, or 30 ¼ square yards =	1 (square) perch	25.28 square metres
40 (square) perches =	1 rood	1011.2 square metres
4 roods =	1 acre	0.405 hectare

Units of square area as used in the rental, with metric equivalents.

Reformatting the survey text

Each entry was reformatted into a spreadsheet retaining only key cartographic information necessary to produce a map. A unique four digit cross reference number for each entry in the rental was used to link the modern transcription of the survey text with this new spread sheet.

Additionally the linear boundary dimensions for adjacent plots were recorded and compared in order to identify any text transcript or survey errors. Areas when available were also compared with actual calculated areas from the linear dimensions.

Database reference number	Property	Plot length in perches	Direction	Adjacent plot length in perches	Overlay plot length in perches
1128	Free School house and garden	5.75	North	5.75	6.5
		2.875	South	(4.25)*	3
		5.75	East	5.75	6.5
		3.0	West	Not available**	3.25
	AREA	17 perches			20.3 perches

* The adjacent plot referred to two plots with a cumulative length of 4.25 perches.
** This side was the frontage on Stoneham Street.

The rental entry for Baumann's Brasserie 4-6 Stoneham as set out in the database.

Reference map

A reference outline map based on the Ordnance Survey Master Map or OSMM at a scale of 1:500 was used. With 5 metres being just in excess of one perch the scale chosen worked out conveniently at 10mm = 1 perch.

Reference buildings

For each street the descriptions in the statutory lists of listed buildings were reviewed. Assuming the dates given in the list descriptions were correct, the age of each house was recorded and grouped into pre- and post- late 16th century in line with the rental date of 1575. This information was marked up on the OSMM reference map.

For each street a reference property was selected, usually the oldest. Examples of reference buildings used are Spooners on the south side of Church Street (no. 30, 1353-86), and 10 on the south side of East Street (1320-86).

The incremental street frontage dimensions from the survey were drawn out on a strip of tracing paper. Starting with the reference property, a best fit was achieved by sliding the strip of paper along the street building frontage on the master map. Where possible, additional reference buildings were used to eliminate cumulative incremental errors within the rental survey.

Draft overlays

Once satisfied with an absolute best fit, a plot overlay in tracing paper was begun. Often these overlays went through a number of versions before the final draft.

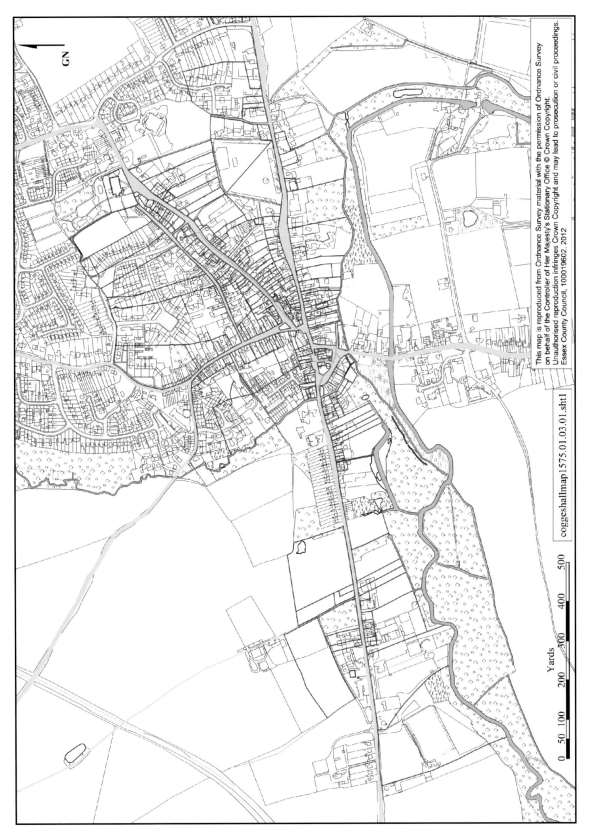

The map of Coggeshall showing landholdings as they were in 1575, recreated from the detail in the rental of the manor of Great Coggeshall, and overlaid on the Ordnance Survey Master Map

The actual dimensions used in the final draft overlay were recorded in the reformatted cartographic-information-only spreadsheet. This was so that the actual plot, adjacent plot, and as-drawn plot dimensions could be directly compared in one single line entry. In other words, there is another visible audit trail from map overlay to the original rental text.

Rental survey plots to current street plan 'look up' table

A second spreadsheet was created recording the unique cross reference number, the current street number, the age of the building given in the statutory list description, and the owner or occupier in 1575. Again this document was primarily used to achieve visibility and an audit trail to the original survey. However it soon became a useful 'look-up table' cross referencing current street numbers with the 1575 rental entries.

The database

Embedded within the rental there are thousands of small bits of important but jumbled up information. What was required is a process that allowed easy access to all those bits of information and in many different ways. The solution was to create a computer database.

Initially key elements from the rental were indentified to be loaded into a database template. Each key element was allocated a field and progressively 25 different fields were identified such as name of the plot holder, street, number of tenements, close, mead, area and so on.

There are 225 entries within the rental, one for each plot. This data was then progressively loaded into the database with each line entry being identified by the four digit unique reference number. A simple calculation of 225 entries multiplied by 25 fields gives a database in excess of 5000 individual cells.

The first application of the database was to rationalise the many spelling variations and subsequently it become a critical input document for digitising the map of Coggeshall. A summary of the contents of the database, listing the details of the plots in the town and their owners, is given in Appendix 1.

Digitising the map

Because of their experience of working with computerised maps generated by geographical information systems, the Historic Environment Record (HER) at Essex County Council was commissioned to digitise the hand drawn maps. From the tracing overlays, another set of 1:500 master maps were drawn up and passed to the HER. What they did was to take the hand drawn draft maps and in effect re-draw them onto a computer screen and then electronically store the data in a large computer memory file, a process called 'digitising'.

The HER have embedded within their mapping computer system the Ordnance Survey Master Map. All the maps they produced are in effect additional layers based on the reference OSMM. Our maps are no different and are constructed in the same way.

The outline of each rental plot is represented by and referred to as a 'polygon'. Each plot or polygon is cross referenced to the database unique number. The large database file was sent electronically to the HER, and using this file, the information for each polygon relating to the relevant database line entry is recorded within the mapping computer system, similar to an additional layer but in text.

Map formats

The scale, size and type of maps capable of being produce are almost infinite, but having considered the end users or markets most likely to be interested in them, a limited range of four different formats have been produced.

For in depth detailed analysis suitable for current and future research by professional and amateur historians, maps have been created with the outline of the rental plots overlain in red on the OSMM in black on a range of AO and A3 sheets at scales of 1:500, 1:1500 and 1:5000. For the largest scale, using a simple grid system, the 1575 rental survey has been represented on seven different sheets including one focused on the town centre.

The second format shows only the 1575 rental outline and is intended for analysis of the town plan at that period without the clutter of 21st century detail. The third format comprises a range of maps in the style of the most famous Essex map maker of the late 16th century, John Walker of West Hanningfield, using period colours and text, but without the illustrations of individual buildings characteristic of his maps. All of these maps can be downloaded from the Discovering Coggeshall website (*www.discoveringcoggeshall. co.uk*). However, if using an A4 printer, some detail will be lost. Lastly, a number of bespoke maps have been produced for specific areas of research, some examples of which appear here.

Property owning and land use in the town

The map of the rental, and the database from which it was derived, contain a great deal of information about Tudor Coggeshall. In particular, it makes it possible to visualise the pattern of property owning and land use in the town. In one sense, the data is not as informative as it might be, as whilst it is clear who owned a property, it is more difficult to say who lived in it. This is because many people owned several properties, and as a result many houses were leased or rented. Although the plots in the town were notionally held of the lord of the manor, there was by this time a fairly free land market, and it is evident that some people had acquired considerable landed property.

Entries in rental	Sum	Area in perches	Area in acres	Average area in perches	Rental value £0.00
Named entries for individuals	204				23.567
Entries for buildings	3				0
Additional entries	18				0
Totals	225	23782	149	106	23.567
Unique named occupiers	95				

A summary of the total data in the rental. The rental value is expressed in decimals of a pound rather than shillings and pence. The total rental value is understated, since no value is recorded for 19 entries.

Analysis of the rental shows that about a dozen individuals, most if not all of them clothiers, owned over 40% of the property listed in the rental, and over 50% of it by area. Some of them had small urban estates, the blocks of land owned by Thomas and John Paycocke in West Street, and by William Saunders behind Stoneham Street and to the north of Church Street, being striking examples. Sometimes land might be acquired for business purposes, as the Paycockes seem to have done in accumulating it for grazing and cloth manufacturing processes such as tentering. Houses will have been acquired through marriage and inheritance, and also with the intention of providing for families. When John Paycocke died in 1506, he left three houses, one to his wife and eldest son, and the others to his two other sons, one of whom, Thomas, rebuilt his as the existing house in West Street in 1509. In 1610, the clothier Robert Litherland left his wife a life interest in two houses, one occupied by her and his son Robert, and the other by the widow of his other son, as well as the rents from a number of other gardens, meads and pieces of land.[3]

	Names	No. plots	Actual %	Cumulative %
1	Thomas Paycocke	15	6.76	6.76
2	Mr Longe	11	4.50	11.26
3	John Paycocke	9	4.50	15.77
4	William Fuller	8	4.05	19.82
5	Richard Sammes	8	3.60	23.42
6	Robert Jegon	7	3.15	26.58
7	George Copsheff	6	2.70	29.28
8	William Saunders	6	2.70	31.98
9	Thomas Ansell	5	2.25	34.23
10	John Clarke	5	2.25	36.49
11	Thomas Clarke	5	2.25	38.74
12	John Ennewe	5	2.25	40.99
13	John Goodaye	5	2.25	43.24
	Total number of plots in rental	225		100

	Names	Area in perches	Actual %	Cumulative %	No. plots
1	William Fuller	2829.80	11.90	11.90	8
2	Thomas Paycocke	2251.22	9.47	21.36	15
3	John Paycocke	2241.65	9.43	30.79	9
4	Mr Longe	1071.44	4.51	35.30	11
5	Thomas Ansell	793.44	3.34	38.63	5
6	John Ennewe	789.57	3.32	41.95	5
7	John Goodaye	787.53	3.31	45.26	5
8	Robert Jegon	778.22	3.27	48.54	7
9	Thomas Till	747.28	3.14	51.68	4
10	Richard Sammes	380.77	1.60	53.28	8
11	Thomas Clarke	300.50	1.26	54.54	5
12	George Copsheff	281.45	1.18	55.73	6
13	Richard Hankins	253.92	1.07	56.79	4
14	William Saunders	217.39	0.91	57.71	6
15	Thomas White	141.23	0.59	58.30	4
16	John Clarke	98.18	0.41	58.71	5
17	John Till	86.47	0.36	59.08	4
	Total area land in rental	23,782		100	

Tables giving the largest landowners by number and area of holdings. As the lord of Coggeshall Hall manor, Mr Longe was a notional landowner; the properties attributed to him in the rental would have been held by others, including no doubt some of the individuals listed in the tables.

---

3   Essex Record Office D/ABW 24/99.

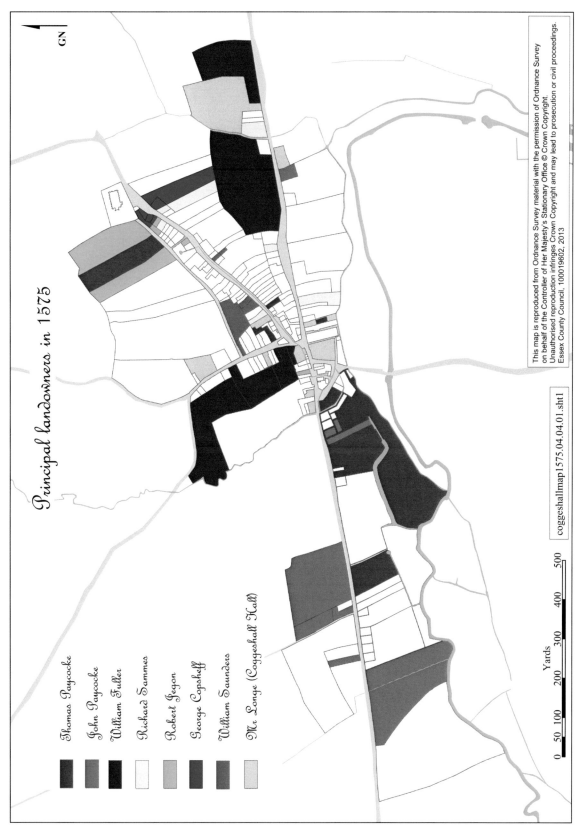

Principal landowners in 1575

Thomas Paycocke
John Paycocke
William Fuller
Richard Sammes
Robert Pegon
George Copshoff
William Saunders
Mr Longe (Coggeshall Hall)

Yards

0 50 100   200   300   400   500

This map is reproduced from Ordnance Survey material with the permission of Ordnance Survey on behalf of the Controller of Her Majesty's Stationary Office © Crown Copyright. Unauthorised reproduction infringes Crown Copyright and may lead to prosecution or civil proceedings.
Essex County Council, 100019602, 2013

coggeshallmap1575.04.04.01.sht1

The 1575 map of Coggeshall showing the property owned by the eight largest landowners

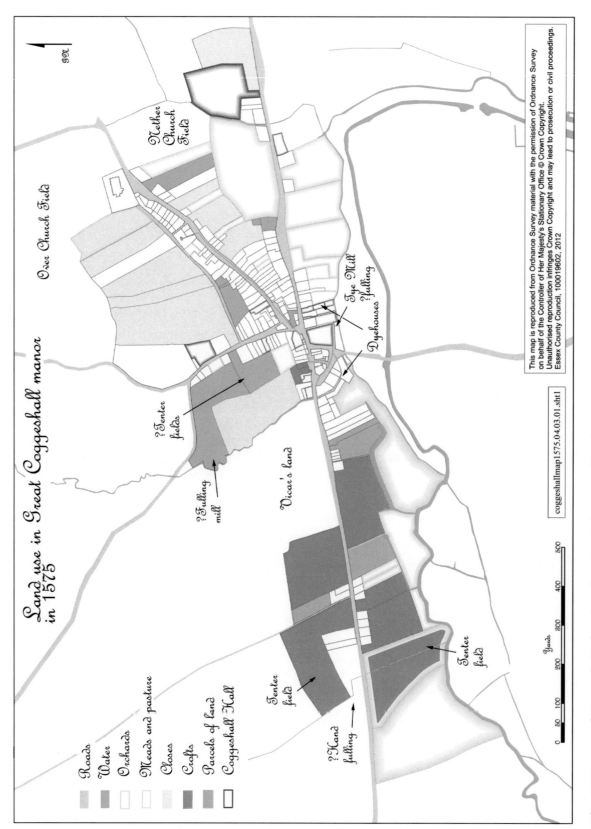

Land use in Great Coggeshall manor in 1575

Over Church Field

Nether Church Field

?Tenter field

?Fulling mill

Vicar's land

Tye Mill ?fulling

Dyehouses ?fulling

Tenter field

Tenter field

?Hand fulling

Roads
Water
Orchards
Meads and pasture
Closes
Crofts
Parcels of land
Coggeshall Hall

coggeshallmap1575.04.03.01.sht1

The 1575 map of Coggeshall showing the principal types of land use

Because of its rentable value, houses and land must also have been acquired for investment, and would have been instrumental in setting the more successful clothiers on their way to leaving trade behind and joining the ranks of the gentry. The largest landowner in the rental was William Fuller. He is probably the same as the William Fuller, clothier of Coggeshall, who the county historian Morant records as acquiring the manor of Paris in North Weald some time after1593, thus setting himself up a gentleman.[4]

Most of the properties were tenements with gardens. In area, they were variable, partly because there was no regular grid plan to the town, boundaries being determined by roads that were not parallel and by watercourses, but the average was 52 perches or about 1/3 acre. Outbuildings are very rarely mentioned, presumably because the term tenement was understood to include more than just the house.[5] Shops must have been considered to be part of the house. Although many houses have been found to incorporate shop fronts, the rental only mentions three, which can be identified today as the pair at 1 Church Street (Black Boy Bistro), and that belonging to John Bacon next to the market hall (now the former Cricketers public house). These were all very small buildings with limited accommodation, discrete structures built for a single well defined purpose. Similarly no kitchens are listed, a type of building which must have been common, although in the study of the timber-framed buildings in the town, only one has been identified. In the same way, commercial or industrial buildings are not mentioned, though a number of non-residential buildings of undefined purpose have been discovered in the town. Three stables figure in the rental. Only one possible one of 16th or 17th date has been identified in the town today, behind 6 East Street. Of interest is a dovehouse, possession of which was normally a manorial privilege. This was on land belonging to the Chapel Inn, a reflection perhaps of the importance of this particular holding and the status of its owners, who probably included John Sewell, sheriff of Essex, at the end of the 14th century.

Some of the larger properties had orchards, crofts and closes. These landholdings, with the parcels of land, are a reminder that however important the cloth industry might have become, many of the inhabitants kept livestock and horses and had an involvement in agriculture. Meadowland and pasture round the valley sides and rivers were a much valued resource for hay and grazing. Crofts and closes were both enclosed pieces of land. A croft is normally interpreted as a plot or smallholding attached to a house site. A close suggests land enclosed from the waste or a larger field. Crofts and closes present a distinct distribution pattern when seen on the map, the crofts being almost all clustered round West Street and the closes round Church Street. The closes are mostly regular strips. Those on the north side of Queen Street (in 1575 known as Church Lane) are said in the rental to be part of Over Church Field, as also is a piece of land on the south side of Queen Street. They seem to represent enclosure of strips in a large open field. The crofts are less regular in shape, and look as if associated with a more rectilinear pattern of fields. Some had names derived from the families which had owned them, unlike the closes, none of which had such names. Not all were attached to tenements though they may have been in the past. The crofts thus seem to have been a feature of house sites in this western part of the town, associated with a more open and spacious settlement pattern than the densely built up area of the town centre, where many of the plots seem to represent what had been strips in open fields.

---

4   Morant 1768, vol. 1, 151. For an analysis of landholding and the property market in Earls Colne in the 16th and 17th century, see French and Hoyle 2007.
5   Cf. Poos 1991, 74.

Property	Count	Sum	Area perches	Area acres	Average area perches	Rental value
Single tenement plots	122	122	6390	40	52	14.171
2 tenement plots	18	36	2414	15	67	3.066
3 tenement plots	4	12	504	3	42	0.55
4 tenement plots	1	4	49	0	12	1
6 tenement plots	1	6	48	0	8	0.1
Tenements total	146	180	9404	59	52	18.887
Garden	140	140				
Close	15	15				
Cottage	5	5				
Shop	3	3	1.99			0.1
Town House	1	1	5.42			0
School	1	1	20.64			0.11
Croft	9	9				
Stable	3	3				
Barn	4	4				
Dovehouse	1	1				
Yard	5	5				
Pond	1	1	50.76			0
Orchard	18	18	1450	9	81	2.13
Mead	8	8	5482	34	685	2.01
Parcel of land	22	22	4323	27	196	2.235

Property and land use in the rental. The entries for plots with tenements have been subdivided according to the number of tenements recorded. These could indicate several buildings, or a building in multiple occupancy.

This insight provided by the apparent difference between crofts and closes, combined with an analysis of the frontage widths given by the rental, makes it possible to draw inferences about changing patterns of land use, and the development of the town and its buildings. In particular, it can shed light on the strips which form the closes and seem to represent the origin of many of the house or tenement plots.

The strips in open fields such as Over Church Field are likely to have been of the order of 1 perch in width, a supposition supported by an analysis of frontage widths. On the south side of Church Street, the most common plot width was 2 and 2½ perches. A plot width of 2 perches by 1 furlong (220 yards, 40 perches, the notional length of a strip in medieval fields and the approximate length of the shorter strips at the east end of Queen Street and the longer ones on the south side of Church Street) would equate to an area of one half acre. The areas given in the rental for the holdings north of Queen Street are all in round acres or half an acre. Elsewhere in Essex, at Witham, the house plots in the new town founded by the Knights Templar in 1212 on Newland Street on the old Roman London to Colchester road were of the order of one half acre, and indeed were known as the *Halfacres*.[6]

The widths of the strip-shaped plots on the north side of Queen Street are approximately 6 – 6½ perches. These seem to be multiples of the narrower plots identified in Church Street, and may represent the original width of discrete holdings composed of a number of strips within the field systems of both Over Church Field and Nether Church Field.

---

6   Britnell 1962.

A typical frontage in much of the town was about 2-3 perches. This would accommodate a standard late medieval house with a parlour, hall, and services, or one with one or more cross-wings. Narrower frontages, of 1-2 perches, can indicate areas of market infill, or smaller houses of a type of which only a few have survived today. The pair of shops at 1 Church Street (now the Black Boy Bistro) have a combined frontage of only 1 ¼ perches. 40 Church Street, Craig Dhu, a 14th century house, comprises a hall and cross-wing 1½ perches or 24ft wide. It is thought that this was one of a pair of such houses. 1½ perch dimensions occur in the rental on the west side of Stoneham and may indicate the existence of similarly small properties, most of which have since been rebuilt in modern times. The six tenements owned by John Paycocke on the south side of the east end of East Street occupied a frontage of 6 ¼ perches and must therefore have been small houses or cottages.

The rental notes the tenurial status of the properties listed, whether they were copyhold, freehold, or held by lease or indenture, also referred to as 'convent seal', or put out to farm. The pattern presented by these tenures when mapped ought to shed some light on the development of the town, but by 1575 there seems to have been too much change over time for clear insights to emerge. Copyholds, which must once have been numerous, were relatively few. There are large blocks of freeholds in Stoneham Street and on the north side of Church Street. Conceivably these may have been offered by the abbey to encourage settlers in the early days of the town, or represent copyholds offered on better terms by the abbey in difficult times when it was difficult to get tenants. The convent seal lands may reflect similar processes or an attempt to let property on more advantageous terms. The closes to the north of Queen Street, which as has been seen represent enclosure of strips in Over Church Field, were all convent seal. The convent seal lands were the most extensive in area and also generated the most rent, a disproportionately high amount when their area is compared to the other types of tenure. This type of tenure may thus represent an estate management policy intended to increase the abbey's rental income.

Tenure	Number	Actual %	GIS area in perches	Rental value £0.00
Freehold	85	37.7	4211.5	3.54
Convent seal	48	21.3	5731.8	8.735
Copyhold	39	17.3	1757.0	5.3
Indenture	12	5.3	1846.4	3.61
Fee farm	3	1.3	1417.2	0.476
Unknown	38	16.8	8818.7	1.906
TOTAL	225		23782.8	23.567

Analysis of the different types of tenure in the rental

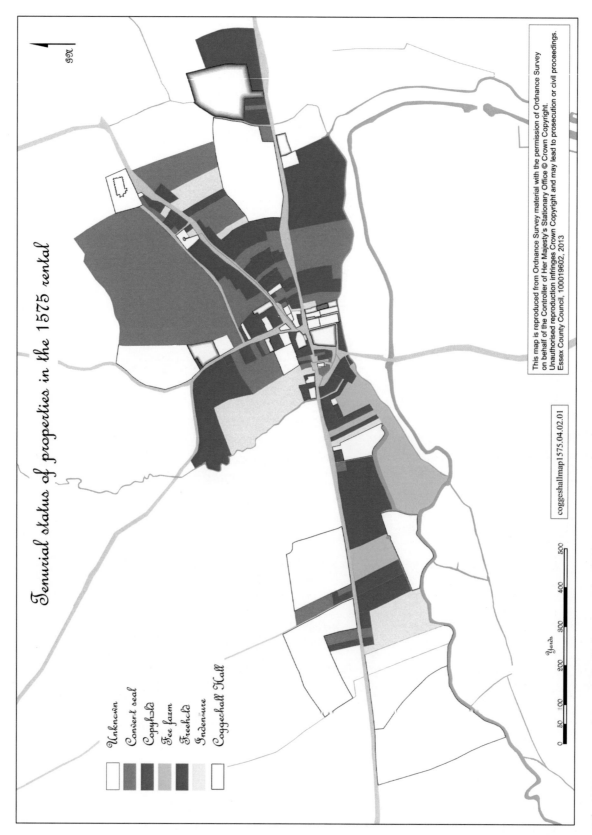

Tenurial status of properties in the 1575 rental

Unknown
Convert seal
Copyhold
Fee farm
Freehold
Indenture
Coggeshall Hall

The 1575 map of Coggeshall showing the different types of tenure

coggeshallmap1575.04.02.01

COGGESHALL AND THE WOOL AND CLOTH TRADES[1]

In the 12th and 13th centuries, England was a major exporter of wool. From the 14th century, the manufacture of cloth developed as a significant industry and its export overtook that of wool in importance. North Essex and south Suffolk was to become an important cloth producing area, and Coggeshall one of the most important towns engaged in its production. Its fortunes were therefore closely related to those of the wool and cloth trades. The availability of work led to an increase in population, but many of these people depended on low paid jobs carried on from home such as spinning, and as a result there were times of great hardship when the export trade was interrupted by warfare and other events. Wool was always produced in Essex and Suffolk, and would have been exported in the early period, but it was not of the best quality and it was not local wool which was primarily being used in the great age of cloth production.

England, with Burgundy and Spain, was a source of the better quality wool prized in the medieval cloth manufacturing centres of the Low Countries and Florence. English wool was being exported there from Norman times. In the trade in English wool, Italian merchants became dominant from the 13th century, and we find them recorded in East Anglia at that time. Wool was the mainstay of the English economy. It paid for wars and other expenses, kings raised money against it, and it was taxed, and as such had an important role in the constitutional developments which saw Parliament assert control of taxation and win enhanced political power.

The monasteries were leading wool producers, and several Essex houses, including Coggeshall, are recorded exporting wool to Italy. They would raise loans from merchants against future sales of wool, one of the ways in which their buildings were financed. Coggeshall Abbey sent wool to its sister house at Stratford Langthorne, now the site of the Olympic Stadium, but the number of sheep at Coggeshall never seems to have exceeded 300, compared with flocks of 25,000 at Yorkshire abbeys like Fountains and Rievaulx. Other Cistercian abbeys in the area present a similar picture: Sibton in Suffolk near Saxmundham, produced even less, whilst Tilty near Dunmow was slightly more active.

In any case, most of Coggeshall's flock was not resident in the abbey meadows but on the marshes between Goldhanger and Tollesbury, an estate acquired in the 1250s. Being marsh sheep, their wool was not particularly good quality. Nevertheless, the annual fair at Coggeshall was noted for its trade in wool.[2] The mighty Grange Barn, on the other hand, bears witness to the fact that the main agricultural interests here were grain. So the image of the abbot surrounded by sheep, as depicted on the Coggeshall town sign by the church, may be somewhat misleading.

There is evidence for cloth manufacture in eastern England from the 12th century and before. Since clothing is a basic requisite, weaving must always have been carried on locally from earliest times. Surnames associated with the cloth trade are found at Coggeshall before the end of the 13th century. William le Fullere and Richard le Webbe (i.e. weaver) appear as witnesses to the charter datable to *c*.1275 which has been mentioned above. Another William Fulur, or possibly the same, is recorded in 1286. By this time, cloth

---

1 These observations on the cloth trade are taken from Beaumont 1890, McClenaghan 1924, Power 1941, Carus Wilson 1967, Quin 1981, Dymond and Betterton 1989, Gervers 1989, Heard 1970, and Thornton 2011. It has also benefited from documentary research by Michael Horne. We are grateful to Sarah Howard for advice on the processes involved in working cloth.
2 Britnell 1986, 45.

production in north Essex and south Suffolk was already serving a wider market. Customs duties were already being paid on cloths of Coggeshall, Colchester, Maldon and Sudbury passing through the port of Ipswich at the beginning of the 13th century.[3]

The increase in cloth manufacture and export can be explained by the settlement of Flemish weavers in north Essex (though the importance of this may have been exaggerated), the changed economic and political circumstances of the big Flemish production centres, the dislocation caused by warfare, favourable tax and trade regulation regimes, and the creation of a larger internal market. The growth of exports nationally in the 14th and 15th centuries is evident from customs accounts at ports. Locally, there was a period of prosperity at the end of the 14th century and in the first decades of the 15th, with the industry centred upon Colchester as the principal manufacturing centre but also dispersed throughout the smaller market towns and large villages of north Essex and south Suffolk. This rural distribution has fascinated historians. It has been attributed to the lack of guild and trade regulation outside the large towns, and the development of fulling mills in rural locations. However, in a country which was not urbanised, there was little option but for expansion to occur in smaller centres. It was assisted by good communications, and a network of closely spaced market towns, often no more than six or seven miles apart. Manorial lords may well have promoted the spread of the industry as they benefited from the prosperity of their tenants, whilst the gradual relaxation of manorial controls made individual enterprise more straightforward.

A tax called ulnage was levied on cloth which was assessed and sealed as being of good quality, fit for sale. It was paid by the seller, who was not necessarily the maker. Although they have the potential to give a picture of how much cloth was being made each year in different places, the ulnage accounts are an unreliable and frustrating source. Nevertheless the Essex figures for 1394/5 are striking. Coggeshall was the third largest producer after Colchester and Braintree. Only nine Coggeshall men are listed, one of whom, Walter Trewe, had made almost twice as many cloths as any of the others. The only approximately contemporary return that may be compared to it is that for 1398 which names only five Coggeshall men who accounted for cloth to much less value, and thus seems incomplete or misleading.

The records of customs duties can also shed light on how the cloth trade operated and the role of Coggeshall people in it. In 1397/8, an Ipswich merchant John Parker imported 50 tuns of wine worth £381 and £5 worth of salt from a ship which had returned from Bordeaux and Bilbao, which he then loaded on the outgoing voyage with £61 of Coggeshall broadcloth. Parker's dealing in Coggeshall cloth is explained by his will, which shows that he came from the town and that his parents were clothiers. It is probable that they lived at Parker's tenement which later became the site of Paycocke's house.

In the absence of satisfactory records, the fortunes of the Coggeshall cloth industry remain largely invisible until the 1460s. In the ulnage returns for 1467/8, Coggeshall was the second largest Essex producer after Colchester, 34 names being entered in the list for that year. The 1464/5 return lists 70 names for Coggeshall, amongst whom no single person was predominant. Many of them accounted for only one cloth. Several women are mentioned, working as individual traders. The impression given is of an industry in which many people were engaged on a part-time or small scale basis. Despite this apparent increase in relative prosperity, Coggeshall like many other towns probably experienced economic stagnation or decline in the middle and later years of the 15th century.

---

3   Twiss1873, 18 7.

In contrast, the striking feature of the cloth industry in the early 16th century is the presence of several notable capitalists who had brought control of the different branches of the industry into their hands on something approaching a factory system and amassed considerable wealth. Of these, the outstanding figure is Thomas Spring III of Lavenham, who was one of the wealthiest men in England when he died in 1523. Lavenham church is ample testimony to his means, and indeed those of his father and the other local clothiers. It was rebuilt from 1486, and Thomas Spring bequeathed what amounted to over £1000 to its completion. Although less rich and his life less well documented, Thomas Paycocke of Coggeshall is another well known clothier whose wealth is visible from the house he built for himself in West Street in 1509.

The cloth manufacturing processes

In its early form the industry was organised by individual trades, each man his own master. By the 15th century, it was increasingly centralised in the person of the clothier, an incipient capitalist who controlled the stages of production, from the buying of wool to its distribution to the spinners and the yarn to the weavers, and finally the finishing processes.

Robert Reyce in the early 17th century estimated that a clothier making 20 broad cloths a week would create work for 500 people, 'what with breakers, dyers, woodsetters (woad), wringers, spinners, weavers, burlers, sheermen, and carriers'.[4] In his will, the Thomas Paycock who died in 1580 left £7 10s 'to and among thirty of the poorest journeymen of the fuller's craft' in Coggeshall.[5] Joseph Buston, a Coggeshall clothier born in 1650, was apprenticed to a Mr Hedgethorne, probably a Colchester clothier, who he said took in 23 weavers, but as many as 60 weavers and 8 combers at the time of his death.[6]

Clothiers such as the Springs of Lavenham, or the Paycocks of Coggeshall, grew to be wealthy capitalists. The raw wool had to be picked and sorted by quality, work often performed by children, and scoured and washed to remove dirt and grease. Spinning was done by women and girls, originally mainly using the distaff, spinning wheels only becoming improved in the 16th century. Oil was used to soften the wool as it was spun into yarn. Typically two types of yarn were produced, one taut for the warp and the other more open for the weft.

Weaving might be done in a shop attached to the house. A Long Melford clothmaker bequeathed his 'loomes standing in the shoppe next the street, with all the sleys and trendlys belonging thereto'.[7]

Dyeing might be done after spinning or after the yarn had been made into cloth. A building was required which would contain cisterns, vats, coppers, hearths for heating water, and which had access to water. A Lavenham clothier, Roger Ruggles, who lived in Water Street, bequeathed 'my dyehouse with the backside as it lieth together to the same dyehouse with the watercourse there'. Woad, fixed with alum, was the most commonly used dye. It was imported from Spain and France in the form of hard balls which had to be ground and fermented. Other shades were reds and violets.

---

4   Hervey 1902.
5   Emmison 1978, 300-02.
6   Beaumont 1890, 219.
7   McClenaghan 1924, 15.

Semur-en-Auxois, church of Notre Dame, the clothworkers' window. The processes illustrated are, clockwise from top: sorting and cleaning the fleece; carding; washing yarn; weaving; fulling; teasing; shearing; and pressing. (Bridgeman Art Library)

Once woven, the cloth had to be fulled, a process involving beating and hammering to close up the fibres, and make them smoother and more felted, and then washed and cleaned to remove any residual dirt and grease. Fulling was originally done by foot in a trough or pit, but after the 12th century water powered mills with hammers activated by the rotating wheel to pound the cloth became widespread. Finally the cloth was stretched out on frames to dry and to check shrinkage, a process known as tentering. Typically the frames would be set out in rows in a tenterfield, the cloth attached with iron hooks, hence the saying 'on tenter hooks'.

The finishing processes encompassed shearing, drawing, dressing or burling, and washing. The cloth was wetted and put on a frame and loose threads were picked out and holes repaired by a 'drawer'. Rough nap was sheared off using cropping shears. The nap was then raised using the heads of teasels, a thistle grown locally for the purpose.

There was a risk of fraud at any stage of the process. The spinner might not return all the wool to the clothier, and the weaver might keep some of the yarn. Clothiers would weigh and seal wool sent to the spinners. Both risked exploitation by the clothier. The clothier could avoid such problems by directly employing craftsmen who might work on his premises. In 1539, Suffolk weavers petitioned against wealthy clothiers who employed weavers and fullers in their own houses and paid them low wages. By this time, the wealthy clothiers were men of substance with a variety of business interests. Some such as the Paycockes seem to have been employing people on their own premises in what resembled factory conditions.

The cloth industry at Coggeshall in the 16th and 17th centuries

The analysis of the 1575 rental of Great Coggeshall manor identified 180 properties in the town, owned by 95 individuals, of whom at least 20, and probably significantly more, were active in the cloth trade. As has been seen, because of the many stages in the manufacturing process, these men had the potential to create work for large numbers of people. There were also changes in the pattern of cloth manufacture in the 16th century which saw an increase in production at Coggeshall. There was a slump in cloth exports in the middle of the century which especially hit those places producing the traditional broadcloth. However, Dutch immigrants who arrived in Colchester and north Essex in the 1560s introduced new, lighter, finer and more economical woollen cloths known as the New Draperies. Of these there was a great variety of types, but the best known were bays and says. Their rapid success saw a further decline in the production of broadcloth, and of those places that persisted in its manufacture, and the enhanced prosperity of those places that adapted to the new ways, notably Colchester, Coggeshall and Bocking. It is possible that Coggeshall benefited from such changes earlier in the century, as it is said that an Italian Bonvise introduced a new type of Coxall cloth in 1528, possibly the white cloth for which the town had a reputation, though Coggeshall whites are recorded at an earlier date.[8]

---

8   Thornton 2011, 39.

TRADE	Documentary reference	Named person	Textile trades
Apothecary	1	1	
Apprentices	4	4	
Bakers	4	3	
Barbers	1	1	
Beer brewers	4	5	
Blacksmiths	6	9	
Butchers	5	6	
Cardmakers	1	1	1
Carpenters	5	3	
Carters	2	5	
Clerks	1	1	
Clothiers	40	41	41
Constables	2	3	
Cooper	1	1	
Currier	1	1	
Draper	1	1	1
Dyer	1	1	1
Fullers	45	60	60
Gentlemen	3	3	
Glovers	1	1	
Husbandmen	35	41	
Innholder	1	1	
Comber ('Kember')	1	1	1
Labourers	30	40	
Lawyers	1	3	
Millwright	1	1	
Officers	1	3	
Physician	1	1	
Servants	4	4	
Shoemakers	5	10	
Singlewomen	6	10	
Soldiers	2	2	
Spinner	1	1	1
Surgeon	1	1	
Surveyors	1	2	
Tailors	4	4	
Tanner	1	1	
Tiler	3	3	
Victualler	1	1	
Weavers	54	63	63
Wheelwright	1	1	
Widows	23	22	
Yeomen	25	21	
Persons with no named trade	64	64	
43 trades or occupations		452	168

Trades and occupations at Coggeshall 1550-1610 compiled by Michael Horne by searching on the SEAX catalogue to the Essex Record Office

As a busy market town, there were a wide range of trades carried on at Coggeshall. An analysis of recorded tradesmen in the second half of the 16th century suggests that perhaps 37% of the town's population was engaged in some aspect of the cloth trade. In contrast most other trades or occupations are represented by a handful of individuals, except for husbandmen and labourers, a reminder that farming and agriculture were significant activities in these small towns.

The main manufacturing centres became proto-industrial towns with large artisan populations dependent on cloth for their livelihood and vulnerable to any downturn in a trade which tended to be cyclical, being very much at the mercy of political events. In 1629 an interruption of the trade caused by war with France and Spain was claimed, no doubt with exaggeration, to risk reducing 30,000 people in north Essex to poverty and causing riots. In 1652, the clothiers of Coggeshall submitted a petition to the government drawing attention to the distress they suffered through the damage to trade caused by war with Holland, and seeking measures to relieve the situation.[9] This petition had 72 signatories, suggesting a significant increase in the number of clothiers over the total in 1575. It is difficult to make accurate estimates of the size of the population, but there can be no doubting that it had grown significantly. The 180 properties recorded in 1575 should be compared with the 460 on which the hearth tax was assessed in 1670, making Coggeshall the second largest town in Essex.[10] This could be taken to imply a doubling of the dwellings in the town, achieved however not so much by new build as by sub-division of existing properties, and a similar increase in inhabitants. The hearth tax returns reflect their precarious economic status, with 50-60% of the population in the cloth producing area of Essex being exempt from the tax. The criteria for exemption were being excused from paying poor rates on the grounds of poverty, or occupying a dwelling with an annual rent of 20 shillings or less, or having goods not worth more than £10. At Coggeshall, 59.8% were exempt.

In the 18th century, the cloth trade went into a slow decline. It did not survive the Napoleonic Wars. In Braintree and Bocking, it was succeeded by the silk industry established by the Courtaulds. Silk mills were set up in Coggeshall in the 19th century but were unsuccessful, presumably failing to compete with Courtaulds.

	Taxpayers/ heads of households	Dwellings/ properties	Families/ occupiers	Actual or estimated* population	Rank in Essex towns
1086 Domesday	59			300*	
1327 lay subsidy (includes Marks Hall)	53			300*	
1524 lay subsidy	118			590*	6
1575 rental (excludes Coggeshall Hall manor)		180		1200*	
1670 hearth tax (excludes Little Coggeshall)	460	460		2300*	2
1801 census				2469	
1861 census				3679	
1881 census		683	704	2998	

Table of Coggeshall's population at different times. The pre-census figures should all be treated as no more than indicative. A multiplier of about 5 has been used for the estimates. The estimated figures are all likely to be underestimates. (Sources include Beaumont 1890, Ward 1983, Petchey 1991, and Ferguson et al. 2012)

9   Quin 1981, 55; Beaumont 1890, 188.
10   Ferguson et al. 2012.

The cloth trade on the 1575 map of the town

The prosperity brought by the cloth trade has left Coggeshall with a heritage of fine timber-framed houses, of which Paycockes is the outstanding example. The industrial processes associated with cloth manufacture also had an impact on the appearance and layout of the town, both on the buildings and the spaces around them. Documents occasionally mention wool halls, buildings which provided storage for the wool prior to processing and the cloth at the various stages in its production. Whereas spinning and weaving could be continuous processes, tentering and drying were weather and season dependent and therefore output was not constant. Provision had therefore to be made to store the cloth at each process stage and at point of sale. Most cloth was sold between Christmas and Whitsun, so to be 'market ready', stocks would have to be gradually built up from the previous summer and autumn.

Within houses used for weaving, in addition to a loom, warp frames were required to store and prepare the long warp threads. Evidence of warp frames can be identified by rows of parallel dowel holes in wall studs. Examples can be seen at 17 East Street, 10 East Street and 18/20 Stoneham Street. At 18/20 Stoneham Street there is evidence for at least three warp frames in two upper floor chambers, suggesting the simultaneous use of several looms in what were approaching factory conditions.

Water would have been a critical resource for processes such as washing, scouring, fulling, finishing and dyeing. Conveniently located fields or gardens would have been required for tentering and drying the cloth. At Lavenham water courses were diverted and channelled into canals and cisterns for industrial purposes, and there was a tenter field area west of the High Street and Water Street in that town. With insights from the 1575 rental and the study of the town plan and its buildings, evidence for similar activity can be identified at Coggeshall.

Hand fulling, or walking and washing, could have been carried out in lower Robin's Brook and the stream to the east of Starling Lees, now the Recreation Ground. Mechanical fulling would require a reasonable head of water, such as at the Back Ditch or up stream Robin's Brook. It is thought that a fulling mill was located on the site of the 19th century teasel mill in Robin's Bridge Road on land appropriately owned by William Fuller in 1575. Tye Mill is recorded in the survey at the confluence of the Back Ditch and the original course of Robin's Brook with its associated flood gates across the Back Ditch at Short Bridge. There is no firm evidence whether Tye Mill was used as a fulling mill or a grain mill or indeed both.

Men washing cloth and a fulling mill from the title page to Chapman and André's 1777 map of Essex

At the site of the old isinglass factory on the north side of West Street, the stream known as the Pissing Gutter that now runs in a culvert would have been ideal in the 16th century for fulling and washing, well away from the town centre polluting industries such as dyeing. The 1575 rental also refers to a 'furnace' being located within this area, possibly used to heat up water for the washing process.

All this wet wool needed to be dried, and after fulling, which shrinks the cloth by at least 25%, the cloths about 30 yards long had to be stretched and hung out to dry on tenter frames resembling football posts in 'tentering gardens' or 'tentering fields'. Tenter Croft is recorded in the 1575 rental survey on the site currently occupied by the Dutch Nursery. The 1838 tithe map identifies the field just to the north of the isinglass factory as Tenter Field. This clothworking activity is the likely explanation for the presence of the group of late medieval houses here, isolated from the main town centre.

Two dye houses can be identified. One was on the site of 3/5 The Gravel south, just north of the Back Ditch at Short Bridge, owned by John Goodaye. The second was behind 8 East Street on land held of the manor of Coggeshall Hall. Although this plot was known as the Dyehouse, it may no longer have been operating by 1575. Dyeing pollutes the water so no other clean wet processes can be undertaken downstream of it.

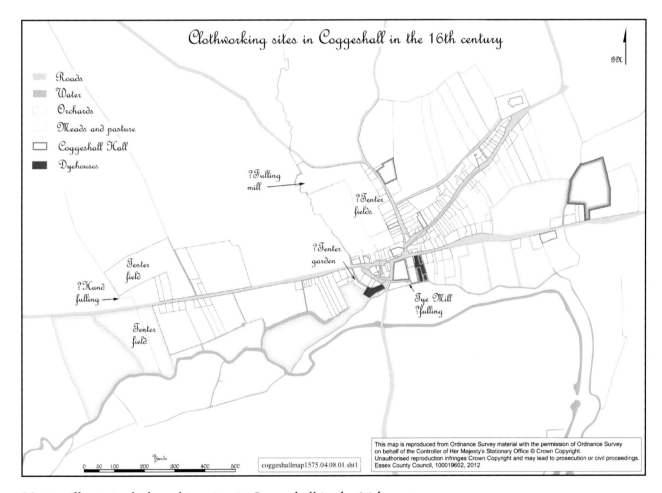

Map to illustrate clothworking sites in Coggeshall in the 16th century

The Thomas Paycocke lands, West Street south and the Gravel west.

In the late 15th and early 16th century, the Thomas Paycocke who built the house in West Street, owned much of the land south of West Street to the Back Ditch and west of the Gravel. The 1575 rental survey shows that much of this land passed into the ownership of his nephews Thomas and John. Historically, the Paycocke family had probably built up this landholding in an area of meadows and pasture because the Thomas Paycocke who died in 1461, and whose brass is in the church, was a *carnifex* or butcher, as was his son John. He would have needed this land for grazing. His descendants were clothiers and they would have found it valuable because it gave them access to water and space essential for carrying out the finishing processes involving washing and drying cloth on a relatively large scale.

It has been argued above that Robin's Brook probably once flowed along the Gravel. The 1575 Rental Survey described two of Thomas Paycockes plots located to the west of the Gravel west as having a 'river to the south'. There is also a record of a water lane running parallel with this 'river' on the west side from West Street towards his land at Horse Lease Pasture. This suggests that the Robin's Brook had been diverted from Hares Bridge to the west of the Gravel, through what is now Brian Tebbit's garden and across Culvert Close, to benefit land which was then owned by the Paycockes, and probably carried out on their initiative.

Bradford Street mill, Bocking. The single storey part to the rear was built as a fulling mill in the late 17th or 18th century. In the 19th century, the front part was raised in height as a corn mill

THE TREE-RING DATING PROGRAMME

Tree-ring dating

Tree-ring dating or dendrochronology is an independent dating technique that utilises the growth pattern of ring widths within a sample of timber to determine the calendar period during which the tree grew. From England there is a large number of oak *(Quercus)* ring-width reference chronologies against which new sequences can be tested. The geographical and temporal coverage of these ring-width reference chronologies is extensive and a series of strong regional chronologies can be produced for almost the entire country. If suitable ring sequences can be obtained, and these can be matched to reference chronologies, precise dates can be provided for buildings for which the date is either unknown or uncertain. It is not intended here to provide comprehensive details of the method as there is an extensive body of literature upon the subject which can be found elsewhere.[1] A dendrochronological study is of greatest value when integrated with detailed building recording.

Trees put their new growth on the outside of their trunk, just under the bark. The most recent rings are therefore those originally nearest the outside of the tree. A series of tree-rings from a sample will run from the oldest which are those nearest the centre through to the most recent which are nearer the outside.

It is necessary that enough annual growth rings are obtained from any one sample in order to be able to find reliable cross-correlation with other tree-ring sequences. For oak the minimum acceptable number of rings is widely held to be 50, although some of the material from each building usually requires more than this number if dating is to be successful. Since not all timbers contain datable sequences, it is necessary to obtain samples from a number of apparently suitable timbers in any building for which a date is sought.

The date of the tree-ring sequence must not be confused with the date when the tree was used. The felling year of a tree can only be determined by obtaining sequences that have complete sapwood and either bark or identifiable bark-edge. Such samples do not survive in every building. In converting trees to structural timber, carpenters square them up, removing most or all of the sapwood and bark. Many dendrochronological studies of buildings only provide felling date ranges or a *terminus post quem*, a date after which the tree must have been cut down.

The date of felling of a tree is not necessarily the date of its use. Observations relating to the toolmarks and conversion distortions can be used to suggest timbers were cut and framed whilst green, which was generally the practice in the Middle Ages. However timbers were sometimes used after an interval of time, and they might also be reused, something that may not be recognised without a full analysis of the building.

An offcut from a house dated to 1435. It has about 100 rings from the centre of the tree to the heart/sapwood boundary. The bunching of narrow rings separated by wider ones probably reflect coppicing cycles

---

1   Schweingruber 1988, English Heritage 1998.

The standard method of reporting the correlation between tree-ring sequences employed throughout European dendrochronology is by use of coefficients calculated using the CROS algorithm of Baillie and Pilcher (1973). This algorithm produces t values. A t value of between -3.0 and 3.0 is normally found for each non-matching position of overlap between any two sequences. Values of between 3.0 and 5.0 may reflect the correct dating position. Values between 5.0 and 10.0 are usually reliable indicators of synchronous sequences. Values of 10.0 and above are usually found between two sequences derived from the same tree. Reference chronologies are composite series mathematically constructed from many separate data series. Reference chronologies correlate more strongly than individual series.

Methodology

The Discovering Coggeshall project attempted to date a sample of the houses within the initial study of the 'triangle' in the centre of the town. Not all timber framed buildings are equally suitable for tree-ring dating. Their timbers may not be accessible enough to be successfully sampled. Their timbers may not have sufficient rings, or show irregular growth patterns which cannot be cross-matched, thus limiting their potential for reliable dendrochronological dating. The carpenters may have removed the original outer surfaces of the tree, limiting the precision of any results obtained. Post-medieval buildings are often constructed of reused timber, or timber of slight scantling, or of timber other than oak, so making dating impossible.

A large group of buildings in the study area were visited and assessed for their dendrochronological potential. Their timbers were carefully examined for indications of the numbers of rings present and the presence of sapwood and bark. This provided a shortlist of buildings with the potential for successful dating.

For the selected timbers within each of the selected properties, the precise location of the sample was determined by factors such as the localised presence of sapwood or bark-edge, and ease of access. The sampling locations were designed to maximise the numbers of rings obtained and, wherever possible, to include all the sapwood and the original bark-edge of the tree. The timbers were sampled using a 17mm diameter hollow corer attached to an electric drill. Despite selecting positions that initially included sapwood and bark the resultant cores do not always retain these delicate structures, since sapwood that has been attacked by woodworm, or other pests, will often crumble during coring. The holes made to take the cores were usually filled with dowels afterwards.

A timber being sampled with the corer

34

In the laboratory the sequence of ring widths in each core were revealed by preparing a surface equivalent to the original horizontal plane of the parent tree with a variety of bladed tools and/or increasingly fine sand papers. The prepared surfaces were then assessed again to determine the suitability of each sample for analysis. The complete sequence of the annual growth rings in each of the suitable samples were measured to an accuracy of 0.01mm using a micro-computer based travelling stage. The sequence of ring widths were then plotted onto semi-log graph paper to enable visual comparisons to be made between sequences. Cross-correlation algorithms were employed to search for positions where the ring sequences were highly correlated.[2] These positions were checked using the graphs and, where these were satisfactory, new mean sequences were constructed from the synchronised sequences.

This initial analysis can obviously only date the rings present in the cores. The correct interpretation of those dates relies upon the nature of the final rings in the individual samples. If the sample ends in the heartwood of the original tree, a *terminus post quem* for the felling of the tree is indicated by the date of the last ring plus the addition of the minimum expected number of sapwood rings that may be missing. This *terminus post quem* may be many decades prior to the real felling date. Where some of the outer sapwood or the heartwood/sapwood boundary survives on the sample, a felling date range can be calculated using the maximum and minimum number of sapwood rings likely to have been present. Alternatively, if bark-edge survives, then a precise felling date can be identified from the date of the last surviving ring. The sapwood estimates applied here are a minimum of 10 and maximum of 46 annual rings, where these figures indicate the 95% confidence limits of the range. These figures are applicable to medieval and modern oaks from England. The dates obtained by the technique do not by themselves necessarily indicate the date of the structure from which they are derived. They need to be set in the context of the analysis of the building fabric, which may be of several phases of construction and also incorporate reused timbers.

Results

Coggeshall was visited over a number of occasions between March 2010 and May 2011. Many buildings were assessed, and timbers from 20 of the properties were selected for sampling. The initial assessment indicated that there was great diversity in the suitability of the timbers in Coggeshall for tree-ring analysis. There are significant differences in the growth rates, scantling sizes and tree-ages of the timbers used, usually within any one structure, and certainly across the settlement as a whole. Most of the apparently original structural timbers in the older buildings are oak *(Quercus spp.)*. Elm occurs as original timber from the 17th century onwards.

A total of 108 timbers were selected for tree-ring sampling from the 20 properties, representing about two dozen phases of construction. The sampling attempted to encompass as wide a range of elements as possible within each building. If a low number of samples were taken, that is because relatively few suitable timbers were accessible. After preparation and re-examination a total of 88 of the samples were found to be suitable for analysis. The remainder variously either fragmented, contained too few rings, or were trees with aberrant anatomical features. 62 of the suitable samples were found to be datable, a success rate which repeats those seen at similar projects in Herefordshire, Worcestershire, & Norfolk. The full results of the dating programme, and the data generated by it, are available in a separate report.[3]

---

2   E.g. Baillie & Pilcher 1973.
3   Tyers 2011.

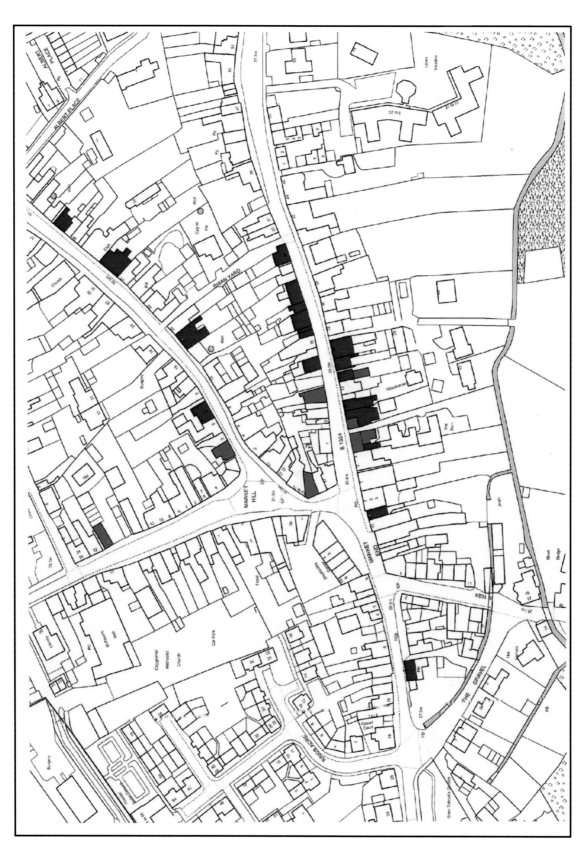

Map showing houses which have been tree-ring dated. Coloured green are houses which were sampled but failed to date

DATED HOUSES	DATE	NOTES
30 Church Street, Spooners	1353-86	In-line house
18 East Street	1361-97	Cross-wing
10 East Street	1386	Cross-wing, ?wool hall
40 Church Street, Craig Dhu	1387-1423	Hall and cross-wing, originally one of a pair
17-19 East Street	1397	H-plan house
The Cricketers, West Street	1403-29	Market and court hall
11 East Street	1404-40	Cross-wing
29 East Street	1418-54	Cross-wing
9 Market End	1422-48	Cross-wing, part of White Hart
18 Church Street	1428	Rear wing only
14 East Street	1435	Cross-wing
6B East Street	1441	Commercial building
5-7 Church Street	1454	Cross-wing
10-12 East Street	1552-88	Rebuilt hall
Paycockes, West Street	1509	Long-wall jetty house
18 Church Street	1545	Frontage building, long-wall jetty
55-63 Stoneham Street	1555	Moved here after 1575
52-54 Church Street	1565	Inscription, long-wall jetty house
32 & 20 East Street	1585	Inscription, long-wall jetty house
23 East Street	1599	Long-wall jetty house
30 Church Street	1608-09	Rear wing
8 East Street	1618	Rear wing
16 East Street	1636	Rebuilt hall

Dated buildings in Coggeshall. As well as buildings dated for this project, this list includes ones dated by inscription, and ones dated on previous occasions. Buildings in which dates were obtained for reused timbers, and hence unrelated to their construction, are omitted

Discussion

An assessment of the buildings in the town in 2004 suggested that many had timbers suitable for tree-ring dating. This was confirmed by dating offcuts from repairs to three buildings before the project began. That 18 out of a total of 22 buildings from which samples have been obtained were dated represents a success rate unusual in Essex, where it often happens that timbers, especially those from urban buildings, have insufficient rings for the technique to work. Thus no buildings in Colchester or Maldon have so far been dated, apart from St. Martin's church in the former and Beeleigh Abbey at the latter. Experience indicates that high status buildings such as these have good dating potential because their owners had access to woodland which was not being intensively exploited and where there were older trees. The woodland available to most Essex towns seems to have been under pressure from local consumers, with the result that trees were felled as soon as they had reached a useful size. Timber was a valuable resource and access to it was controlled by the lord of the manor.

Today there is still extensive woodland to the north of Coggeshall, extending eastward from Great Monks Wood to the Markshall estate. Parts of this are still managed in the traditional way as coppice and standards. Monks Wood as its name suggests belonged to the abbey, and this exceptionally large timber resource no doubt explains why tree-ring dating works so well in the town. Another factor in its success is presumably

Managed woodland in Great Monks Wood today

the woodland management regime: relatively slow grown timbers would have more rings than intensively managed fast grown ones.

Although the timbers in medieval buildings are generally similar in dimensions, they could come from trees of very variable age, presumably reflecting what was available to the builder. The timbers in the Coggeshall buildings range from as little as 55 years to well over 100 years old. Typically they were 60-90 years old. The timbers in the Cricketers, however, were from 150-200 year old trees. This was a market and court hall built for the abbey, which would have had access to the best timber in the manorial woods. For the other inhabitants of the town, sourcing timber suitable to build a house would not have been so straightforward.

If the dates of all the buildings in Coggeshall, including those with dates carved on them, are plotted, there is a striking peak at the end of the 14th century and in the early 15th. Numbers fall off in about the mid 15th century and in the early 16th century, to rise again in the second half of the 16th. This peak between about 1350 and 1450 is also repeated if the tree-ring dates obtained so far for Essex are plotted out in the same way. The pattern of building activity mirrors that obtained in a chart of national tree-ring dates from urban buildings, but not those for rural buildings which tend to show sustained activity from about the middle of the 15th century until the end of the 16th.[4]

---

4   Pearson 2001.

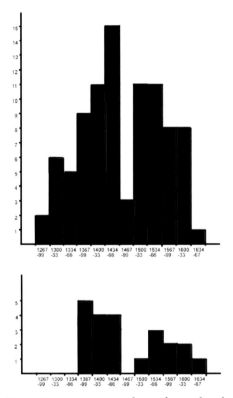

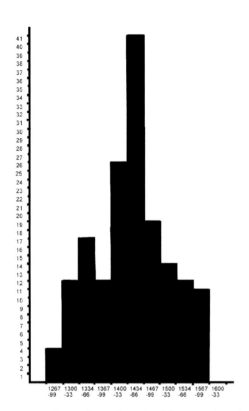

Top: Essex tree-ring dates for individual buildings and major phases of buildings of all types.
Bottom: the dates of 23 buildings from Coggeshall

Tree-ring dates for urban buildings in England obtained during 1980-2001 (after Pearson 2001)

Admittedly the Coggeshall and Essex statistics are a very small sample, but their consistency must be of some significance since building activity must be linked to the general state of the wider economy. A detailed study of late medieval Colchester reveals it to have prospered in the second half of the 14th century, especially from the 1360s and 1370s.[5] The tree-ring dates suggest this trend was paralleled at Coggeshall. In this apparent economic growth there can be no doubting the role of the cloth trade. Statistics for cloth exports show them rising dramatically from a low base in the middle of the 14th century through to 1400 after which they reach a plateau with occasional peaks and troughs. While it is commonplace to talk of 'wool churches' built on the proceeds of the trade, the dates reveal that the timber-framed houses of Coggeshall also reflect the prosperity brought by cloth manufacturing, and that this was not just a Tudor phenomenon but a late medieval one. Building activity seems to have dropped at the end of the 15th and in the early 16th century, the latter being a time when towns are known to have been experiencing economic difficulties. The increase in activity at the end of the 16th and in the early 17th century fits in the period of the 'great rebuilding' identified by W. G. Hoskins.[6] This renewal of the housing stock may have been made possible by increased prosperity, but also was partly motivated by improvements such as the flooring over of halls and insertion of chimneys. Similar factors may have been at work in the late 14th century, in-line houses being adapted to more densely occupied urban conditions and commercial requirements by having cross-wings added to them to provide workshop and storage space.

5   Britnell 1986.
6   Hoskins 1955.

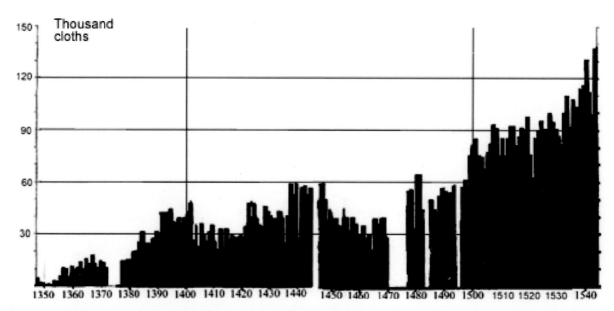

English cloth exports 1347-1544 (after Carus-Wilson 1967)

COGGESHALL HOUSES AND THEIR CARPENTRY

The 1575 survey provided a most wonderful snapshot of the town in regards to ownership, extent of land-holding and tenure. However what is lacking is any information on the buildings extant at that time. Were they relatively new, had older buildings been modernised and how were they positioned on the plots? These were some of the questions that had to be answered and many more besides in the course of the Discovering Coggeshall project. The original aim of the project was to survey in detail the buildings contained within the triangle of land bounded by Market Hill to the west, Church Street to the north, East Street to the south and Swan Yard, a later lane to the east. Reports on these buildings are contained in Appendix 2. An opportunity was also taken to study most of the timber-framed houses within the 1575 survey area, with the aim of presenting an over view and providing information that might provoke further research. This wider survey has been published as the first volume of the Discovering Coggeshall project.[1]

The co-operation of the owners was essential to the success of the exercise. For the most part they were extremely enthusiastic, but in an urban situation with rented properties in multi-occupancy, the consent of both the owner and the tenant was required. The sub-division of these older and larger buildings often resulted in 'flying freeholds' which also added to the complexity of producing a complete survey. Changes through the centuries have also resulted in exteriors and interiors being covered, making the recording of the timber-frame more difficult. Original features have been altered or lost, and large pieces of furniture often hide that clue which will solve the mystery of the development of the building. These problems are very obvious when the surveys of two empty fire damaged buildings, The Cricketers and 8 East Street, are compared with occupied buildings. Given all of the difficulties, there are bound to be some errors in the recording and interpretation of the buildings, and unanswered questions which it is hoped will spur on successive generations to continue to study and rectify any discrepancies that they find.

Materials

Early buildings are built from readily available local materials and it is not until the age of countrywide transport that the sense of place produced by the vernacular materials is broken. In simplistic terms Essex is a county with a surface of geology consisting mainly of thick deposits of Boulder Clays to the north of the A12, with a central mixed band of wooded hills and heaths and heavy London Clays to the south following the coastal zone. River valleys contain deposits of sand and gravel. The chalk, which outcrops in the north-west and south of the county, contains good deposits of flint. The presence of no good free stone led to the use of earth generated materials such as the brickearths for brick and tile, clay for infill and daub, timber for timber-framing, boarding, and shingles, wattles and staves for infill, and straw and reed thatch for roofs.

Timber-framing in Essex has been studied in depth over the last 40 years by individuals too numerous to mention, with the backing of the former Historic Buildings and Conservation Section of Essex County Council. Although no physical survey and study of timber-framed buildings within an urban context such as that at Coggeshall has been previously undertaken in Essex, the involvement of the Essex Historic Buildings team in both the government's accelerated listing process of 1984, and in giving listed building advice to the local planning authorities, has resulted in various publications. Conferences organised by

---

1   D.F. Stenning, *Discovering Coggeshall. Timber-framed buildings in the town centre*, 2013.

Essex County Council and the Essex Historic Buildings Group saw the publication of two seminal books, *Regional Variation in Timber-framed Building in England and Wales down to 1550,*[2] and *The English Medieval Roof. Crownpost to Kingpost.*[3] These publications set the scene for the development of plan form and the regional spread of framing and roof style. Another Essex County Council conference addressed the development of the county's historic landscape, its proceedings published as *The Essex landscape. In search of its history.*[4]

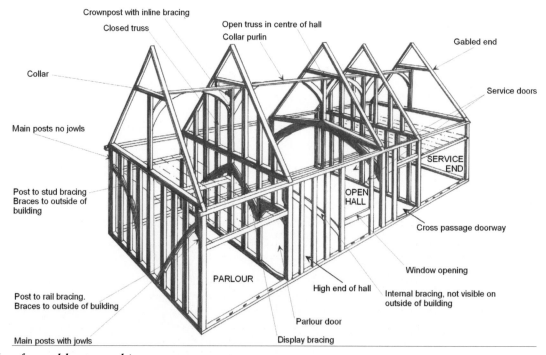

A timber-framed house and its component parts

Timber conversion

During the medieval period the strict management of woodlands was important to produce the timber required. Considerable areas of woodland still exist today to the north of the town, and timber may have been supplied from Monkswood by the Abbey up to the Dissolution, and afterwards by private owners.

The main method of management was by coppicing, cutting down to ground level on a regular rotation leaving a set number of 'maiden' trees to grow through the coppice to provide the larger timbers. Most of the early buildings in Essex tend to have a majority of small timbers of relatively square section with larger trees for the main structural frame.

In the buildings inspected there was a mix of relatively slow grown timber and some that was exceptionally fast grown. It is unusual in Essex to find such a high ratio of slow grown timber, rather than the fast grown timber which is what is produced by regular woodland management. However this did result in a higher number of successful tree-ring dates.

2　Stenning and Andrews 1998.
3　Walker 2011.
4　Green 1999.

The tree-ring dates obtained with terminal dates show that most of the timber was felled in the winter-spring period followed by conversion. This involves hand hewing with an axe after felling when the first stage would be to notch along the length of the timber to a line to remove excess and sap wood. The excess between the notches can then be easily removed and a broad axe used to produce a flat smooth surface. Larger section timber could be further reduced by sawing. The earliest system is known as single trestle or see-sawing as the timber had to be pushed up the trestle to the mid point and then turned over to start from the other end. Each time the timber was moved up the trestle a change of angle was noticeable in the cutting lines. Where these two cuts meet the last section will usually shear leaving a small triangle as a signature. No evidence for single trestle sawing was found in the study area but it was noted at Spooners, 30 Church Street (1353-86), in 1999.

Axe conversion of timber: notching to a line (left) and finishing with a broad axe (Carpenters Fellowship at Cressing Temple)

In general see-sawing changed to double trestle or pit sawing in the early 15th century. This leaves a relatively consistent kerf line from the saw. One of the earliest dated examples was at 18 Church Street (1428) where an apotropaic or protection mark intended to ward off evil on the converted timber was severed by the process of long sawing to produce a pair of joists.

See-sawing (left) and trestle sawing (Carpenters at Fellowship at Cressing Temple)

Apotropaic mark on joists dated 1428 from 18 Church Street

Once converted the timber would have been used green and the various elements for the timber-framed house produced either in the woods, a framing yard or on site. Joints would have been predominantly of

mortice and tenon type and cut with a chisel after initial marking out and boring with an auger. All components of the timber frame would have been marked at the framing stage ready for assembly on site. These carpenter's marks can be made in various ways with tools such as a race knife or later a chisel. Based on Roman numerals they can sometimes be clearly seen but are often hidden inside timber joints or below floor boards. One set that can be clearly seen are those to the replacement 17th century hall of 5 Church Street where there are external chiselled marks to the studs above the jetty.

Timber-framed buildings in the east of England are described as being of box-frame construction and formed of bays. The width of the building is limited by the length of timber available. Typically it is 15-

Chisel cut carpenters' marks at 5 Church Street

16ft (5.0-5.3m), rarely does it exceed 20ft (6.1m). The bays are marked by full height timbers, storey posts, along the length of the building at an average of 10ft (3.05m) centres but this could vary. They could contain one full depth room such as a parlour, or be divided to provide combinations of shop, workshop, service rooms and parlour. These uses are usually contained within the floored ends of the building. The hall of one or more bays occupied the full height and depth of the building.

The full height storey post evolved from a straight post positioned under the wall plate, sometimes with an upstand against the side of the plate, into a jowl post made by turning the tree upside down to provide adequate timber for a jowl or swelling at the top which made it possible to create the ultimate three-way locking joint between storey post, wall plate and tie-beam. By the early 1300s it would normally be expected to find jowled posts. However, Coggeshall generally follows the Colchester tradition that can also be found in Maldon and other coastal regions of having mainly unjowled storey posts in the early buildings. Carpenters are usually quick to adopt changes that improve the structural qualities of the building, so was there a limit on the availability of suitable timber of adequate width to make jowl posts? Looking at the timber used for the sizeable unjowled storey posts, 1ft 2ins (356mm) square at the three storied Cavendish House, the service cross-wing to The White Hart, it would appear unlikely, but here sapwood erosion is clearly visible on the arrises of the posts and the mouldings to the service doors, which are usually carved out of the solid, had to be applied, all of which implies that the timbers were barely large enough for the carpenters' requirements.

Early tie-beams are of steep cambered profile with arched braces to the storey posts. In the earliest examples, there might be spandrel struts as at 19 East Street (1397). By the late 16th century, with the introduction of attic floors, the profile is virtually flat, although a cranked tie-beam is used at 32 East Street (1585).

Service doors with applied decoration at the White Hart

Framing of the houses is in the typical close studded pattern of the region with variations in the spacing of the studs and the style of bracing. Coggeshall exhibits the expected pattern with the early buildings having wider spaced studs and the spacing reducing through the 15th and 16th centuries. Both the frontage range of 10 East Street (1386) and the cross-wing at 19 East Street (1397) have studs set at 2ft 6ins (760mm) centres. At the 18 Church Street rear range (1428) they are at 2ft (610mm) centres. Closer studding can also be found on the early buildings ruling out the temptation to make generalisations. In the hall of the Through Inn, 19 East Street (1397) the spacing is at 1ft 6ins (460mm) centres, as also at the later shop range to the rear of 6 East Street (1441) and the front elevation of the cross-wing at 7 Church

Street (1454), although there the side and rear elevations have studding at 1ft 9ins (533mm) centres. The semi-detached shops at 1 Church Street dated stylistically to the second quarter of the 15th century had a marked difference between the front and rear stud centres. Whilst the studs to the front elevation were at 1ft 6ins (460mm) centres, those to the flank and rear were at 2ft 6ins (760mm) centres. Was this a conscious attempt to save expenditure on this speculative development or just that more timber used in the front elevation implied higher status? The same hierarchy of materials and finishes can be found in 19th century architecture, with expensive bricks used to the front and cheaper ones to the flank and rear walls.

Example of a cranked tie-beam, and a crown post with in-line and down bracing

From the later 17th century most buildings were being constructed with both the interior and exterior of the building covered in plaster. With the framing now hidden, the quality of timber conversion and size decreases together with an increased use of elm for structural timbers. This reduction in timber size used in the buildings can be seen right through to the middle of the 19th century when brick takes over as the main building material for the area. This can be seen in Coggeshall initially in higher class buildings such as 10 Church Street, The Curtain Exchange, Market Hill, and 1 East Street for a smaller but high class building.

Reused timber is also a characteristic feature of 17th century and later carpentry. Normally in Essex reused timber never occurs in late medieval houses, but one surprise was the discovery of it in several of the Coggeshall properties, such as the roof of Spooners (30 Church Street), and the rear parlour at 6 East Street. In the later period, buildings could also be moved, as was found at 55-63 Stoneham Street, a property tree-ring dated to 1555 but not recorded in its present position in the 1575 rental.

Bracing

Coggeshall lies within the main area of Essex where tension or down braces are the norm. In the area to the south-west of Chelmsford and a small area to the south of the Suffolk border, north of Colchester, arch bracing is more common. Tension bracing is described as joining a horizontal and vertical timber. In the study area there are a number of buildings where Colchester or Suffolk style bracing is used. This is bracing that connects vertical timbers without joining a horizontal. It does not achieve full triangulation but would still be sufficient to stabilise the building during construction.

In the early buildings the braces are trenched into the external face of the studs with the exception in the study area of 18 East Street where the east wall has internal bracing. Normally braces are 1-1½ inches (25-38mm) thick, but the early bracing, 2 inches (51mm) thick, at 14, 16, 18 and 19 East Street, is both trenched across the studs and the brace halved at stud positions. By the 16th century, the pattern starts to reverse with the braces shown internally to better reveal the close studding externally, as at 8 East Street (1618) and 23 East Street (1599). With the advent of wider windows and closer studding in the late 16th and early 17th century, braces are often omitted. By the early 17th century primary bracing becomes the norm. In this type of timber-framing the brace is the main structural element in the stud wall with the studs being set to either side of the primary brace. No dates were obtained for primary braced framing due either to the use of elm (which cannot be tree-ring dated) or unsuccessful tree-ring cores.

Floor joists

Floor joists are set flat in the earlier buildings and average from 6x4 inches (150x100mm) to 7x5 inches (178x125mm). They are commonly produced in pairs by sawing in half the converted tree so that the outer half with any sap wood is to the top and the heart wood at the bottom. This can be clearly seen at 18 Church Street (1428) where an apotropaic mark, applied to the initially converted timber, has been sawn through in the production of two joists. The early common joists were well converted and seldom chamfered or decorated, even in the parlour.

The earliest joint housing for the common joists is the central tenon, as found at 10 East Street (1386), 18 East Street (1357-1393) and 19 East Street (1397). It was still being used at Cavendish House (1422-48), a two bay cross-wing jettied to both front and rear. The Cricketers (1403-29) gives a firmly dated joint of the more unusual profile of central tenon with soffit spur. 7 Church Street (1454) has bare faced soffit tenons

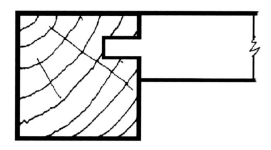

Central tenon

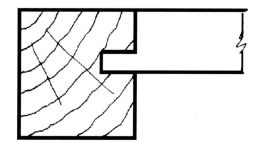

Bare faced soffit tenon

which develop into the soffit tenon with diminished haunch in the 16th century. Unlike other areas of Essex the preference at Coggeshall appears to be for the shouldered central tenon joint that continues through the 16th and 17th centuries.

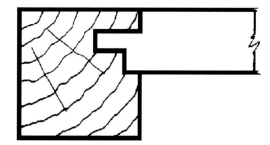

Shouldered central tenon

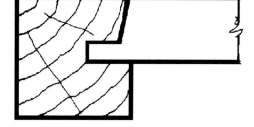

Soffit tenon with diminished haunch

Flat section joists are still being used at 32 and 34 East Street (1585) housed with soffit tenons and diminished haunches. By 1618 at 8 East Street the change has been made to vertical section with soffit tenons. The 17th century also marks the change to the use of more elm for floor joists.

Jetties

6b East Street (1441) and 7 Church Street (1454) have the jetty overhang exposed clearly showing that the joists rest on the jetty plate with the bressumer above. The joists normally have the lower end finished with quarter round ends and are usually supported on brackets to the posts and some of the studs. At 6 and 14 East Street (1435) only the moulded soffit of the bressumer can now be seen but the mid rails and joists appear to be housed into the bressumer as is common in later examples such as 32 and 34 East Street (1585) when carved fascias also become fashionable. 14 East Street also has a jettied gable with moulded tie-beam and it is assumed that many examples of the early framed jetty also had moulded bressumers. At 10 East Street (1386) and 18 East Street (1357-1393) evidence survives for the joists having been pegged to the jetty plate. At 18 East Street they were also housed into it to locate their position. At 6b East Street (1441) the top surface of the joists was rebated to house the bressumer.[5] There seems to be evidence for jetties being underbuilt to create a flat façade as early as the 17th century. This may have occurred at 8 East Street when it was remodelled in 1618, and at 23 East Street when the brick chimney was erected in its present position in the 17th century.

---

5   Further examples of jetties can be found in the study by Richard Harris (1990).

Jetty to the 1441 rear range of 6 East Street

Many jetties have been underbuilt, leaving clues in the floor joists for the position of the jetty plate and bracket

Roofs

The earliest surviving intact roofs consist of paired rafters linked by a collar for narrow spans, or the addition of a collar purlin and crown post for wider spans. Evidence for earlier roof forms, such as scissor braced trusses, survived as reused timbers in rebuilt roofs, such as that at Spooners. As expected some of the early crown posts are four-way braced with minimal curved braces up to 4ins (100mm) thick set at a steeper angle than those of the 16th century that are two-way braced at a slack angle, curved and from 1 inch (25mm) thick. In common with the lack of decoration in Essex buildings, many of the crown posts are of square section, even in the high end cross-wing of 7 Church Street.

East Street with moulded crown post and four way bracing

In the hall of 19 East Street (1397) the crown post is of cross-quadrate form with moulded base whilst at 14 East Street (1435) it is of octagonal section with moulded base and capital. This was clearly a roof structure that was meant to be seen with moulded wall plates, ashlar pieces between wall plate and rafters, and soulaces from collars to rafters, although the timber used is of smaller scantling than normal with rafters 6x3ins (150x75mm). Foot braces occur on the early crown posts in the open trusses at 10, 11, 12 17 and 29 East Street at a similar date to the four-way braced form. Whilst the service cross-wing (Cavendish House) of the White Hart has a plain crown post, the hall has a queen post roof with the octagonal posts having moulded capitals and bases. The queen post form, rare in Essex, is common over a large area of Suffolk. It is interesting to note that most of the cross-wing roofs are gabled to the front and rear rather than the more usual form of a hip with gablet to the rear.

The gradual change to clasped side purlin roof type in Coggeshall can be plotted by the early example for Essex at 18 Church Street where a principal rafter of the long-wall jetty building

Clasped side purlin roof at 5 Church Street

was dated to 1545. 10-12 East Street, where the hall was rebuilt 1552-88, 32-34 East Street (1585) and 23 East Street (1599) are other early examples of the clasped side purlin roof with wind bracing. One of the main advantages of a side purlin roof is that it opens up the attic space, something that would have been appreciated as the attics became used for storage. Further height for storage was gained at 8 East Street (1618) where the tie-beam was dropped down the storey post to below the wall plate. Unfortunately this created later structural problems caused by the lack of an effective tying joint. Additional attic space formed by having a half storey roof at second floor level was to be found at Paycockes (1509). This top storey was later removed but not before it had been echoed by the adjacent building, The Fleece public house.[6] 16 East Street (1636), a rebuilt hall, has a double butt purlin roof with two principal trusses strengthened with arched braces marking the possible position of a dormer or lucam used to load goods into the attic.

Scarf joints

Through the centuries scarf joints change and develop mainly to simplify their manufacture, but they are not always as strong as many of the earlier designs. In Coggeshall scarf joints follow the expected pattern as defined by Cecil Hewett from early splayed types (e.g. Chapel Inn), to edge-halved and bridled ones.[7] This standard form which tended to replace splayed joints from about the middle of the 14th century was still in use at 8 East Street (1618). An early variation with sallied abutments and face peg is found in the rear outbuilding (1397) at 19 East Street. Another variation, with under-squinted abutments, is found in an interesting position on the mid-rail of the rear commercial building to 6 East Street to add a small length to form the jetty. The face-halved bladed scarf is the type most commonly used from the 17th century. It was used in the hall between 10 and 12 East Street built 1552-88. It also occurs at 9 East Street and Flat 2, 14 Market Hill, both 17th century buildings. At 13-15 East Street, a late 16th century or early 17th century building, a housed variety was found.

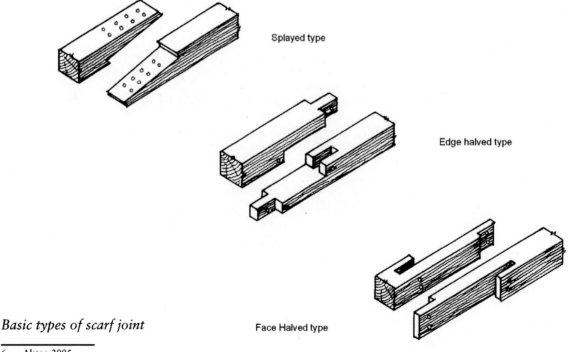

Splayed type

Edge halved type

Basic types of scarf joint   Face Halved type

6   Alston 2005.
7   Hewett 1980.

Windows

Many medieval windows have been destroyed during refurbishment and others are still hidden under plaster, but where there is evidence it is usually for unglazed diamond mullioned windows with shutters. At 19 East Street (1397) evidence survives for moulded mullions to the front hall window with diamond mullions to the rear. Shutters are usually housed into a groove under the wall plate with an applied bearer across the cill and adjacent studs to house the bottom edge. A rare example survives at 6b East Street. Large diamond mullion windows were to be found at the market hall at the Cricketers, and in the rear wing of 8 East Street,

Most early windows would be diamond mullion with no glass but a sliding shutter to cover the window. The slot for the shutter is now often the only clue to a previous window. This 16th century example is from the Great Dunmow Boyes Croft malting before restoration

where light was probably needed for a space being used as a workshop. The upper shutters to the open halls were normally hinged with the lower shutters housed into applied bearers. The rear parlour extension to 6 East Street had a 6ft (1.8m) wide glazed window with moulded mullions of front roll and ogee. At 16 East Street (1636) the wide central window had ovolo mouldings and was flanked by frieze windows of similar design, both features which had appeared in the second half of the 16th century. Glazed windows with ovolo moulded mullions also occur on the rear stair tower to 14 Market Hill and as a secondary feature in the remodelled hall of 6 East Street.

There are a number of shop or workshop windows with evidence for brackets at the corners as at 1 Church Street, but they can also have arched heads or, as at 6B East Street (1441), just be defined by the timber frame.

Stairs

Although there is usually enough evidence to locate the stair position by the survival of a fully framed stair trap formed within the floor joists, the original stairs rarely survive. However a relocated solid tread stair comprising triangular bulks of oak pegged to the side bearers survives in the range to the rear of 6 East Street. At 14 East Street (1435) the front cross-wing is accessed from the truncated older rear range through an arch headed doorway at first floor. The stair position in the front cross-wing of 6 East Street is problematic as the floor joists in the two bay cross-wing are complete. Was access to the first floor gained by a stair in the rear range as at 14 East Street?

A 15th century solid tread stair survives at the rear range of 6 East Street, now restored for normal use

More often the only clue to a stair position is an infilled stair trap as here at the Cricketers. The smaller size timbers to the right are the infill

Chimneystacks and fireplaces

On the west wall of the cross-wing at 14 East Street (1435) there is a stack constructed from tile, brick and miscellaneous pieces of stone. The stone surround to the fireplace has a four-centred arch with foliate carving in the spandrels and attached shafts. A later and simpler stone surround was used for the first floor fireplace to the replacement hall at 6 East Street. A framed opening and later wall plate infill for another early stack were found at 18 East Street (1357-1393), whilst the very elaborately decorated hall of the White Hart still had an open hearth and louver although dated 1422-1448. Although brick was used

The stone fireplace at 14 East Street (1435) and the simpler one associated with the 16th century remodelling of the hall at 6 East Street

briefly in the 12th and 13th century at Coggeshall Abbey, and then became more widely used from the first half of the 15th century, it does not appear to have been used for stacks at an early date in the Coggeshall houses. It is just possible that 23 East Street did not have a brick stack when first built in 1599. 15 East Street contains an interesting brick stack with the remains of lined out or ashlared plasterwork within the hearth area. At the back of the hearth are three openings or 'nostrils', a device thought to improve the draught. This is one of a small group of 'nostril' fireplaces known from central Essex, probably all much the same date and built by the same contractor or group of contractors. At 16 Market Hill (17th century) the first floor hearths in the brick stack have four centred arch openings and typical canted sides to the hearths.

'Nostril' fireplace at 15 East Street

Doors

Whilst the early doors have not survived door openings framed into walls can be found in various positions. At 19 East Street (1397) a four centred arch headed doorway gives access to the parlour, whilst there was an unusually wide arched entrance of 7ft (2.13m) to the cross passage. Another wide arched opening is also found at 11 East Street where it unusually provides access to the rear from the side wall of the cross-wing rather than the usual opposed position. At 14 East Street (1435) the doors giving access from the cross passage to the cross wing have four centred arch heads with moulded jambs and a wide arched opening at first floor gives access to the first floor chamber from the rear range. The cross-wing at 6 East Street has

The two service doors at 6 East Street before restoration with the spere truss opening from the cross passage to the hall clearly visible. The door opening to the left on the service wall is a later insertion

three-centred arched openings serving the service rooms from the undershot cross passage. The adjacent rear range (1441) has a flat headed opening to the shop, and the 15th century range next to it on the south side has external four-centred arch openings. Cavendish House (1422-1448) has flat headed openings for the service rooms which are decorated with applied mouldings to the hall side now in the White Hart. The openings to the rear latrines found at 17-19 East Street (1397) had the usual flat head.

In many instances where studs have been removed there is no indication of door position as the head was dropped and not part of the structural frame. At 7 Church Street a small mortice for a door jamb is the only evidence for the door to the parlour in the back of the high end recess.

Infill

Where infill has been noted it is the traditional style of the area with vertical staves of either riven oak (frontage range of 8 East Street) or rods such as hazel tied back to horizontal wattles fitted into V-shaped nicks, or square or round housings. Prior to the restoration of the rear range of 6 East Street the scratch design on the daub was clearly visible. At ground floor the vertical panels of daub were precisely lined out and then saltire crosses added either in a vertical pattern or placed into squares to provide a key to a skim coat of lime plaster. At first floor the design was more modest consisting of a simple diamond pattern.

Spere or draught screens at 6 and 8 East Street had rebates for board infill with evidence for a horizontal fixing rail at 6 East Street. In both of these properties the spere was part of the side wall of an undershot cross passage whereas at The White Hart the remnant of the spere was defining the cross passage from the hall.

Infill panel at 8 East Street

Paycockes (1509) has original brick infill or nogging between the studs but no evidence for this was found elsewhere in the study area.

Chamfers and mouldings

In most of the buildings simple chamfers with or without stops can be found on the structural timbers. In the earlier buildings such as 6, 8, 18 and 17-19 East Street hollow chamfers are used. At 14 East Street (1435) the wall plates and transverse beam are moulded with a series of hollows, ogees and bowtells with the lower hollows having simple stops. As expected from the mid 16th century lamb's tongue stops are used. They continue into the 17th century when the typical addition of an end notch was found at 25 East Street and 14 Market Hill. 16 East Street (1636) had a mix of quarter round mouldings to the ground floor whilst lamb's tongue stops were used at first floor level where the 3 inches (75mm) wide chamfer was unusually double faced.

Double faced and single faced chamfers both at 16 East Street

Double ogee chamfer at 6 East Street and at 14 Market hill a 17th century lamb's tongue stop with a notch

Decoration, moulding and carving

Coggeshall houses as we see them today, are typical of Essex in being mostly plain, presenting a contrast with the more decorative timber-framed buildings of the North and West of England. The exception is Paycockes, the extravagantly carved timbers of which must have seemed as striking in the 16th century as they do today.

Moulded high end dais beam now visible in rebuilt hall at 5 Church Street but part of the structure of 7 Church Street where it was the outer side of the undershot high end recess

A characteristic decorative feature of some 14th century East Anglian houses was bracing arranged in fan-shaped patterns. The only building in the town where this can be seen externally is the older cross-wing of the Woolpack near the church in Church Street. Bracing that was intended to impress can be seen in the flank walls of halls, for instance two tiers of down braces at 16 East Street, and saltire or X-shaped bracing at Craig Dhu (40 Church Street), the Woolpack and 12 East Street. Serpentine bracing is found in the front of the 14th century Spooners (1353-86) in Church Street. It was also fashionable in the 16th century, and in Coggeshall can be seen in the façade of a house of that date at 53-55 Church Street.

Spooners also has a rare example of decorative carving in the spandrels of the arched heads of the former front door. They are carved with conventional 'daggers' which clasp a trefoil containing a leaf pattern, reminiscent of the foliate carving found in 14th century stonework. The parlour door inside Spooners is one of the two true ogee arches surviving in Coggeshall, a type of arch not found in Essex after *c*.1420.

Wall paintings, be it very simple patterns or more elaborate schemes, would have been common but have not survived. Suggestive but very fugitive traces of paint can be detected for example on the wall of the old hall inside 16 East Street. There are also remnants of a floral design on the wall plate of the cross-wing of 6 East Street where it represents a later decorative scheme related to the later hall.

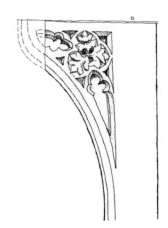

Carved spandrel from the front door of Spooners in Church Street, one half of a 'durn' door made of two pieces of timber

Octagonal crown posts with moulded capitals and bases are to be found in the roofs of one or two of the grander older buildings (e.g. 14 East Street, 1435). Queen posts similarly octagonal with mouldings occur in the White Hart. The presence of a grotesque head with lolling tongue

Carved jetty bracket and top of shaft at 6 East Street

on a jetty bracket at Cavendish House comes as a surprise, because this remarkable three-storey building (originally part of the White Hart) is otherwise totally plain. This type of head is a not uncommon motif, found on church roofs and elsewhere. The jetty bracket here descended into an engaged shaft with a capital. Similar shafts with capitals occur on the truss dividing the ground floor of 14 East Street and the remaining post of its front wall, on the front of the cross-wing at 6 East Street, and on the front of 29 Church Street, a jettied building of *c.*1500. They were a feature of many higher status 15th and early 16th century houses of the cloth working areas of north Essex and Suffolk.

A rare example of richly moulded floor joists can be seen at 13 East Street where, curiously, the timbers have been reused in a 17th century building, their impressive craftsmanship clearly being valued. In contrast are the very simple quarter round mouldings systematically used at ground floor of 16 East Street built in 1636, a moulding that was to become increasingly common in the 17th and 18th centuries.

Decorative fascias and bressumers are an attractive feature of the Coggeshall streetscape. Probably the work of specialist carvers, it would be interesting to know how they interacted

Grimacing head from Cavendish House

with the carpenters. Paycockes House of 1509 is the earliest surviving example and the only planted fascia with carving. This skilled craftsman probably also carved the two repositioned mantel beams inside the house. The fascia is the only one in the town with an 'inhabited' vine trail, although the leaves are varied and include oak. The carving clearly carries messages that are personal to the Paycockes. Thomas Paycocke's initials flank each side of his merchant's mark and are deliberately sited in front of the important parlour. The vine trail motif unifies the fascia and looks back to gothic motifs also found in illuminated manuscripts.

Carving on the façade of Paycockes, from the top: bressumer with vine scroll, with enlarged details below; arch to the blocked doorway to the right of the carriage arch; and figures either side of the carriage arch

Inhabiting the vine trail are grotesques which have a variable parentage with just a hint of Renaissance influence. Thomas Paycocke seems to have wanted to associate himself with the London Weavers Company. The leopard and the rose are long established emblems of the Company's arms. On the left, the trail begins with an upside down ferocious wyvern, and there is another on the mantel beam. In 1611, the wyvern was approved as the supporter of the London Weavers Company arms, but was clearly commonplace before that date. The old spelling of wyvern is closer to weaver; thus it became a kind of trade rebus or visual pun.

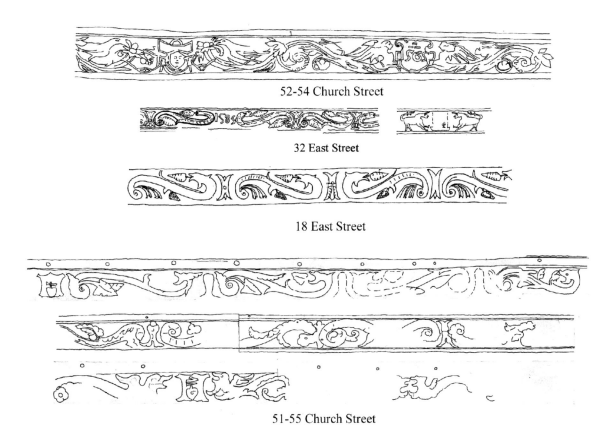

52-54 Church Street

32 East Street

18 East Street

51-55 Church Street

Carved fascias from Church and East Street

Perched on the vine trail is a peculiar bird which might, inaccurately, represent a pelican or a peacock. There are also mysterious human legs and profile heads which are favoured motifs of the period. Some of the grotesques defy interpretation, but they may all contain a message. Paycockes also displays a pair of full length figures carved in the round, located on pedestals flanking the carriage arch. Excellent examples of wooden sculpture, it is possible that they are 'mummers', one being St. George. Above their heads are capitals with pronounced concave cusping, similar to the capitals of the engaged shafts noted above. In one of the spandrels of the blocked door to the right of the carriage arch, there is a pomegranate, the badge of Catharine of Aragon and a motif often found on carved timbers in church roofs.

The decoration at Paycockes is like so many other features of the house quite exceptional, but it can be paralleled at the Marquis of Granby in North Hill, Colchester, a house built a little later in the 16th century by another wealthy clothier, a Mr Webb, where there is also an inhabited vine scroll.

The contrast between Paycockes and the plainness of other houses presumably reflects the high cost of such decorative carving, as well as Thomas Paycocke's image of himself and his standing in the town. However, the bressumers and fascias covering the ends of the floor joists in long-wall jetty houses of the second half of the 16th century were often carved, though in a way that represented a complete break with the tradition of vine scroll decoration found at Paycockes. This later carving made use of a heterodox collection of motifs that could be combined in any manner the carver fancied. But as well as a fondness for decoration, these jetties offered an opportunity for self-expression on the part of the owners or tenants, as merchants' marks, dates and initials are a feature of these carvings. The merchant's mark was treated as a kind of pseudo heraldry, providing status for the mercantile class.

52-54 Church Street has a well preserved bressumer which is usually taken to be a later replica. However the carving is of exceptional quality and seems likely to be authentic. The design may have a graphic source such as a North European mannerist engraving. The date ANO DMI 1565, and initials TC for Thomas Clarke who owned the house in 1575, are placed on shields and there are cornucopias and mannerist faces.

The wyvern, a mythical two-legged dragon which was a popular motif in England and the Continent, is a common feature of other surviving bressumers. It is possible that the Coggeshall wyverns, being so popular, do represent the dwellings of people engaged in the textile trades and are a valuable indicator of their ownership. But it is also possible that they were simply an attractive motif which could be found on anyone's house. The wyvern was a popular and widespread motif in the 16th century. Elsewhere it is found where there were rebus-like connections, as with the rivers Wye and Weaver. The Stockwell Arms in West Stockwell Street, Colchester, has a much eroded three-dimensional wyvern on the capital of its dragon post. It is suggestive that it is in the Dutch Quarter, the weavers' area of the town.

The bressumer dated 1585 at 32-34 East Street is of the standard wyvern design which uses scroll-like forms to provide a linear unity. The wyverns face each other to provide an interesting classical pattern. Towards the right hand side, a pair of unicorns face a much damaged merchant's mark which resembles that of Thomas Paycock. The little that survives shows the Paycocke merchant mark in its bottom right hand corner. This house and 18 to the west were originally one though now separated by an alleyway. 18 has a short length of fascia with similar wyverns.

Bressumer dated 1585 at 32-34 East Street

51-55 Church Street have a very long fascia made up of three pieces which look as if they represent successive phases of rebuilding which are not evident in the structure. The left hand part has a slightly more varied standard wyvern pattern and a shield with a heart-shaped merchant's mark. Then follows a short length of unrelated design based on a scroll-like pattern. The third section at the east end has a quite different and more complex wyvern pattern. Despite missing areas, two shields can be seen. One is a merchant's mark with a similar heart motif overlain with the number 6. The right hand side shield seems to contain superimposed initials but is partly concealed by a later planted timber.

Plan form

The earliest surviving timber-framed buildings identified in the town were aisled. One had previously been found at 45-47 Church Street, outside the study area, where there are the remnants of a two-bay aisled hall.[8] Within the study area, an aisled hall is inferred at 29 East Street and it is suggested that there was formerly a hall with a single aisle to the rear at 12 East Street.

Analysis of buildings depicted on some of the late 16th and early 17th century Walker maps which depict mainly rural situations indicates a high percentage of single storey cottages or in-line hall houses.[9] No surviving examples of either were found within the study area but the presence of in-line houses could be inferred by the pattern of alternate rebuild at 6 and 14-18 East Street, where pre-existing rear ranges have been shortened when one end of an in-line house was rebuilt as a cross-wing. To the rear of 6 East Street is a commercial building of 1441 which appears to have been truncated to allow a later two bay cross-wing to be built. Similarly at 14 a rear range has been truncated for the later and longer two bay cross-wing of 1435. It is also suggested that the existing narrow form of the cross-wing at 18 could be due to the restrictions of the site or an earlier in-line form. Spooners, 30 Church Street (1353-86), is a remarkably complete and interesting example of an in-line hall house with the typical three cell layout comprising floored service or low end, open hall and floored parlour or high end. The cross passage is contained within the volume of the open hall and expressed by the spere truss that creates a narrow bay at the low end of the hall. A central door off the passage gives access to a single service room with the first floor chamber above it apparently accessed by a ladder stair from the hall. The floored high end extended into the volume of the hall creating a recess housing the high end bench which was flanked by draught screens and doors. The door against the front wall gives access to the parlour whilst that to the rear opens onto the stair to the first floor. The high end recess can be echoed in form in a low end cross-wing by the creation of an undershot cross passage. Both of these features are common in urban situations where a compact plan was necessary due to the limitations of plot size. That Spooners has survived and escaped significant rebuilding is almost certainly due to its height, given that the average eaves height of 16th century rural buildings in Ingatestone was 7-9ft (2.1-2.7m) whereas Spooners is 14ft (4.27m) to wall plate.[10]

The characteristic late medieval three cell plan form comprising parlour, hall and services continues with variations and improvements into the 17th century. One of the main improvements was the use of the cross-wing form at the floored ends which gave increased height and more fenestration than that usually available in the flank elevations in an in-line plan.

Two properties, 8 and 10-12 East Street, have been identified as comprising an open hall with a probable single cross-wing form. At 8 the two bay low end cross-wing had an undershot cross passage that gave

8   Stenning 2003.
9   Edwards and Newton 1984.
10   Ryan 2000.

access to two separate rooms with the spere opening to the hall framed by boarded draught screens. At 12 the cross passage appears to have been against the west wall of the two bay hall with the high end cross-wing on its east side. This was of two uneven bays, undivided at both ground and first floor with the longer rear bay housing the stairs. It has been suggested that the hall may have been aisled to the rear to provide the required space for domestic services, the cross-wing at no. 10 being interpreted as a commercial building.

To both the south and north sides of East Street there would have been a striking pattern of gabled cross-wings interspersed with the low hall roofs parallel to the street. Whilst many of these appear to be of hall and double cross-wing or H-plan, none of these houses were originally built like this and instead this streetscape was the result of a process of alternate rebuilding, each element having been replaced on different occasions.

Reconstruction of the south side of East Street in 1575 (D.F. Stenning)

In plan form 17-19 East Street, the Through Inn (1397), is a good example of a hall with two cross-wings or H-plan house. The three bay low end or service cross-wing contained an undershot cross passage of unusual 7ft (2.13m) width. The front bay was a shop or workshop as evidenced by the half arch windows with service use within the rear bays. The stairs were located in the rear bay giving access to the first floor

A similar view of East Street in 2012

with latrine door to the rear wall. The hall is of two unequal bays and trapezoidal in plan constrained by the line of the street frontage. The parlour door, against the front wall leads to the east high end cross-wing which was changed from two to three bays during construction. The stairs were housed in the north-west corner of the separate rear bay giving access to the undivided three bay first floor chamber with latrine door in the north-east corner. A single bay of an outbuilding was interpreted as a contemporary kitchen and its tree-ring date (1397) is thought be valid for the main house.

When viewed externally 14-18 East Street looks like a text book example of an H-plan house but this has been achieved by alternate rebuild which appears to have started with the new high end cross-wing of 1357-1393. In 1435 the low end was replaced by a cross-wing that could be contemporary with the replacement of the earliest hall. Finally this hall was replaced with a full two storey jettied building containing a hall and hall chamber of 1636. Alternate re-building at 6 East Street achieved the urban plan form of a parlour set to the rear of the hall, a plan form favoured in urban settings where the street frontage was restricted.

The low end cross-wings to both 6 and 14 East Street are of two bays positioned to the front of truncated rear commercial ranges accessed from the cross passage. At 6 the cross passage was undershot giving access through the traditional paired doorways to a shop or workshop in the front bay and service bay to the rear. The hall was accessed through the central spere opening flanked by boarded draught screens like the arrangement at 8 East Street. The position of the stairs is not clear and could have been from the truncated rear range. At 14 the cross passage was contained within the hall and access to the cross-wing was through two elaborately moulded doorways into an impressive high ceilinged single space with moulded timbers and a stone fireplace. Access to the first floor is through an arch opening from the rear range. A contemporary cellar, taking advantage of a drop in ground level, is sited towards the rear and was accessed externally.

11 East Street (1404-40) was another low-end cross-wing of three bays with an undershot cross passage and paired doors to the front service rooms. However the passage was interrupted by a door to the rear bay giving access to another room, and also had a wide arch opening to the east rather than an opposing door. The hall and high end have been rebuilt.

Text book examples of medieval house plans show two service rooms entered from the cross passage, with the stairs either in the rear room or also accessed from the cross passage. The examples above and others in Coggeshall show that people were quite ready to adapt this conventional layout to their individual circumstances.

High-end cross-wings do not survive in the same numbers as low-end ones but 7 Church Street (1454) represents a good example of one of three bays with a recessed high end to the parlour of two bays. A comparatively wide stair trap was situated in the rear bay but insufficient evidence meant that means of access and purpose are unknown.

The dates obtained for the insertion of a floor into an open hall (1552-1588, 10-12 East Street) and the rebuilding of an open hall (1636, 16 East Street) give a wide range for the change to the 'closed' house, fully floored with chimney and glazed windows. Within the study area the preference appears to have been to remodel the hall parallel to the street, such as the complete rebuilds at 5 Church Street, 13-15 and 16 East Street, and the roof raises undertaken at 10-12 and 19 East Street. At 8 Church Street the hall was rebuilt in cross-wing form with a gable to the street, an urban feature often found in larger towns. 1636 is a late date for the rebuilding of an open hall to one of two storeys but it is suggested that, as shown by the height of the trapped former hall frame, a previously inserted floor could possibly have been heated by a rear wall stack. The 1636 rebuild at 16 East Street appears to have been prompted at least in part by storage needs.

The long wall jetty building that provided a full two storey form throughout is found in commercial buildings earlier than domestic examples. Dated commercial ranges are those to the rear of 6 East Street (1441), 14 East Street and the semi-detached 15th century shop or workshop range (1 Church Street). Domestic examples that are dated are 18-18A Church Street (1545), 32-34 East Street (1585), 21-23 East Street (1599), and 8 East Street (1618) which appears to be part domestic and commercial. Plan form in some of these buildings could not be fully recorded but appeared to follow the three cell layout with 21-23 East Street soon being adapted from cross passage plan to lobby entry with central door. Two examples of the long wall jetty form, 9 and 25-27 East Street, both of 17th century date, appear to have been built for a commercial use and then adapted to domestic use by the addition of a rear range.

The lobby-entry plan form provides the entrance, stack and stairs as a unit either offset or in the centre of the house as at 2-4 East Street, the entrance being to the front of the stack and the stairs behind it. Here the central stack was flanked by a parlour to the west and hall to the east with kitchen to the rear. Access to the two first floor chambers appeared to be gained by a rear stair tower. This building was modified in the 19th century to form two separate houses with a central passage tunnelled through the brickwork of the stack, something which also happened at 23 East Street.

Commercial buildings

Shops

Shops or workshops contained within domestic buildings are not included as separate entries in the 1575 rental survey. Only three shops are listed in it, two of which are in the triangle study area at 1 Church Street. These consist of a speculative development of two 15th century semi-detached shops/workshops which unfortunately failed to give a tree-ring date. In the absence of documentary evidence, it is unclear how they were used, whether they were entirely commercial or combined that function with residential accommodation, and why there is a variation in the design of the shop windows.

Rear ranges

The surviving buildings span in date from the early 15th century through to the 17th century and range from relatively complete buildings to a single surviving bay. There is a lack of internal features that can be associated with a particular function other than storage, and this means that little can be said about their original use. Most towns have a considerable number of rear ranges to buildings suggesting that many houses were always a combination of living and commercial uses of some kind.

At 18 Church Street a single bay remains of a longer range behind the later long wall jetty house. This bay dated to 1428 had evidence for an external door at first floor and was thought to have been an early commercial building at right angles to the street. It was truncated when the present long wall jetty building was constructed. East Street provides other examples, especially the long range behind 6 where the truncated range of 1441 contains three flat headed shop or workshop windows to the south of the entrance door. A first floor door gave access to the jettied first floor apparently for storage use. To the south is a later building of three bays with a central narrow bay which contained a timber chimneystack. Access to the first floor was in the south bay where the remnants of a re-sited solid tread stair still survive. A contemporary brick sub-basement appears to have had internal access from the otherwise self-contained north ground floor bay and external access from low openings adjacent to the north and south doors. Further ranges continuing to the rear are mainly constructed from reused timber including moulded floor joists, a cambered tie-beam and a coved window head. The most southerly of these buildings is interpreted as a stable.

The rear range to 14 East Street was truncated in 1435 by the new cross-wing which appears to work in conjunction with the rear range as evidenced by the connecting arch doorway at first floor level, with the possibility of the ground floor functioning as a merchant's showroom. The cellar contemporary to the cross-wing may have had either a commercial or service function and was accessed from the rear.

The building of commercial ranges continued through the 16th and 17th centuries. They take the form of either attached rear extensions (10 East Street) or free-standing buildings (33 and 36 East Street and 11-15 Church Street). 9 and 25-27 East Street were both unheated two bay buildings converted to domestic use at a later date by the addition of stacks and rear ranges. Many of the domestic buildings appear to have had mixed uses as evidenced by shop/workshop windows to the front bays. Commercial storage could also have been accommodated either in the roof space or on the upper floor. At 8 East Street (1618) the attic space appears to have been designed to increase storage capacity. 16 East Street has an A-frame roof originally with a front dormer or lucam to provide ease of access for storage. The three storey cross-wing to the White Hart (1422-48) had an unusual framed opening in the joists to the front bay of the second floor which could have facilitated the use of the top storey for storage.

Church Street looking north-east, with the pair of shops at no. 1 in the foreground (Dave Stenning)

OVERVIEW

Before the building of the bypass, when all traffic would have passed through the middle of the town, Coggeshall would have seemed to the traveller to be a straightforward case of ribbon development along a Roman road. The work presented here, based on the reconstruction of the map of the town from the 1575 rental and the analysis of the buildings, shows that to be a simplification. A pattern of north-west to south-east boundaries has been recognised which are of at least Roman origin and probably earlier, and indeed are not at right angles to Stane Street. If the site of the church is of Saxon origin, then it can be inferred that the main settlement focus at the time was also set back from the road, a pattern that can be seen at many other places where the medieval churches are distant from the Roman roads.[1]

A shift in settlement towards the main road and the bridge on the river Blackwater can be attributed to the Cistercian abbey which was founded in the 12th century. The monks took an active interest in the management of the manor and its resources. This is most vividly seen in the cutting of a new channel for the river, leaving its old course, the Back Ditch, as an overflow stream. If the abbey could do this, there is no reason to doubt that they reshaped the settlement pattern at Coggeshall. Evidence for the pull of the abbey and its marketplace can be seen in the way Church Street is aligned on them, cutting across the older topographical framework represented by the pre-existing boundaries.

An early feature of the local topography was the open fields. One of these was Church Field, which occupied the area north and south of the church, and was divided by Church Street (and the stream running down it) into Over Church Field and Nether Church Field respectively. The study of the rental suggests that the house plots in Church Street were set out within the framework of the strips into which the field was divided. If so, then this implies an element of settlement planning, presumably by the abbey. Church Street is densely built up with old houses, and it is there that the oldest types of houses in the town have been identified. It seems to represent an initial phase in the development of the medieval town. However, the stages in which the town developed are not totally clear. There may well have been setbacks too, when it shrank back and there were empty houses and plots, most predictably in the years after the Black Death of 1348.

It is possible to point to parts of the town which look as if they represent discrete phases of development. In Church Street itself, there is a striking difference between the long plots on the south apparently related to the strips in Nether Church Field, and the shorter ones on the north side, confined between the street and the back lane Queen Street, formerly known as Church Lane. The row of very small plots with gardens on the north side of Church Street, at the east end between Vane Lane and the churchyard, look like the building up or infill of a green or early marketplace close to the church.

On the rental map, it is possible to trace a continuous curving boundary running north-south about 60-80m east of Stoneham Street. This looks like the sort of classic S-shaped boundary formed at the side of a medieval field by the ploughman manoeuvring his team of oxen to turn round at the end of the strips. If so, then it marks the western edge of Church Field, and the house plots on the eastern side of Stoneham Street were established between the street and this boundary. The medieval houses on this side of the street are confined to the area between Queen Street to the north and Church Street to the south. Similarly on the west side of the street, the medieval houses did not extend north of the line of Queen Street. Here the rental reveals the existence of a row of house plots which, at about 1½ perches according to the rental, were

---

1   E.g. Bradwell-iuxta-Coggeshall, Stisted, Kelvedon and Witham.

unusually uniform in width, and about half the average width of the plots elsewhere in the town. This looks like an episode of planned development. Interestingly, the buildings in this area today are all post-medieval, suggesting the houses proved under-sized or in 1575 were already old, or both.

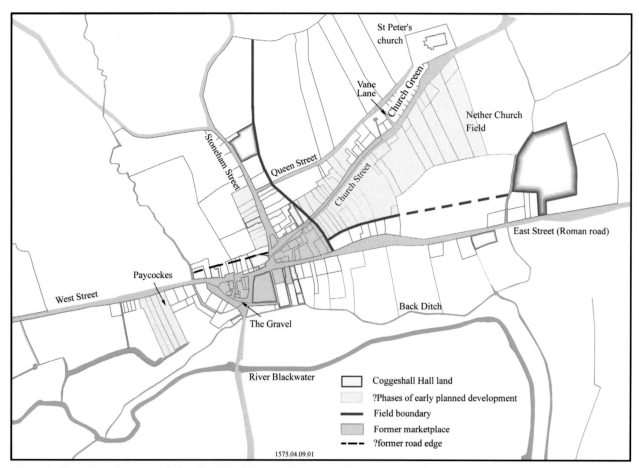

Map to illustrate aspects of the development of the town

The two sides of East Street show the same contrast as Church Street, with long plots on the south side extending to the Back Ditch, and short ones on the north. These shorter plots occur to the east of the probable field boundary described above, the position of which corresponds approximately with the Through Inn (nos 17-19). Their northern boundary forms a continuous line which can be traced as a cropmark running east-west across the recreation ground (Starling Lees), and apparently representing the southern edge of Nether Church Field. The smaller plots on the north side of the road would seem to have been accommodated on roadside waste between this boundary and the side of the road. They can be seen as part of a process of encroachment on the highway which has left East Street very narrow at its western end.

An East Street location brought access to the traffic along the main road and must have been good for business. The buildings at the west end of it were well adapted for commercial purposes. They have wide service cross-wings. No. 10 was probably a wool hall, and there was a row of commercial buildings behind no. 6. The plots on the south side of East Street also had access to the river which could have had advantages for industrial purposes and no doubt explains the presence of a dyehouse here in the area of nos 6 and 8.

West Street west of the Gravel gives the impression of being a peripheral and less densely developed area with later housing. To some extent this is reinforced by the presence of the grandest house in the town, Paycockes, built in 1509. But this occupies the site of an older house plot called Parkers and 14th century pottery has been excavated in its garden. There are several medieval houses beyond it further to the west. The rental map shows Paycockes to be one of a row of four fairly uniform long plots, which look like strips in what had been pasture fields or meadows, a situation comparable to the long plots south of Church Street. The rental also reveals the existence of crofts concentrated around West Street, apparently reflecting a different settlement process at work in this part of the town. This may be an area where medieval settlement had shrunk back from its furthest extent. Houses here had access to fields and water which were useful to merchants and others engaged in the cloth trade. The isolated group of late medieval houses at the west end of West Street near the present nursery can be considered an industrial suburb so located because of the shortage of space in the town centre and the presence of a water source in the form of the Pissing Gutter.

The *Discovering Coggeshall* project was initially focused on the marketplace. Marketplaces in English towns are relatively predictable. They start as large spaces which became smaller as they were infilled, stalls becoming permanent and then replaced by houses and buildings. Less predictable is the way they can shift and expand before contracting again. They can completely disappear and be revived, as happened at Coggeshall where in recent times the market in Stoneham Street was resurrected by the lord of the manor. The infilling process has usually left marketplaces recognisable in town plans because the house plots are small and have very little land attached to them. Marketplaces are most evident today when they were rectangular. When formed around streets and junctions, as at Coggeshall, their shape is less recognisable. Even when irregular in shape, they had to be laid out to a regular plan because otherwise chaos would ensue. Thus stalls came to be arranged in rows, as in modern markets. In Colchester at the St. Dennis' fair, stalls had to be set out along the street, not at right angles to it. In rectangular markets, row buildings can be striking survivals today, as at Saffron Walden and Bury St. Edmunds. To work out the extent of the market at Coggeshall, the clues would seem to be the presence of small plots, of row- type buildings, and commercial or non-standard buildings.

The triangle of land at the junction of Church Street and East Street on Market Hill, west of Swan Yard, was expected to be market infill, and so it has proved. The plots are irregular and the buildings are 17th century or later. The pathway through the cross-passage of the Through Inn (17-19 East Street) from East Street to Church Street, is the sort of feature that might develop where there was a permeable space in a partly infilled market. The eastern limit of the market was probably just beyond the Through Inn, approximately on a line with no. 27 and just before Swan Yard. The Through Inn has been dated to the end of the 14th century, and by this time permanent infill must have been well developed here, extending at least as far west as 11 East Street which is dated 1404-40. Further west, the junction between the two streets was not built up until the 16th and early 17th century. In this area, 9 East Street and 17 Market Hill are identifiable as commercial buildings. A final stage in the infilling of this area was the building up of the frontage on the northern side of it, from 12 Market Hill to 7 Church Street, which did not take place until the 18th and early 19th century.

On the north side of Church Street, the market may at an early stage in its development have occupied much of the southern end of Stoneham Street, before the latter became fully built up. The pair of shops at 1 Church (Black Boy Bistro) at the junction with Stoneham Street look like row buildings which could perpetuate the location of stalls laid out in a spacious market area, but once again the infill process must

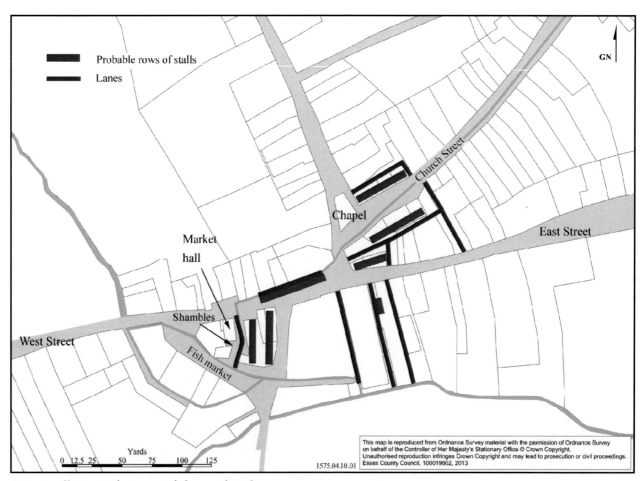

Map to illustrate features of the marketplace

have begun at least in the 14th century. These shops were on much the same alignment as the chapel which once stood in the road at the southern end of Stoneham Street. In the 16th century this building became a market house with a clock and bell tower, and was used for the corn and butter market, with a wool hall at an upper storey. The building was pulled down in 1787.

On the south side of East Street, there is a north-south 'row' of two commercial buildings behind no. 6. The northern one, dated to 1441, was truncated by the construction of a cross-wing and hall on the street frontage. These buildings could be interpreted as vestiges of a market row in this area. To the east of them, there is still a lane, Pettits Lane, from the street down to the Back Ditch. The rental reveals a parallel lane to the west, at what is now 2-4 East Street, on land belonging to the Coggeshall Hall manor. This seems to have linked to the large area of Coggeshall Hall land in Market End, between the White Hart and Bridge Street. This landholding occupied a strategic position in the market area, and suggests that the lord of Coggeshall Hall had acquired rights in this commercially important location in an arrangement with the abbey. Cavendish House (1422-48), the cross-wing of the White Hart, is jettied on both sides. It would be easy to fit it into a row development where initially there had been market stalls.

The most recognisable row buildings in the town are close to each other on the north side of West Street (nos 2-4) and Market Hill (no. 10). These were narrow buildings jettied on both sides, laid out parallel to the street. Their existence implies there were once more of them. Indeed, their alignment is shown continuing to the east on the first edition OS map of 1875, in front of the 20th century shopping parade at Doubleday Corner, where the 1575 rental records two small plots about 1 perch square which were probably row type structures. The presence of these buildings shows that there has been significant encroachment on the street. Opposite them, the irregular shaped block of land between West Street and the Gravel is the site of the market and court hall dated to 1403-29, the former Cricketers, and hence clearly part of the marketplace. Here too there must have been rows, possibly north-south to judge from the existence of Pellory Lane which runs in that direction just to the east of the Cricketers. Historical sources reveal that this was the site of the shambles and fish market, functions that were able to exploit the nearby stream for the disposal of waste, and a reflection of the zoning of trades characteristic of markets.

The marketplace at Coggeshall can thus be shown to have been very extensive, with focal points at the chapel in Stoneham Street and the Cricketers in West Street, but stages in its growth and contraction remain unclear. There would have been many rows of stalls and shops, few of which are identifiable today. Indeed, the 1575 rental only listed three purpose built shops, and the process of infilling with substantial buildings and houses was clearly advanced by the time of the earliest dated buildings in the second half of the 14th century, and largely completed by the later 17th century.

The tree-ring dating programme dated eighteen buildings, a success rate so far not matched in other Essex towns, and a reflection presumably of the existence of relatively abundant timber resources and the local pattern of woodland management. The oldest buildings date back to the second half of the 14th century, and seem to relate to a period of increased prosperity as the local economy, underpinned by the newly flourishing cloth trade, recovered after the Black Death and other crises of the earlier part of the century. The tree-ring dates obtained seem to reflect a building cycle linked to the fortunes of the cloth trade and local economic trends, things which have been most closely studied at Colchester.[2]

In towns, the typical medieval tripartite house plan of parlour, hall and services assumed a variety of forms, adapting when necessary to the more confined conditions. They might be parallel with the frontage with a full tripartite plan or a reduced one with a hall and single end; or the hall might be located behind the frontage buildings, or set at right angles to the street; or a courtyard plan might develop.[3]

In Coggeshall, the houses are all parallel to the street and there is no evidence of them being turned round at right angles to it and accommodated on narrow plots as happened in major cities. No example was found of a hall set behind the frontage. In this, it was typical of small towns with populations of less than about 2000. Spooners in Church Street is a well preserved example of a large in-line house of early date (1353-86). There is evidence for some 14th century houses with aisled halls which as such seem even less urban in character. But the later houses were not as spacious as these and there is evidence for growing pressure on space. A contracted plan, comprising a hall and another unit contained in a cross-wing, was common, and can be recognised as the typical local response to more cramped conditions. The cross-wing was usually a service end with a shop at the ground floor. Halls were compact, sometimes quite small indeed, and to preserve the maximum amount of usable space within them, the cross-passage was usually of the undershot type located within the cross-wing. Such properties might be small, as at 40 Church Street (Craig Dhu, 1387-1423) which seems to have been one of a row of small hall-and-cross-wing houses, probably built for rent, or larger as at 6 and 8 East Street.

---

2   Britnell 1986.
3   See Pearson 2009 for a discussion of medieval urban buildings.

The only examples of houses which did not have halls are the semi-detached pair at 1 Church Street. These were shops, and their limited accommodation raises the question of whether originally they had a residential function at all. They are the only very small houses to be identified in the town, apart from structures which originated as market stalls. As such, the question arises as to whether more modest accommodation actually existed or not. Small one-cell houses survive in large cities such as York and Canterbury, but have not yet been recognised in Essex towns or the countryside before about 1600. Smaller dwellings units could be created through sub-division of larger houses, something for which there is evidence from the 17th century at Coggeshall but which almost certainly had been going on long before. If there were small medieval houses for the urban poor, they have not survived. A hint at their existence can be found in the 1575 rental which records six houses on a plot of John Paycocke at the east end of East Street with frontages only about 1 perch long. These cottages are indicated on a map of 1639 but do not survive. They may have been of recent construction in 1575 and one presumes that they were built to accommodate people who worked for the Paycockes in the textile trade.

One response to the shortage of space in towns was to erect taller buildings, typically on three storeys. Again this was more typical of cities than small towns, but Cavendish House (1422-48), the service end cross-wing of the White Hart, a hall and cross-wing house, has three storeys. This building seems quite exceptional at this period. In the 16th century there is more evidence of taller buildings, sometimes like Paycockes and the Fleece next door with only an attic half storey at the top of the house.

Although reasonable to assume that the cloth industry would have left its trace on the building stock of Coggeshall, there is nothing today like the 'bay and say factory' at Southfields, Dedham, a large courtyard complex of buildings. All the processes involved would have required a great deal of storage space, but as a function this is too unspecialised to have left any distinguishing features. Weaving required looms and good light. Wills indicate the presence of them in shops or workshops, but looms could be assembled and dismantled without leaving any structural evidence for their existence, unlike the peg holes for warp frames that are found in timber studs.

Paycockes is an impressive example of a clothier's house. 14 East Street and the White Hart are possibly other examples. The so-called barn, to the rear of the Chapel Inn, was probably a wool hall, as so too was 10 East Street. 27 and 49 Church Street are peculiar buildings, not fitting the normal residential pattern and hence candidates for having had some manufacturing or commercial function. The two narrow 15th century buildings behind 6 East Street were also commercial or industrial buildings of some sort. 37-41 Stoneham were built in the 17th century originally as a shop or warehouse. The attic storeys at, for instance, Paycockes, the Fleece, 8 and 16 East Street, and 18-20 Stoneham Street, were clearly intended for storage. The relatively large first floor spaces in the service cross-wings could also have provided useful storage space. It is frustrating that this once thriving industry, which brought prosperity to Coggeshall and the surrounding region, should have left so little recognisable architectural evidence today, and that in cases where unusual buildings survive, our knowledge of the manufacturing processes involved is too limited to be able to understand them fully.

With its multi-disciplinary approach, the Discovering Coggeshall project has made it possible to outline a picture of the town in the later Middle Ages which however inaccurate aspects of it may prove to be, should bring it to life for people today as well as serving as a useful base for future research. The documentary sources are what have the most potential for telling us more about the town and its people, but where building work occurs there is an opportunity for learning more about the town's houses and topography.

POSTSCRIPT

Today the centres of historic market towns like Coggeshall may often seem unchanged and unchanging. If that is so, it is because of a planning system which has evolved to ensure their conservation and to manage change in such a way that the character of historic places is not damaged. It is worth remembering that this is something which has happened relatively recently, and what the alternatives are. Indeed, most towns have stark reminders of this, in the form of unfortunate 1950s and 1960s developments. At Coggeshall, Doubleday Corner is such an example. It was dismay at the appearance of such unsympathetic buildings that led locally to action by civic societies and nationally to the introduction of conservation areas from 1967 and to the strengthening of protection for listed buildings.

At Coggeshall, the damage could have been worse. In the 1960s, 32-36 East Street, described as 'a series of very sub standard cottages', were threatened with demolition under a Clearance Order. They were however listed and a Building Preservation Order gave them a reprieve. Braintree Council undertook not to enforce the Clearance Order if the County Council would purchase the buildings and restore them. Listed building consent was granted by the Minister for Housing and Local Government in 1970, and the houses were restored by Birkin and Sons. This initiative was carried out under the County Council's Revolving Funding programme which enabled it to act as a building preservation trust, acquiring, restoring and selling on a series of threatened buildings.[1] If residents and visitors alike find the town an attractive place today, that is due in large part to the commitment of the Braintree District Council and the County Council working together to look after it, and the existence of a planning system that enables them to do so effectively.

Contemporary drawing showing how 32-36 East Street would look when restored

1   Essex County Council 1994.

Reconstruction of market rows in West Street, Cavendish House in the foreground on the left, and the Cricketers in the background (Dave Stenning)

APPENDIX 1

The 1575 rental survey summarised in database format[1]

Ref. no	Forename	Surname	Street	Current house number	Trade	Building units	Land units	Area in perches	Tenure	Rental £
1001	Thomas	Hopper	Market Hill South	14/15/16 and 3 East St. North		2	1	23.19	?	?
1002	John	Dyer	Market Hill South	11/12/13 and 2W Church St. South		1	0	6.82	?	?
1003	Richard	Browne	Church St. South	2E/4/6		1	0	11.09	?	?
1004	George	Lawrence	Church St. South	8/10W	Clothier	1	0	5.96	c.s.	0.13
1005	William	Cock	Church St. South	10E/12W		1	0	8.83	copy	?
1006	John/Geo.	Ansell	Church St. South	12E		1	0	3.69	c.s.	?
1007	House	Alms	West St. South	11W/13, at rear		na	na	8.37	na	na
1008	William	Cock	Church St. South	14/16		0	1	4.8	copy	?
1009	Thomas	Paycocke	Church St. South	18	Clothier	1	0	15.76	?	0.066
1010	Ellen	Scarlett	Church St. South	20		1	0	12.85	copy	0.08
1011	John	Clarke	Church St. South	22E and Lane	Clothier	1	0	20.25	free	?
1012	William	Clarke	Church St. South	22W/24		1	0	24.28	free	0.05
1013	William	Adams	Church St. South	26		1	0	18.05	copy	0.09
1014	John	Pond	Church St. South	28		1	0	22.96	c.s.	0.2
1015	William	Spooner	Church St. South	30		1	1	29.84	copy	0.25
1016	William	Adams	Church St. South	32/34		1	1	36.04	copy	0.2
1017	John	Clarke	Church St. South	36/38		1	0	47.59	copy	?
1018	William	Ridley	Church St. South	40/42		2	0	65.24	c.s.	?
1019	Ellen	Scarlett	Church St. South	44/46		2	0	24.2	c.s.	?
1020	Thomas	Clarke	East St. North	57/59		0	1	45.71	copy	?
1021	Thomas	Clarke	Church St. South	48/50/52/54 and 1/3 Albert Close		2	1	221.01	free	0.22
1022	Thomas	Clarke	Albert Gardens	2 Front Garden		0	1	11.6	copy	?
1023	Thomas	Clarke	Church St. South	56		1	0	9.58	free	0.02
1024	William	Saunders	Church St. South	58/60, at rear	Clothier	0	1	6.68	copy	?
1025	William	Saunders	Church St. South	58/60	Clothier	1	0	7.76	free	0.03
1026	Widow	Trewe	Church St. South	62/68, at rear		0	1	47.16	indent	0.05
1027	Widow	Trewe	Church St. South	62/68		1	0	8.19	free	0.01
1028	William	Till	Church St. South	70	Weaver	0	0	28.96	free	0.04
1029	Hilary	Johnson	Church St. South	76		2	0	10.64	free	?
1030	Thomas	Till	Church St. South	78	Yeoman	1	1	240.76	c.s.	0.5
1031	John	Trewe	Church St. South	80	Clothier	1	1	80.96	copy	0.05
1032	John	Goodaye	Church St. South	82	Fuller	3	1	136.55	indent	0.18
1033	Wylis	Fuller	Church St. South	84		1	0	11.25	free	0.01
1034	Richard	Sammes	Church St. South	84, at rear		0	1	124.47	indent	0.18
1035	Richard	Sammes	Nunns Close	Road entrance		2	0	0	free	0.01
1036	George	Copsheff	Nunns Close	1 West		1	0	28.96	free	0.01
1037	George	Copsheff	Nunns Close	1 East		1	1	24.59	c.s.	?
1038	George	Cockerell	Church Green South	2/4		3	1	242.72	c.s.	0.04
1039	Thomas	Till	Market Hill South	17	Gentleman	1	0	256.56	free	?
								3.13		

1 The information presented here is based on transcriptions of the 1575 rental by Michael Horne and Leigh Alston. It should not be considered definitive: in particular, the names are often not very legible and could be read differently.

Ref. no	Forename	Surname	Street	Current house number	Trade	Building units	Land units	Area in perches	Tenure	Rental £
1040	George	Browning	East St. North	1		1	0	6.37	free	0.05
1041	Building	Church	Church St. North			na	na	37.14	na	na
1042	John	Clarke	East St. North	5		1	0	6.91	indent	0.08
1043	Thomas	Felsted	East St. North	7/9	Barber	1	0	9.26	copy	0.04
1044	Peter	Ryce	East St. North	11/13/15	Clothier	1	0	26.51	free	0.1
1045	John/Geo.	Ansell	East St. North	17/19		1	0	37.58	c.s.	0.6
1046	Mead	Cocke	West St. South	Vineyard, at rear		na	na	453.93	na	na
1047	Mr.	Buck	East St. North	2½/3		2	0	19.8	copy	0.1
1048	Edmund	Hills	East St. North	25/27		1	0	14.9	free	0.02
1049	Robert	Webb	East St. North	29/35/37/39W and Stable		4	0	48.83	c.s.	1
1050	John	Ennewe	East St. North	39E/41		1	0	28.72	free	0.1
1051	Augustine	Crackstone	East St. North	43/45		1	0	20.14	c.s.	0.16
1052	John	Ennewe	East St. North	47/49/51/53		1	0	17.12	c.s.	0.11
1053	Richard	Sammes	East St. North	55		1	0	22.45	c.s.	0.08
1054	William	Fuller	East St. North	59E Stable/61 and Recreation Field		0	2	1167.46	?	?
1055	William	Till	East St. North	1 Parklands	Weaver	1	0	38.44	c.s.	0.1
1056	Richard	Sammes	East St. North	67		1	1	76.57	copy	0.1
1057	Thomas	Ansell	East St. North	65W	Clothier	1	0	21.77	c.s.	0
1058	Master	Smith	East St. North	65 driveway		1	0	30.58	free	0.01
1059	William	Fuller	East St. North	69E/71		1	1	510.7	free	0
1060	Mr.	Longe	Market End South	1-15 and 1 Bridge St. East		na	na	102.59	na	na
1061	Christopher	Wade	Market End South	1/3/5/7		1	1	61.35	?	0.16
1062	Mr.	Longe	East St. South	4		na	na	18.51	na	na
1063	Robert	Litherland	East St. South	6	Clothier	1	1	37.18	?	0.01
1064	Mr.	Longe	East St. South	8 and Lane	Clothier	na	na	30.87	na	na
1065	Thomas	Paycocke	East St. South	8, at rear	Clothier	0	1	10.84	c.s.	?
1066	Yard	Church	Church St. North			na	na	182	na	na
1067	Robert	Revey	East St. South	10/12		1	0	15.52	indent	0.16
1068	Richard	Warner	East St. South	14/16/18W		1	1	76.9	c.s.	0.76
1069	Richard	Warner	East St. South	18E and Lane		1	0	19.64	free	0.03
1070	Richard	Sammes	East St. South	32/34/36		1	1	97.74	free	0.03
1071	John	Ennewe	East St. South	38/40		1	1	99.5	free	0.18
1072	John	Ennewe	East St. South	42/44/46 and ½ Lakes Meadow		0	1	153.46	c.s.	?
1073	John	Cowell	East St. South	52/66 and 3/4/5 Lakes Meadows		0	1	429.27	c.s.	0.23
1074	Thomas	Till	East St. South	58/60/62	Yeoman	0	1	472.48	free	0.23
1075	Thomas	Till	East St. South	64 Telephone Exchange	Yeoman	2	0	30.91	free	0.02
1076	Mr	Longe	East St. South	68/70		na	na	53.7	na	na
1077	John	Ennewe	East St. South	66a/66W		0	1	490.71	free	0.02
1078	John	Paycocke	East St. South	66E/68 Garden	Clothier	6	0	48.1	?	0.1
1079	Thomas	Ansell	Bridge St. East	15/17	Clothier	1	0	34.47	copy	0.18

Ref. no	Forename	Surname	Street	Current house number	Trade	Building units	Land units	Area in perches	Tenure	Rental £
1080	Thomas	Ansell	Bridge St. East	15/17, at rear	Clothier	0	1	3.16	copy	0.22
1081	John	Webb	Bridge St. West	14		1	0	7.2	copy	0.04
1082	Mr.	Buck	Stoneham St. East	46 north, Tilkey Rd. to Jaggards Rd		na	na	634.37	na	na
1083	John	Goodaye	Gravel South	3/5	Fuller	1	0	58.71	copy	1
1084	Henry	Johnson	Gravel South	2aE/3W		1	0	12.94	copy	0.33
1085	Thomas	Paycocke	Gravel South	½/2a	Clothier	1	0	29.55	free	0.054
1086	Thomas	Paycocke	Gravel South	1 Culvert Close and Garden East	Clothier	2	0	34.14	free	0.066
1087	Mr.	Longe	West St. North	20		na	na	16.9	na	na
1088	John	Smith	West St. North	20, at rear		0	1	7.01	copy	0.05
1089	William	Cowell	West St. North	Road entrance Kings Acre		1	0	28.75	copy	0.5
1090	Mr.	Longe	West St. North	18 and Gravel Court West		na	na	13.54	na	na
1091	Barnard	Bishie	West St. North	Gravel Court 1-5 East		1	0	6.95	copy	0.05
1092	John	Borrowe	West St. North	14/16/Lane and Back Land		1	3	869.53	indent	1.66
1093	Richard	Hankins	West St. North	8/10		3	1	12.04	c.s.	0.63
1094	Mr.	Brockman	West St. North	6W		1	0	8.65	free	0.05
1095	Robert	Jegon	West St. North	6E Yard	Clothier	1	0	11.87	c.s.	0.66
1096	John	Carter	Market End North	10W and 2/4 West St. North		1	0	20.22	copy	0.33
1097	John	Bruckhouse	Market End North	8/10E		1	0	10.93	copy	0.46
1098	Richard	Valentine	Market End North	9/10 Doubleday Corner Forecourt		1	0	1.14	free	0.04
1099	John	Litherland	Market End North	7/8 Doubleday Corner Forecourt		1	0	1.22	free	?
1100	Richard	Sammes	West St. South	Gable End 2 Bridge St. East		1	0	6.95	copy	0.5
1101	Henry	Purkis	West St. South	Sub Station		1	0	5.93	c.s.	0.33
1102	Widow	Rand	West St. South	1/3		1	0	20.05	free	0.25
1103	John	Carter	Gravel North	4, at rear	Yeoman	1	0	1	free	?
1104	Widow	Hankins	Gravel North	4		0	1	2.56	c.s.	0.38
1105	Richard	Hankins	Gravel North	Rear of Cricketers		1	0	3.96	c.s.	?
1106	House	Town	West St. South	7E		1	0	5.42	?	?
1107	Shop	Bacon	West St. South	7W		1	0	0.66	indent	0.1
1108	Heugh	Whiting	West St. South	7, car park		1	0	15.14	c.s.	0.21
1109	William	Fuller	Market Hill West	½/3		2	0	22.2	free	0.1
1110	William	Fuller	Market Hill West	5/6/7 and Back Land		3	1	134.46	?	0.05
1111	William	Fuller	Stoneham St. West	29/31/33 Road and Back Land		0	1	273.7	c.s.	0.22
1112	William	Fuller	Robinsbridge Rd. Sth.	Entire Road and Back Land		0	1	708.9	free	0.01
1113	William	Fuller	Stoneham St. West	1		1	0	12.38	free	?
1114	London of	Burrell	Stoneham St. West	3		1	0	9.68	indent	0.6
1115	Thomas	Damat	Stoneham St. West	5		1	0	13.89	free	0.05
1116	Mr.	Longe	Stoneham St. West	7/9		na	na	15.84	na	na
1117	Thomas	Damat	Stoneham St. West	11/13		1	0	16.62	c.s.	0.18
1118	Robert	Damat	Stoneham St. West	15	Fuller	1	0	14.14	free	0.01
1119	Thomas	White	Stoneham St. West	17		2	0	21.72	c.s.	0.01
1120	Thomas	White	Stoneham St. West	19/21/23/25/27		3	0	46.98	free	0.01

Ref. no.	Forename	Surname	Street	Current house number	Trade	Building units	Land units	Area in perches	Tenure	Rental £
1121	Mr	Longe	East St. North	65W/69E		na	na	641.53	na	na
1122	John	Till	Stoneham St. West	37/39/41		1	0	17.82	copy	0.01
1123	John	Till	Stoneham St. West	43/45/47/49/51/53/55/57/59/61/63		0	1	49.79	free	0.01
1124	Edward	Goodey	Stoneham St. West	65/67	Fuller	1	0	10.75	free	0.03
1125	William	Cole	Stoneham St. West	69/69a		0	1	15.2	copy	0.03
1126	John	Till	Market Hill East	10		1	0	18.26	free	0.1
1127	Thomas	Paycocke	Market Hill East	7/8/9	Clothier	1	1	31.74	free	0.03
1128	Free	School	Stoneham St. East	2/4/6		1	0	20.64	?	0.11
1129	Thomas	Clarke	Stoneham St. East	8/10		2	0	12.64	free	0.03
1130	George	Tayller	Stoneham St. East	12/14		1	0	31.75	free	0.05
1131	William	Clarke	Stoneham St. East	16/18/20	Clothier	1	0	34.78	free	0.05
1132	John	Farthinge	Stoneham St. East	22		1	0	13.66	?	0.05
1133	William	Saunders	Stoneham St. East	24/26	Clothier	1	0	13.12	free	0.05
1134	William	Lewis	Stoneham St. East	28 and 3-25 Queen St. North		2	3	1163.67	c.s.	0.95
1135	Humfry	Lyllie	Stoneham St. East	30/32/34/36		2	0	56.61	?	0.23
1136	Mr	Longe	Stoneham St. East	38/40/42		na	na	113.59	na	na
1137	John	Hardinge	Stoneham St. East	44		2	1	8.17	copy	0.13
1138	John	Till	Church St. North	1W		1	0	0.6	free	?
1139	Richard	Browne	Church St. North	1E		1	0	0.63	?	na
1140	George	Lawrence	Church St. North	3	Clothier	1	0	5.26	?	?
1141	John	Guyon	Church St. North	5/7	Fuller	1	0	5.55	free	0.05
1142	Mr.	Longe	Church St. North	9/11/13		na	na	29.22	na	na
1143	Richard	Sammes	Church St. North	15		0	1	23.14	c.s.	0.03
1144	Robert	Clarke	Church St. North	19		1	0	27.07	c.s.	0.01
1145	William	Saunders	Queen St. South	21	Clothier	0	1	145.46	c.s.	0.16
1146	William	Saunders	Church St. North	23/25	Clothier	1	0	27.97	free	0.03
1147	William	Saunders	Church St. North	27/29	Clothier	2	0	16.4	free	0.05
1148	John	Saunders	Church St. North	31	Clothier	1	0	8.38	free	0.01
1149	John	Clarke	Church St. North	31, Driveway		1	0	7.35	na	?
1150	John	Clarke	Church St. North	33		1	0	16.08	free	0.01
1151	Nicholas	Chefer	Church St. North	35/37 Driveway	Clothier	1	0	18.97	free	0.05
1152	Nicholas	Chefer	Queen St. South	30E	Clothier	0	1	5.73	c.s.	?
1153	Thomas	Cobs	Church St. North	37E/39		1	0	17.84	free	0.02
1154	Thomas	Cobs	Queen St. South	30/32/32a		0	1	17.18	c.s.	?
1155	Thomas	White	Church St. North	41/43		1	1	28.42	free	0.01
1156	John	Goodaye	Church St. North	45/47/49 and 36-40 Queen St. North	Fuller	1	1	69.75	free	0.01
1157	George	Cockerell	Church St. North	51/53/55		1	1	13.89	free	0.06
1158	John	Goodaye	Queen St. South	57/59	Fuller	1	0	10.48	free	0.03
1159	Mr.	Smyth	Church St. North	61W		1	0	8.18	free	0.05
1160	Thomas	White	Church St. North	61E/61a/63		1	1	44.11	free	0.03

Ref. no	Forename	Surname	Street	Current house number	Trade	Building units	Land units	Area in perches	Tenure	Rental £
1161	Pond	Church	Church St. North	65		0	1	50.76	?	?
1162	George	Cockerell	Church St. North	67/67a/67b/67cW		0	1	11	indent	0.01
1163	Robert	Jegon	Church St. North	67cE and Vane Lane West	Clothier	1	0	9.6	free	0.01
1164	Robert	Jegon	Church St. North	Vane Lane East (pavement)	Clothier	?	?	10.43	c.s.	?
1165	John	Sutton	Church St. North	69	Weaver	1	0	20.36	free	0.01
1166	John	Sutton	Queen St. South	Rear 69 Church St. North	Weaver	0	1	7.25	c.s.	0.05
1167	William	Graye	Queen St. South	Rear 71 Church St. North	Weaver	?	?	5.02	free	0.01
1168	William	Graye	Church St. North	71	Weaver	?	?	12.31	copy	0.02
1169	John	Borrowe	Church St. North	73		1	0	10.86	free	0.02
1170	John	Borrowe	Queen St. South	Rear 73 Church St. North		?	?	5.82	copy	0.02
1171	Thomas	Symon	Church St. North	75/77	Weaver	1	0	8.17	free	0.01
1172	John	Hatch	Queen St. South	46a		0	1	3.98	copy	0.02
1173	Richard	Sammes	Church St. North	79/81/83		2	0	14.52	indent	?
1174	Robert	Jegon	Church St. North	85/87	Clothier	1	0	9.52	free	0.01
1175	Robert	Jegon	Queen St. South	48/50/52W	Clothier	0	1	12.79	c.s.	?
1176	George	Copsheff	Church St. North	89		1	0	7.09	free	?
1177	George	Copsheff	Church St. North	91		1	0	10.1	free	?
1178	George	Copsheff	Church St. North	91 Car Park		2	0	11.71	free	0.01
1179	George	Copsheff	Queen St. South	52E and Car Park		0	3	18.25	c.s.	?
1180	Robert	Jegon	Queen St. North	79/89	Clothier	0	2	444.01	c.s.	0.16
1181	Thomas	Paycocke	Queen St. North	53-75	Clothier	0	2	365.42	c.s.	0.16
1182	Robert	Jegon	Queen St. North	49-51	Clothier	1	1	280	c.s.	0.125
1183	John	Goodaye	Queen St. North	33-37 and 6/7 Gardeners Row	Fuller	0	2	550.19	c.s.	0.33
1184	William	Clarke	Queen St. North	27 and 1-5 Gardeners Row	Clothier	0	2	292.8	c.s.	0.16
1185	Thomas	Paycocke	West St. South	37W	Clothier	1	0	6.88	copy	0.3
1186	Mr.	Hollyer	West St. South	39E		1	0	6.04	free	0.01
1187	Thomas	Paycocke	West St. South	39	Clothier	1	0	6.18	free	0.01
1188	Thomas	Paycocke	West St. South	39W	Clothier	0	1	3.91	copy	?
1189	Thomas	Paycocke	West St. South	37		2	1	210.94	?	0.26
1190	Thomas	Paycocke	West St. South	31/33/35	Clothier	3	1	63.69	indent	0.32
1191	Thomas	Paycocke	West St. South	29	Clothier	1	0	54.9	free	?
1192	Thomas	Paycocke	West St. South	27	Clothier	1	0	63.06	fee farme	0.166
1193	Thomas	Paycocke	West St. South	11-65, at rear, Mead to Back Ditch	Clothier	0	2	1069.35	fee farme	0.25
1193	Thomas	Paycocke	Bridge St. West	14 Driveway and Back Land	Clothier	R	R	R	R	R
1194	John	Bacon	West St. South	Brian Tebbit's Garden W/11E		1	0	18.77	free	?
1195	John	Bacon	West St. South	Brian Tebbit's GardenW/11E at rear		0	1	26.35	copy	?
1196	William	Cheer	West St. South	11W/13/15/17/19E		1	0	22.23	free	?
1197	John	Paycocke	West St. South	19W/2½3	Clothier	1	0	25	free	0.03
1198	John	Paycocke	West St. South	25	Clothier	1	0	82.57	free	0.25
1199	John	Paycocke	West St. South	15/17/19/2½3, at rear, Garden	Clothier	0	1	19.27	copy	0.01

Ref. no	Forename	Surname	Street	Current house number	Trade	Building units	Land units	Area in perches	Tenure	Rental £
1200	John	Marsh	West St. South	43/45/47		1	0	21.48	c.s.	0.2
1201	Henry	Ennewe	West St. South	49-65 and Vineyard	Weaver	1	1	754.23	copy	0.06
1202	Thomas	Paycocke	West St. South	Vineyard, new	Clothier	1	1	284.86	fee farme	0.06
1203	John	Saunders	West St. South	Vineyard, new	Clothier	1	1	82.73	free	?
1204	Thomas	Warner	West St. South	Vineyard, new		1	1	83.36	free	?
1205	William	Wetherson	West St. South	85		1	0	15.44	copy	?
1206	Richard	Hankins	West St. South	87		1	1	217.53	copy	?
1207	John	Tourner	West St. South	89		1	0	19.44	free	?
1208	Charles	Belfield	West St. South	91/93/95E		1	0	19.95	free	?
1209	Thomas	Warner	West St. South	95W-103		1	0	22	c.s.	?
1210	John	Goodaye	West St. South	105/Pine shop	Fuller	1	0	20.56	free	?
1211	Richard	Ray	West St. South	Nursery East		2	1	467.78	indent	0.26
1212	John	Pursey	West St. South	Nursery West		0	1	88.61	indent	0.61
1213	John	Paycocke	West St. South	123/125	Clothier	0	2	1041.32	?	0.05
1214	John	Pursey	West St. South	127/129/Football Field		0	1	1735.95	?	0.62
1215	Cudboard	Wall	West St. North	Not on map		0	0	0	free	?
1216	John	Paycocke	West St. North	Field	Clothier	1	2	820.67	?	0.2
1217	John	Paycocke	West St. North	Field	Clothier	0	1	122.4	c.s.	?
1218	John	Paycocke	West St. North	Field	Clothier	1	0	38.08	free	?
1219	Richard	Hankins	West St. North	Field		0	1	20.39	c.s.	?
1220	Thomas	Ansell	West St. North	Garden and Lawn	Clothier	0	2	954.27	?	?
1221	Thomas	Ansell	West St. North	104/106	Clothier	1	0	79.77	c.s.	?
1222	John	Paycocke	West St. North	108/110	Clothier	1	0	44.24	copy	?
1223	Mr.	Longe	Market End North	Doubleday Corner 1-10		na	na	35.15	na	na
1224	House	Church	Church St. North	Church Yard West		na	na	4.46	na	na
1225	Old	Chapel	Market Hill West	Flower bed roundabout		na	na	10.69	na	na
								23767.9		23.577

Notes

Tenure	?	Not recorded
	na	Not applicable and not within the rental survey.
	c.s.	Convent seal
	free	Freehold
	indent	Indenture
	copy	Copyhold
Rental		In whole and decimals of a pound. Originally in £ s d
	?	Not recorded
	na	Non Applicable and not within the rental survey.
All	R	Repeat entry, two frontages
Building units		Includes all individual buildings recorded. Examples include, tenement, cottage, shop, school, town house, stable, barn and dovehouse.
Land units		Includes all separate land and open spaces recorded except for gardens when recorded with a building. Examples include, stand alone garden, yard, pond, mead, pasture, orchard, parcel of land, close and croft.

1 Church Street[1]

Brenda Watkin

The building

Despite the removal of walls and partitions the plan and form of the building can still be readily understood. It consists of two self-contained shop units each with an upstairs room jettied to the front facing Church Street. This form of a long-wall jettied building is much favoured for rows of shops in towns. The building is constructed from well converted oak in the traditional close studded style of the area, with tension braces expressed externally. At first glance the units appear to be a mirror image with the entrance doors against the central division flanked by two shop windows. However, with closer study, it becomes evident that internally the western unit would be 21ft 6in. x 10ft 6in. (6.50m x 3.32m) and the eastern slightly larger at 21ft 6in. x 11ft 0in. (6.50m x 3.35m). The additional length is only really noticeable by the use of an additional pair of rafters in the roof construction. The main difference is in the treatment of the shop windows as the western one is undivided, i.e. from corner post to door jamb, whilst on the eastern side a central stud defines two shop windows.

---

1   This account of 1 Church Street is an edited version of one published by Brenda Watkin in *Essex Archaeology and History* vol. 35 for 2004.

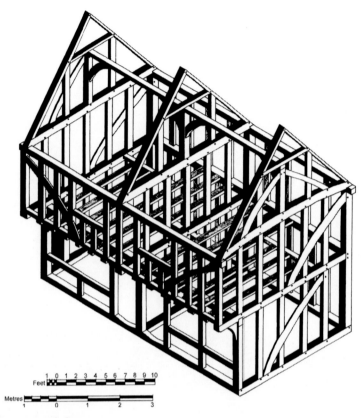

The timber frame of the pair of shops

The timber frame of the pair of shops

The wall studs to the flank walls and central dividing wall average 6-6½ inches (150-165mm) wide by 4 inches (700mm) deep and are placed at 2ft 4in. (710mm) centres. The rear wall is of similar size studs at 1ft 6in. (450mm) centres. There is a tension brace, trenched externally, falling from the corner post on the western flank wall. However on the eastern wall the brace starts at the first stud leaving a gap of 2ft (610mm) that could have been used as an entrance for goods. A narrow 'coffin' door is frequently found on the front elevation of Essex shops.[2] It would allow goods to be taken into the rear area of the shop or, depending on the direction of the stair, directly upstairs if this was being used as a workshop. It also provides a clue to the layout of development within the town as it implies that there was a passage on the eastern side whilst there was continuous development to the west. The end wall frame of an adjacent building is visible on the west side of the ground and first floors where studs have been removed, and in an upstairs cupboard daub panels are visible. The daub is applied to vertical riven oak staves and where there has been a repair, hazel rods are used. This frame is the only remnant of the property between the Black Boy and Market Hill, which according to Beaumont's *History of Coggeshall* was known as the Corner House in 1708. The building was recorded in the Royal Commisson on Historical Monuments survey of Essex (May 1914) and described as an L-shaped building of timber construction jettied on both fronts. A note that at the corner there was a mitre beam taking the joists of the overhang on both fronts suggests that there was a diagonal dragon beam at the corner, indicating the ranges were contemporary.

2   Cf. Stenning 1985.

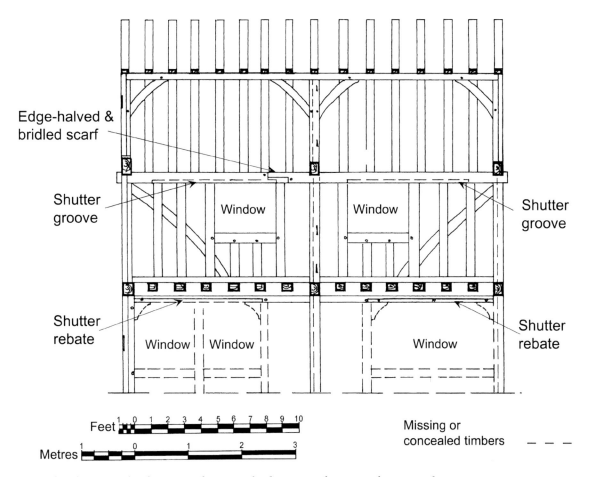

Longitudinal section looking south towards the street frontage from inside

Common floor joists are flat section and average 7½ inches (190mm) wide by 4 inches (100mm) deep at 1ft 9in. (530mm) centres, jettied to the front, with no intermediate brace support, and housed into the rear midrail with central tenon joints. The midrails and central transverse beam are of similar width but 9 inches (230mm) deep. The 5 inches (125mm) wide by 4 inches (100mm) deep trimmer for a stair trap is housed into the side midrails and the fourth common joist. This provided an opening for a solid tread or ladder stair in the rear corner furthest from the door giving access to a single first-floor room

On the ground floor, the jetty plate, 7½ inches (190mm) wide by 8 inches (200mm) deep, is exposed internally and mortices are visible for the door jambs, leaving central door openings of 2ft 6in. (750mm). A stud is placed centrally between the eastern door jamb and corner post forming two window openings that have braces, with angled entry, to the outer corners only. The western window also has braces to the outer corners but no central post. A rebate, 2 inches (50mm) by 2 inches (50mm), is cut into the lower internal face of the jetty plate running from the corner posts to the door jambs of each unit for shop shutters. Evidence has been found in Saffron Walden for a hook fixing that would have held the hinged shutter open during trading hours, but in this instance, although the underside of the floor joists contained many nail holes, a fixing position could be not identified. Externally, the plate was chamfered to the inner face of the western corner brackets and from the eastern corner brackets to the central post, emphasising the window openings.

The first-floor rooms were each lit by a window in the southern elevation to Church Street, with shutter grooves in the underside of the wall plates. As modern windows have been inserted into the original openings, it was impossible to determine the profile of the mullions. The front wall plate is two lengths of timber joined by an edged-halved and bridled scarf, whilst the rear wall plate is one timber 24ft (7.3m) long. There is no evidence that the rooms were heated and no signs of smoke blackening on the timbers. They may have been used for storage although Brian Ayers found in his statistics for Norwich that 30% of upstairs rooms were used for working with 50% used for sleeping. The problem of interpreting buildings without fireplaces is also discussed by J. T. Smith.[3] The studding of the rear wall at first-floor level is at 710mm (2ft 4in.) centres, consistent with that of the flank walls. Were the closer studs on the ground floor a statement of status, or purely a practical way of giving more support to the rear midrail that had been weakened by the mortices cut for the common floor joists? Tension braces, falling from the corner posts, are trenched into the external face of the studs to the flank and front walls where the studs are again at the closer spacing of 1ft 6in. (450mm). The bay divisions are marked by unjowled posts; the tie-beams to the western side wall and central bay are flat whilst that in the eastern wall has a slight camber.

The roof is of typical paired rafter, crown-post construction with the braces 3in. (75mm) in width. The rafters have sawn faces internally showing that two have come from one tree rather than in earlier buildings where one rafter equates to one tree. It appears that the changes to the method of conversion take place after the Black Death due to the lapse in the regular management of the woodlands. The date accorded to the building in the list description is late 15th-century and the style of carpentry and the conversion of the timber are compatible with a mid to late 15th-century date. Three cores taken from the building failed to give a tree-ring date.

History

In the 1575 rental, there is a marginal note that John Till, owner of the southernmost property on the east side of Stoneham at the Church Street junction, also had two shops in Church Street. However, the rental's account of the properties at the corner of Church Street and Stoneham (or what at this point is the corner of Market Hill and Church Street) is not very clear, and in the analysis of it for the purposes of constructing the map, the two shops have been identified as belonging to John Till and Richard Browne. The shops are on a cramped site with very little adjoining land, a typical indication of market infill, and it is likely that they originated as a row

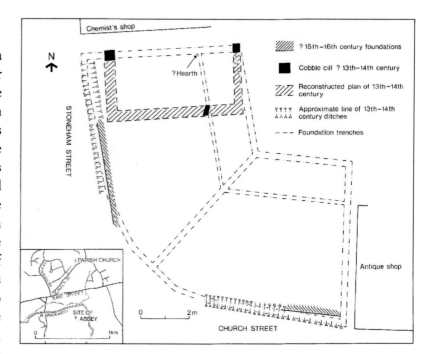

Interpretation of archaeological features seen at the corner of Stoneham and Church Street when the site was rebuilt. The antique shop is no. 1 Church Street, now a café

---
3   Ayers 1994; Smith 1992.

of stalls built in the street and later rebuilt in the more substantial form in which they are found today. Inspection of the foundation trenches for the construction of the existing building to the west of no.1 Church Street in the 1980s suggested that there was evidence for roadside ditches along Stoneham and Church Street, possibly with wooden revetting to the their sides. The ditch in Church Street seemed to have been filled in when the shops at no. 1 were built.[4]

Documents relating to 1 Church Street consist of wills, indentures and conveyances relating to The Corner House, The Black Boy sometimes called Plough and Sails, Argentum Antiques, and also a building to the east in Church Street.

The will of John Shetelworth, baker, dated 29 May 1758 and proved 10 October 1761 left to his son, Henry Shetelworth, baker, several messuages and tenements near the Market Place and in several tenures. Unfortunately none of the property is named. The will of his son, Henry Shetelworth, dated 16 December 1803 and proved 25 January 1804, left property divided between his brother-in-law, John Wright of Feering, farmer, son-in-law John Durrant of Great Coggeshall, collarmaker, and son-in-law John Adams of Finchingfield, farmer. The first property was known by the name of The Black Boy and included outhouse buildings, '*butters*', stables, yards, gardens and premises in Church Street and then in the tenure of John Seex. Another property mentioned adjoined the Black Boy 'on the part of the west' in Church Street and comprised two tenements in the tenure or occupation of Robert Furlong and John Rainer.

The Tithe Award for Great Coggeshall dated 7 March 1854 recorded the landowner of the Black Boy Public House as John Richmond and the occupier Reuben Smith.[5] During the late 1800s there were several conveyances of the property called the Black Boy within a very short period, with yearly leases on the property. For a period up to March 1889 it was owned by Messrs Beard and Bright who were brewers in Coggeshall. In 1896 the property was conveyed by Messrs. T. J. Adams of the Halstead Brewery to the Stamford Hill Brewery. By 1898 it had passed from Stamford Hill Brewery to The Brewery Stratford, and then from Mr. Fred Keep, Black Lion, High Street, West Ham to Mr. H. J. M. Simmons, draper. No doubt the fact that there were about twenty inns and beerhouses competing for custom played a significant part in the demise of this public house, and provided an opportunity to Mr. Simmons (Simmons Bros. general drapery and millinery store was already in existence in Church Street in 1886, as noted in *The Coggeshall Year Book*). In February 1913, when Mr. Simmons had moved to Ramsgate, the property was conveyed to Mr. S. Simmons of Halstead, gent. A photograph, attached to the original Inspector's report, taken at the time of the Royal Commission on Historical Monuments survey of Essex in 1914, shows that the building was then occupied by the Colonial Meat Stores. When Mr. S. Simmons died on 26 March 1918, his niece, Susanna Annie Tyler, inherited the property and it was sold to the Smith family in whose ownership it remained until it was sold in 1994 to Mrs. Diane Carr.

Discussion

Limited documentary evidence gives an insight into the use and owners of the building during the 19th and 20th centuries. Unfortunately it does not give any insight into the original use, owners and tenants that would further the understanding of how this building functioned in terms of trade and use of the upper floor. However, in plan type, it conforms to the standard type of small shop unit that was being built and rented out as a commercial speculation. Its form is the natural progression from the temporary market stall

---

4   Andrews 1987.
5   Essex Record Office D/CT 87.

and represents the first phase of permanent shop building. The long-wall jetty form of the building is typical of many urban examples, and in Essex can be found in the rear range to 6a East Street, also in Coggeshall, and 13-15 (formerly Bonds), North Hill, Colchester. The arch headed shop windows, so often depicted in early manuscripts, still survive in some instances and examples can be found at the Woolpack in Coggeshall and in towns such as Saffron Walden and Lavenham. However, the shop window defined by corner braces, as at 1 Church Street, Coggeshall, and the flat heads to the rear range of shops at 6a East Street, Coggeshall, are equally common. The purpose of the different styles is obscure but other examples of the corner braced shop windows have been noted at the George Hotel, High Street, Colchester, and The Village Shop, Lexden, in unpublished drawings by Richard Shackle. Why in this instance was there also the need to provide a single wide opening to the western unit whilst the eastern unit had a divided opening? Was this to make for a more flexible speculative development or were there already tenants and trades in view? What is certain is that this building represents a rare survivor of the type of medieval shop defined by David Clark in his article as A2a and on a par with rows of shops such as are to be found in York, London and Oxford. [6]

The crown post roof

---

6 Clark 2000.

5-7 Church Street

Brenda Watkin and Elphin Watkin

Introduction

5-7 Church Street comprises two main phases of build, a high end cross-wing gabled to the street and a later two storey hall/service range, parallel to the street, that replaced the original open hall. The ground floor of the front elevation contains modern windows and shop fronts whilst the jettied first floor has exposed timber-framing. The cross-wing was one of the buildings to be successfully tree-ring dated with a firm terminal date of 1454 spring. A core taken from a common joist gave the terminal date with other cores giving a range of 1444-1482. Although cores were taken from the later hall these were not successful. Its carpentry suggests a date in the first half of the 17th century.

The cross-wing (7 Church Street)

The cross-wing is constructed of well converted oak in the typical close studded style of the area with external trenched braces of Colchester type i.e. from vertical to vertical instead of vertical to horizontal. The storey posts are unjowled, a feature that has been noted around Colchester and the coastal area of Essex and in more than one building in Coggeshall. Jettied to the front it is of three unequal bays totalling 28ft 8ins (8.76m) in length and 15ft 6ins (4.7m) wide with a jetty overhang of 1ft 7ins (0.5m) supported on three brackets. There is not a central bracket in this instance as it appears to have been positioned to the left side of a window. A fully studded partition divides the rear bay from the front two which have supporting braces to the transverse beam. Evidence survives in the form of open mortices in two in-line common joists for a high end recess intruding into the ground floor of the front two bays with a door at the north end giving access to the parlour. The evidence for this is the small mortice for a door jamb against the transverse partition wall. The midrail to the hall, across the recess, is moulded with the following elements: hollow chamfer, bowtell, step and bottom hollow chamfer. There is evidence for a pegged bracket at the north end of the recess but the south end is covered. The average size of the common joists is 7½ x 5½ins (0.19 x 0.14m) and they are unchamfered with bare faced soffit tenon housings. The south transverse bridging joist is 10 x 11ins (0.25 x 0.28m) with chamfers and run-out stops. It is shouldered and housed into the storey post. In the rear bay, against the partition, a 3ft 7ins (1.10m) wide stair trap is framed into a common joist. Unfortunately, due to later changes, its length could not be determined. As the partition between the parlour and rear bay appeared to be fully studded, access to the rear bay is uncertain. Many of the studs to the side and rear walls have been replaced but the position of a window could be determined in the central bay against the south storey post. The rear wall appeared to be fully studded with one trenched brace falling from the west storey post to the mid rail.

At first floor level the division of the three bays is as the ground floor with most of the internal surfaces covered. The front two bays were lit by a window to the gabled front and another to the east side above that to the ground floor. The rear bay has one window to the west where the cross-wing overran the hall; as its east side has been rebuilt, no evidence survives there. The west wall plate is joined with an edge-halved and bridled scarf.

The roof is of typical undecorated crown post construction with narrow axial braces, collar purlin, paired rafters and collar. Unlike the majority of cross wing roofs in Essex both the front and rear elevation are gabled. The inner crown posts only have an axial brace to the front.

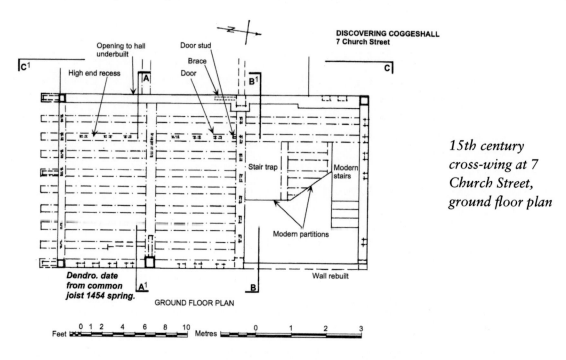

15th century cross-wing at 7 Church Street, ground floor plan

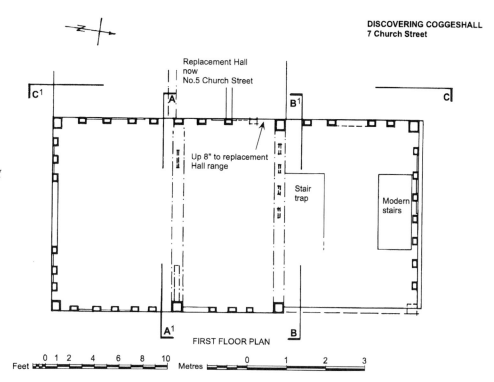

15th century cross-wing at 7 Church Street, first floor plan

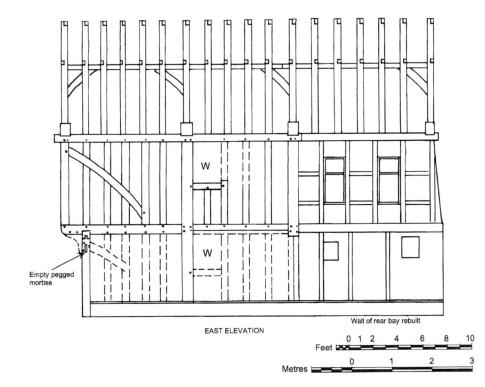

15th century cross-wing at 7 Church Street, east elevation

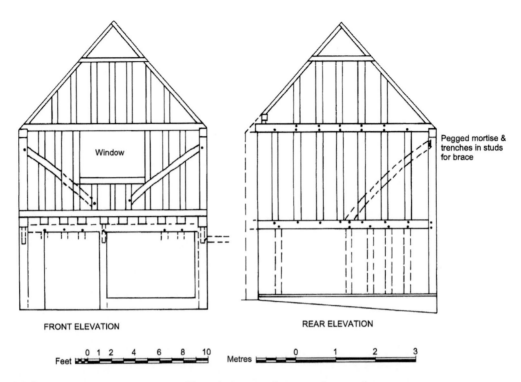

15th century cross-wing at 7 Church Street, front and rear elevations

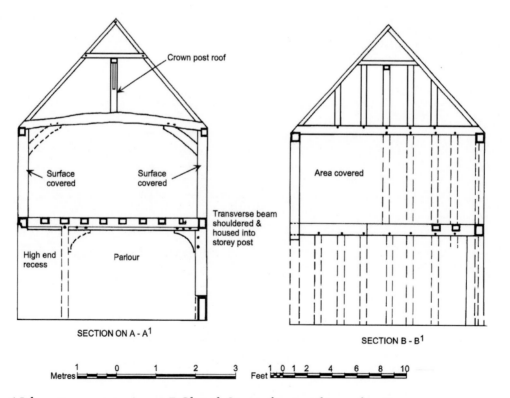

15th century cross-wing at 7 Church Street, front and rear elevations

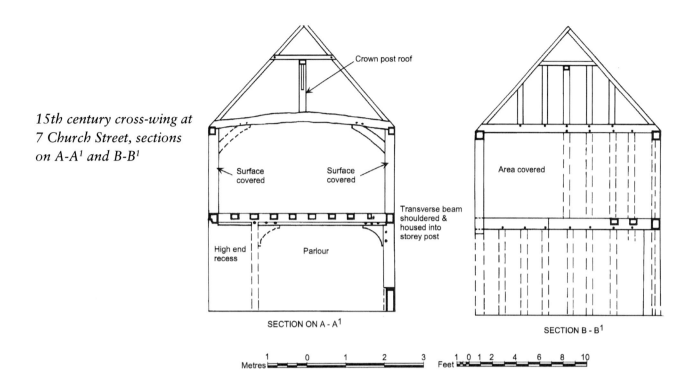

15th century cross-wing at 7 Church Street, sections on A-A¹ and B-B¹

15th century cross-wing and rebuilt hall at 7 Church Street, section C-C¹

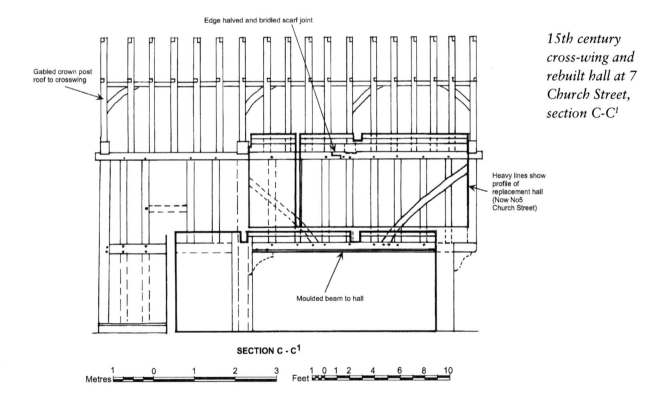

The rebuilt hall (5 Church Street)

The replacement to the original open hall and service end at 5 Church Street measures 24ft 0ins x 15ft 6ins (7.3 x 4.7m) wide internally, is two storied, and of two bays with open frames to both the east and west ends. It is constructed from oak, elm and reused oak possibly from the demolished hall. Oak is used for the main frame, external studs and main axial beams with the common joists and transverse beams of elm. The rear wall of the first floor has reused oak studs and the inserted ceiling joists and most of the roof is elm. The front is jettied continuing the line of the cross wing although the joist ends are covered with a moulded bressumer. Oak studs to the first floor on the street elevation have chiselled carpenter's marks in the usual Roman numeral form with number nine as a V (five) with an additional down stroke rather than IX. A brick stack is positioned to the east of the central truss in the hall but it is not defined by a stack bay. There appear to be doors in both the rear and front elevations of the ground floor with that to the rear positioned against the west wall of the cross-wing. A gap in the peg holes of the front jetty plate, against the west open frame, represents another. Due to the changes to the front wall only part of a small window to the east of the central post is visible. Evidence for small windows in the rear wall of each bay is visible and a large window as evidenced by the wider gap in the studding to the front wall of the west bay. It would appear that the two bays were minimally divided by the brick stack thus forming a hall 12ft 2½ins (3.9m) long, and a service room, 11ft 10ins (3.6m) long . The brick stack, now reduced to just a support on the ground floor, would have intruded into the hall. The floor joists are of vertical section and housed into the axial beams with shouldered soffit tenons and diminished haunches. There is no clear evidence for a stair trap but this is likely to have been placed to the front or rear of the stack.

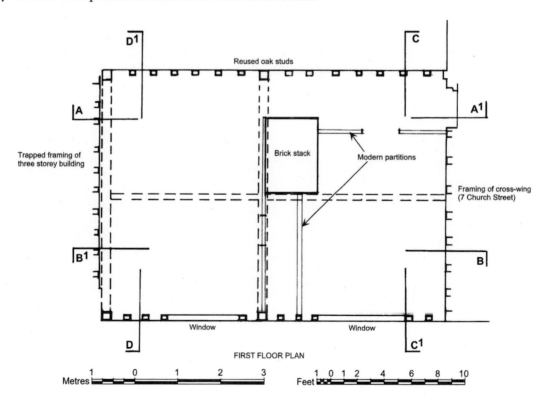

Rebuilt hall at 5 Church Street, first floor plan

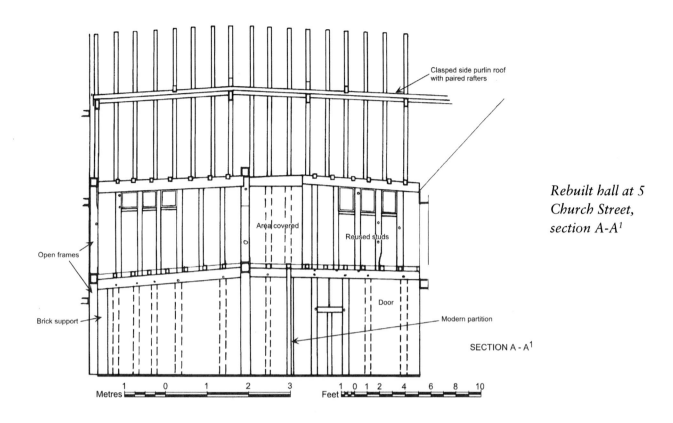

Clasped side purlin roof
with paired rafters

Area covered

Reused studs

Open frames

Door

Brick support

Modern partition

*Rebuilt hall at 5
Church Street,
section A-A¹*

SECTION A - A¹

Metres

Feet

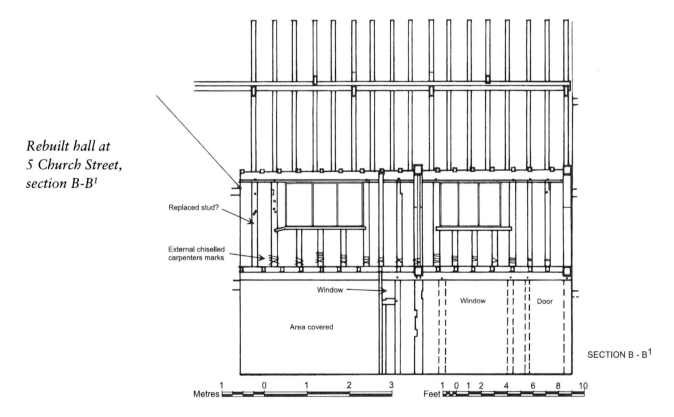

*Rebuilt hall at
5 Church Street,
section B-B¹*

Replaced stud?

External chiselled
carpenters marks

Window

Window   Door

Area covered

SECTION B - B¹

Metres

Feet

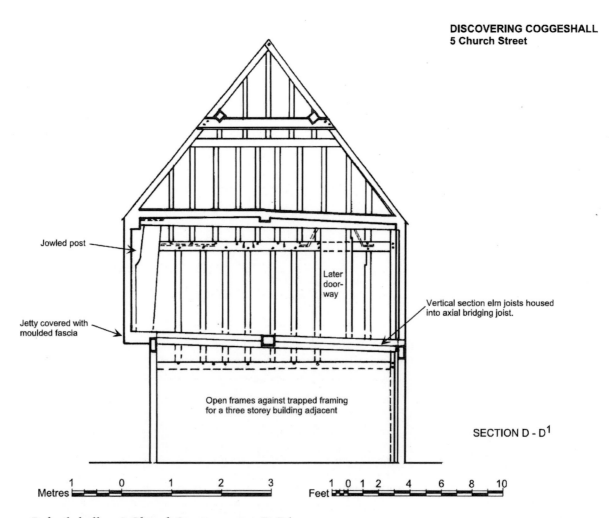

DISCOVERING COGGESHALL
5 Church Street

Jowled post

Later door-way

Vertical section elm joists housed into axial bridging joist.

Jetty covered with moulded fascia

Open frames against trapped framing for a three storey building adjacent

SECTION D - D^1

Metres

Feet

Rebuilt hall at 5 Church Street, section D-D¹

At first floor level two chambers are formed to the same length as the rooms on the ground floor but 17ft 2ins wide (5.23m). There is a large window in the front wall to each of the bays but no evidence of mullion profile. The ground floor windows appear to have been glazed but again a mullion profile is not discernible. The open frame at the west end has the trapped exposed framing of a pre-existing adjoining three storey building whilst the east end has the framing of the earlier cross wing. Whilst new oak is used for the close studding of the front wall the rear wall is of reused oak. The ceiling joists and beams are in elm and appear to be a later insertion suggesting that the upper floor was originally open to the roof.

The roof is a clasped side purlin with collars housed and pegged to the principal rafters that do not coincide with the bay divisions. The rafters are paired and additional collars are bird's mouthed over the top of the purlin.

Discussion

The terminal date of 1454 gives a firm insight into the carpentry style and mouldings of the era. Unfortunately, due to the replacement of the earlier hall and possible service end, the original purpose of the building whether purely domestic or part commercial cannot be answered. The replacement hall/service end is open framed against a now trapped three storey frame to the west of the replaced hall. Whilst this indicates that there was an existing building there at that date it does not offer any evidence for the original length of the hall/service end. The recessed high end is a feature often found in urban situations where there is a limited plot width. It serves to extend the length of the hall in a similar way to that of the under-shot cross passage of 19 East Street. The door from the recessed high end into the front two bays of the cross-wing appears to be at the north end where there is a narrow mortise for a door post. As the door has a dropped head the wattle groove continues either side of the mortise for the short central stud to the door head. The partition between the parlour and the rear bay appears to be fully studded and the height suggests that a dropped head would not be practical. If there is no door in the cross partition the existence of direct access to the stairs from the parlour has to be questioned. Evidence from other buildings suggests that access to an upper storey was sometimes via a stairs directly from the rear of the hall. In the replacement hall a door is positioned in the rear wall adjacent to the high end recess. Did this building function in a similar way?

History

In the 1575 rental survey John Guyon was the owner of the plot with George Lawrence to the west and Coggeshall Hall land belonging to Mr. Longe to the east.

18 and 18a Church Street

Brenda Watkin and Elphin Watkin

Introduction

These buildings are located on the south side of Church Street between the passage to the Through Inn in East Street and Swan Yard. 18 and 18a were originally one property, a 16th century long-wall jetty building on the street frontage with an earlier 15th century range behind. This was subdivided with the formation of a shop, 18a, in the western half with a flat over it. An 18th or 19th century building to the rear which was detached is now joined to the other buildings and forms part of the first floor flat.

18a is the premises of Buntings Butchers. A modern shop front now occupies the front of the ground floor. The first floor elevation has a 19th century sash window and is rendered with a tiled roof with a ridge line parallel to the street.

Successful tree ring dates were obtained for the rear range of 18, and the roof of the long-wall jetty building in the flat over the shop.

Buntings shop, 18a Church Street

The overall dimensions of the long wall jetty frontage range, orientated north-east to south-west, are 32ft 8ins x 19ft 6ins (9.95 x 5.94m), with rear wings to the south. As the interior of the ground floor shop is covered by modern finishes, this report only describes the first floor flat. The frontage range of the flat consists of the original end west bay of 18 Church Street. It measures 11ft 6ins x 18ft 2ins (3.5 x 5.54m) wide internally and is constructed from oak in the typical Essex close studded style, with evidence for external braces. The heads of the storey posts are jowled and all the studs in the close studded construction are pegged. The covered ceiling joists, forming the attic, are housed into a chamfered axial beam that appears to have been inserted to give attic space as evidenced by the iron straps to the slightly cambered end tie beam. To the east side of the rear wall is a window, 3ft (0.92m) wide and 3ft 2ins (0.97m) high, with four surviving diamond mullions set at 9 inch (0.23m) centres. Access to the attic is now by a modern stair against the west wall. The roof is constructed from paired rafters with side purlins clasped by collars, now removed. The principal rafters do not respect the bay divisions with a coupled pair 4ft (1.2m) from the west end frame.

A late 18th or early 19th century free-standing timber-framed building at the rear, measuring 26ft 10ins x 14ft (8.17 x 4.26m) wide internally, and of primary brace construction, has now been integrated with the frontage range.

Discussion

Two cores taken from the roof structure both gave terminal tree-ring dates: a principal rafter dated to winter 1545, and a truncated purlin to winter 1588, a discrepancy which gives rise to concern over how they are interpreted. The first floor ceiling is thought to have been inserted at a later date to create the attic space. A large dormer window now exists between the principal rafter and truncated purlin and the bay division between 18a and 18 Church Street. Changes to create the dormer window have involved removal of the collar and cutting the purlin. It is suggested that the date of the principal rafter is correct and fits with the features that are visible, whilst the date of the purlin be disregarded as this could have been a replacement timber, and if reused could have been placed there at anytime.

18 Church Street

18 comprises the eastern part of the long-wall jetty house on the frontage where successful tree-ring dates of 1545 and 1588 were obtained, and a range at right angles to the rear where floor joists gave a felling date of 1428.

The frontage range has most of the timber-frame covered but at ground floor the transverse beam, with a deep chamfer only to the west, is visible creating a narrow bay at the eastern end. This narrow bay has an axial beam, possibly not original, offset to the rear whilst the axial beam to the west bay is central. This has deep chamfers that mitre into the transverse beam. The chamfers stop at an inserted wall to the west but would have continued for approximately another 3ft (0.92m) to a bay division. A lateral brick stack against the rear wall intrudes into the room with a coved support for a first floor hearth. There is an 18th century door with cock's head hinges to the east of the stack.

At first floor most of the frame is covered but where there is a flying freehold over Buntings shop, the rear wall plate is exposed. This has an edge halved and bridled scarf joint 2ft (0.6m) long, and mortises where studs and storey post have been removed. The studs were set at 1ft 4ins (0.41m) centres and of 5 x 4ins (0.13 x 0.10m) section, with the storey post 9ins (0.23m) wide. Close studding and a window position are visible in the front, north wall.

The rear wing is of medieval date and is the rear bay of a longer cross-wing, the front part of which was removed when the long-wall jetty range was built. The evidence for this statement is the existence of a pseudo jowl on the north-west storey post supporting the transverse beam, and the lack of pegs for infill studs at the west end of the beam suggesting an opening through to another bay.

The wing is two storey with the original joists to the upper floor lodged on the midrails. The joists are from whole trees, converted to square section and then sawn in half to give heavy flat section joists. An apotropaic or ritual protection mark was scribed onto the face of a converted section which when sawn in half has left matching elements of the mark on each joist.

It would appear that there was close studding on all four sides of the building but the evidence in the form of peg holes or studs is clearest at ground level on the east, north and west sides and for first floor on the east and west walls. At first floor the frame is covered by modern finishes. Evidence for a window survives at ground floor in the form of a shutter groove and corresponding lack of pegs towards the north end of the west wall. On the east wall the pegs in the mid rail for first floor studs are evenly spaced at 2ft (0.6m) centres. However the spacing on the west wall is more erratic and lack of studding over a 2ft 8ins (0.81m) gap suggests a door opening that could have been for a garderobe. At the north east corner joists change direction but only one is pegged. This suggests that there has been a trimmed stair trap along the north wall but with later changes the original configuration is unclear.

The roof is of simple paired rafter form with collars, as often found on narrow spans, and appears to be original.

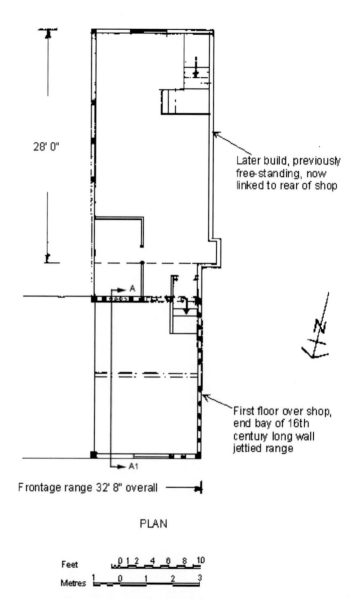

18A Church Street, Coggeshall, Essex. (Buntings flat)

28' 0"

Later build, previously free-standing, now linked to rear of shop

First floor over shop, end bay of 16th century long wall jettied range

Frontage range 32' 8" overall

PLAN

Feet   0 1 2 4 6 8 10
Metres 1   0   1   2   3

Plan of the western end bay of 18 Church Street, the flat at first floor over Buntings shop

Discussion

The rear wing is of interest as it appears to have been part of an earlier frontage building, possibly the rear bay of a cross-wing adjoining an open hall. Evidence is insufficient to say more about its layout other than to suggest that it shared the same frontage line as the existing building, in which case it would have been a three bay cross-wing.

Apotropaic marks have been studied in depth in East Anglia but it is very rare to find one that can be so precisely dated. Its presence on the timbers before they were fully converted excludes the possibility of it having been made at a later date.

History

When the frontage range was built, it was clearly all in the same ownership, the earlier building being integrated into the new build. At the time of the 1575 rental survey it was in the ownership of Thomas Paycocke.

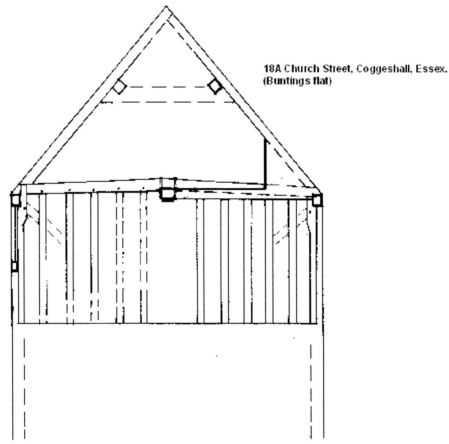

18A Church Street, Coggeshall, Essex.
(Buntings flat)

SECTION ON A - A¹

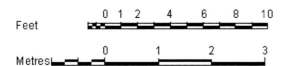

Feet

Metres

*18A Church Street,
Buntings flat,
section on A-A1*

99

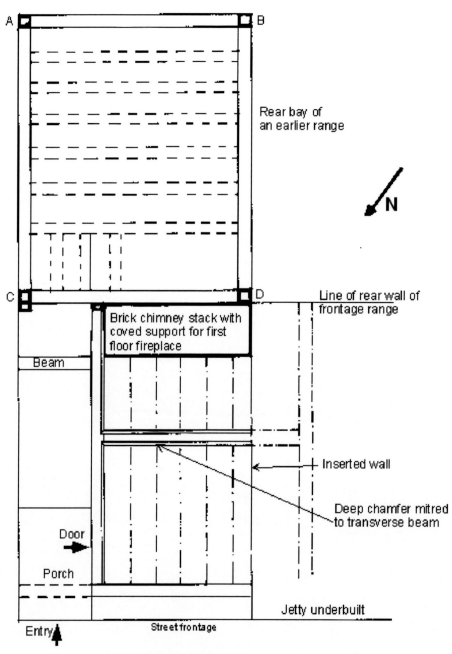

18 Church Street, Coggeshall, Essex.

Rear bay of
an earlier range

N

Line of rear wall of
frontage range

Brick chimney stack with
coved support for first
floor fireplace

Beam

Inserted wall

Deep chamfer mitred
to transverse beam

Door

Porch

Jetty underbuilt

Entry

Street frontage

GROUND FLOOR PLAN

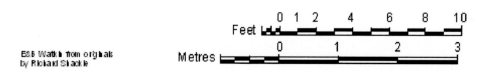

ESB Watkin from originals
by Richard Shackle

18 Church Street, ground floor plan

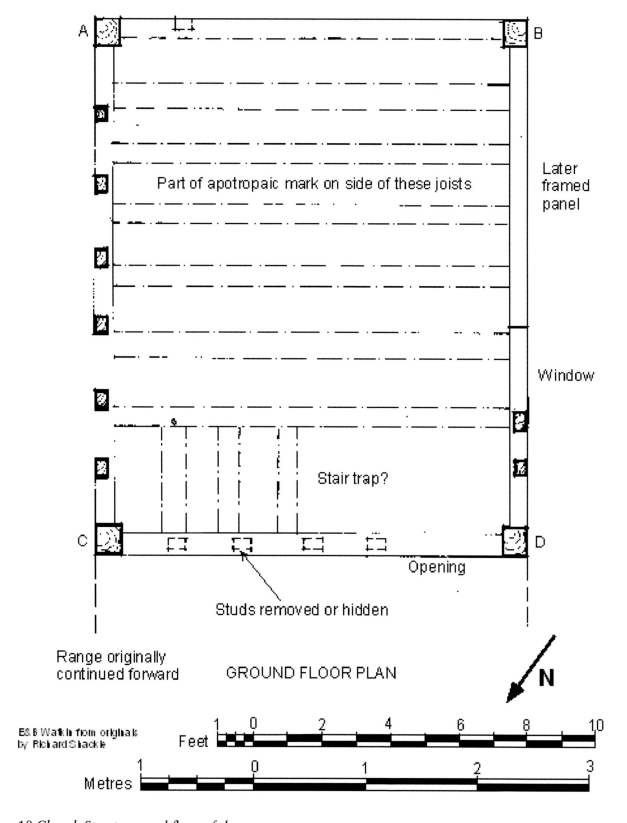

18 Church Street, ground floor of the rear range

18 Church Street, Coggeshall, Essex.

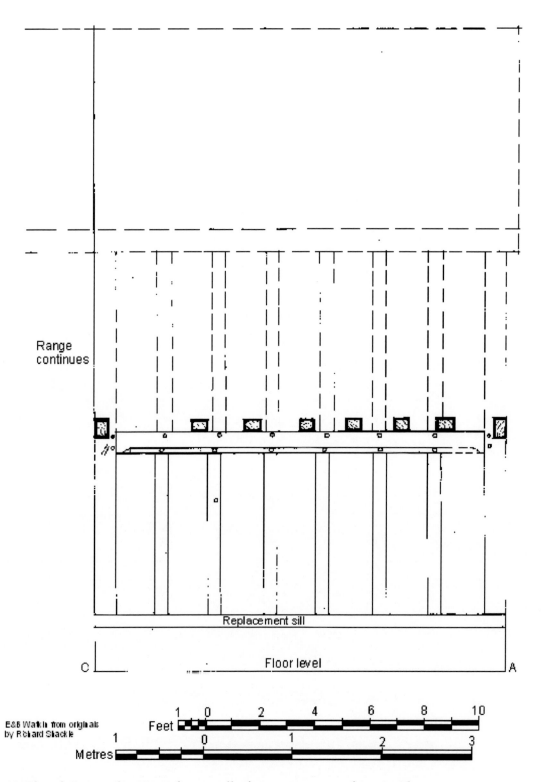

18 Church Street, elevation of east wall of rear range, seen from inside

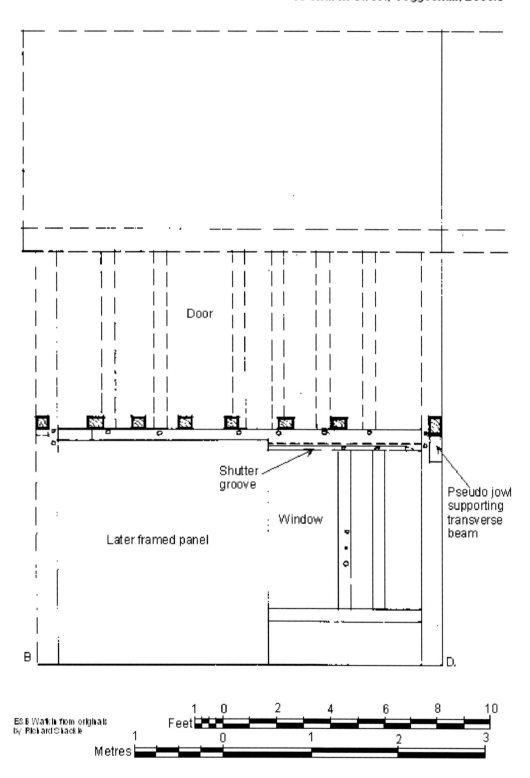

18 Church Street, Coggeshall, Essex.

Door

Shutter groove

Pseudo jowl supporting transverse beam

Window

Later framed panel

B   D.

E&B Watkin from originals by Richard Shackle

Feet

Metres

18 Church Street, elevation of west wall of rear range, seen from inside

30 Church Street, Spooners

David Stenning and Richard Shackle

Spooners is the oldest house to have been dated in Coggeshall. The only house which has been identified in the study of the buildings which may be older than it is 47 Church Street. Cores taken from three timbers, a tie-beam, a post, and a rafter, gave an estimated date between 1353 and 1386.

This is an unusually large in-line house. In its proportions, with its tall hall, it looks forward to the Wealden houses that would be popular a few years hence. For this kind of standard accommodation, a house with its two cross-wings would have been the standard accommodation.

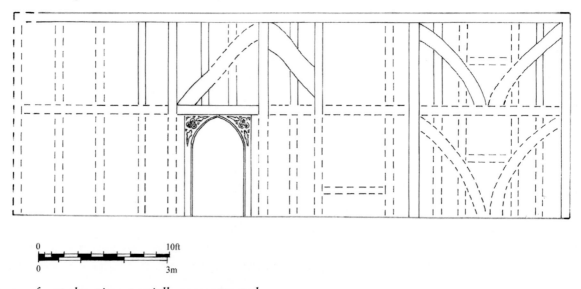

Spooners, front elevation, partially reconstructed

The front elevation is much rebuilt, but the position and features of the four bays remain legible, although the cross-passage door and hall window are now blocked. The framing was characterised by large braces, including one of serpentine or ogee shape. The door was formed of two large curved timbers or durns, with foliate carving between traceried motifs in the spandrels. The left hand durn has reproduction carving, but because the durn is such a good match for the other it may have come from a dismantled doorway at the rear of the house. There is a suggestion, from the presence of marks and pegs, that the high end mid rail may have carried a moulded superimposed fascia, hinting at an implied jetty and making it look like a cross-wing house.

The hall is of two unequal bays separated by a truss with long but modest braces. The hall windows are surprisingly narrow, suggesting that this space would have been relatively dark. The owner's bench was set within a high end recess (a fairly popular feature in Coggeshall) but this has been lost as a result of the moving of the high end partition. All the storey posts have substantial jowled heads. In this respect, the house differs from the Colchester style of carpentry prevalent in Coggeshall, possibly suggesting the work of a non-local carpenter.

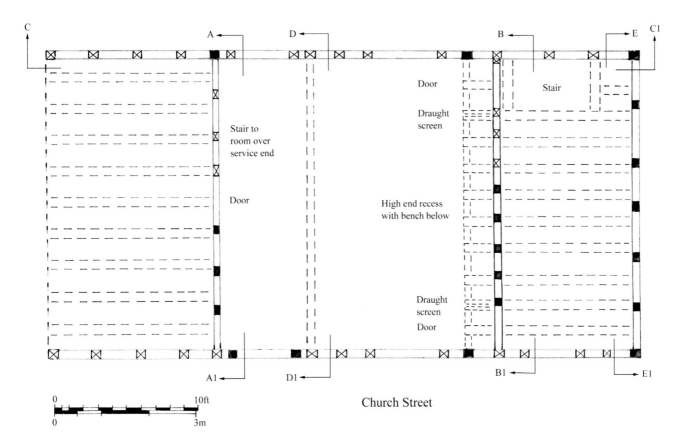

Ground plan of Spooners, 30 Church Street

Both ends of the house are relatively narrow, determined by the limited space on the street frontage. Access to the stair to the solar over the parlour was gained by a door with an ogee head in the high end partition. A first floor window is so positioned as to light the stairwell below.

At the east end, there is a single undivided service room accessed by a central ground floor door. This plan arrangement is unusual, as normally there is a pair of doors leading to the service end. A parallel for a single door can be found at Appletrees Farmhouse, Cressing. The evidence of the timber frame suggests that the chamber over the service room had a similar central door, reached via a ladder up from the hall. The east wall of the service end has been lost. The side of the house here is formed by the framing of the adjoining Conservative Club, a 16th century wall three-storeys high, jettied on both upper floors. The roof has tall simple crown posts and includes a number of reused timbers.

The carving on the door, the curved bracing, and the door with an ogee head, of which there may have been more examples, now lost, identify the house as belonging to the Decorated style of architecture.

*Spooners, longitudinal
section C-C1*

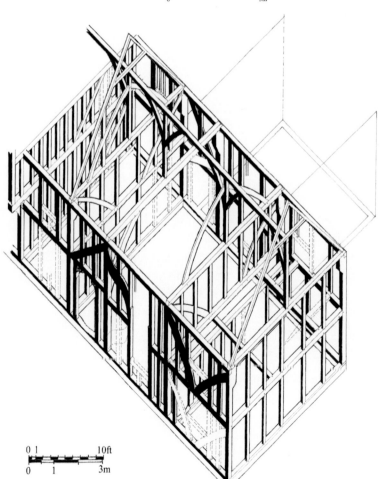

*Spooners, axonometric
reconstruction*

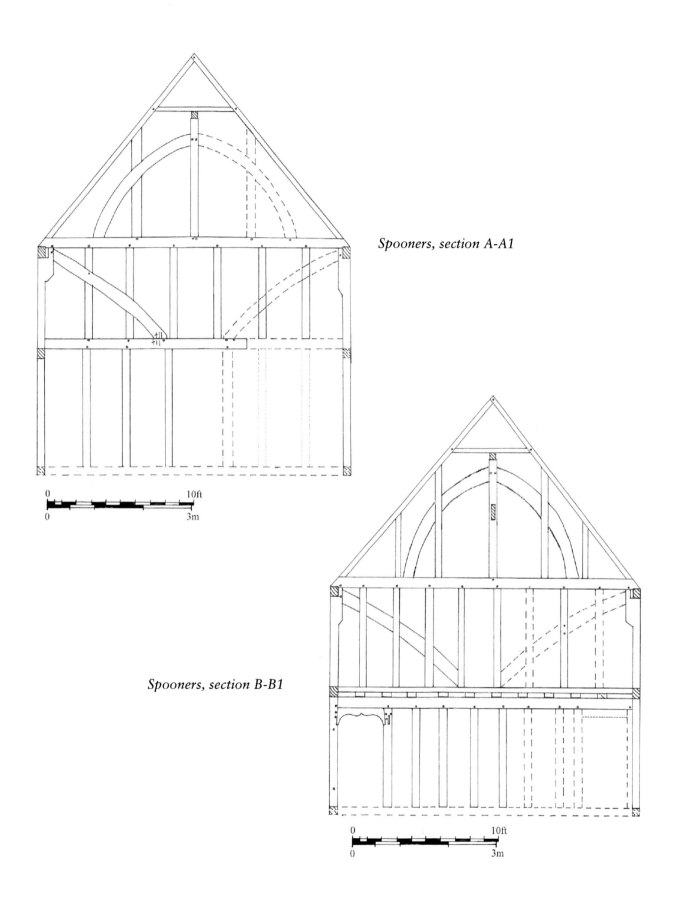

Spooners, section A-A1

Spooners, section B-B1

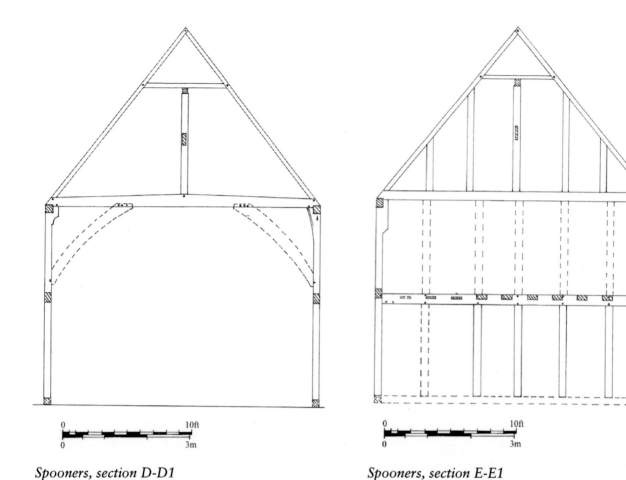

Spooners, section D-D1   *Spooners, section E-E1*

The rear parlour/solar extension

In 1608/9, the date obtained from a core from a storey post, Spooners was given a rear two storey parlour/ solar extension, as occurred elsewhere in Coggeshall. The parlour was heated, there were a number of windows, and the roof has wind-braced side purlins.

History

At the time of the 1575 rental, Spooners was a copyhold property belonging to William Sponer and had an orchard attached to it. No Spooners are recorded at Coggeshall in the 1670 hearth tax returns, but the house has retained the family name until the present day.

40 Church Street today. The timber frame was exposed when plaster was removed in the 1960s

40 Church Street, Craig Dhu

Richard Shackle and David Andrews

This is an important early house, one of the oldest to have been dated in Coggeshall. An offcut supplied by the owner from former repairs to the timber frame gave a date of 1387-1423.

On its front elevation, the timber frame is exposed, revealing it to be of two unequal bays, with a cross-wing to the right and a single bay hall to the left. The cross-wing was jettied, but the first floor has been cut back flush to the line of the rest of the façade, the pattern of the framing with its two braces being retained. The wing has an undershot cross passage, a necessary space saving measure in view of the small size of the hall. The door formerly had an arched head. The front of the wing was occupied by a shop with a window to the front which had short curved braces between the posts and jetty plate. The room to the rear may have had a service function or been a parlour.

Between the undershot passage and the hall there is a spere truss, with arched braces to mid rail of the cross-wing. This wall is smoke blackened. The wall on the other side of the hall has a striking pattern of saltire or X shaped bracing. A feature of the house is the straightness of the braces used in its frame. In the front wall of the hall there was a large almost full height window with diamond mullions.

To the east of the house, adjoining the hall, there was a similar two bay house comprising a cross-wing and hall. It thus formed part of a terrace of compact dwellings with shops which had been built as a single development.

In the 17th or 18th century, the hall was raised in height and the two bays were brought together under a clasped purlin roof parallel to the street, replacing what would have been crown-post roofs. The house was also at about this time extended to the rear.

In the 1575 rental, Craig Dhu was a copyhold tenement belonging to Ellen Scarlett.

*Reconstructed view
of Craig Dhu*

*40 Church Street,
front elevation*

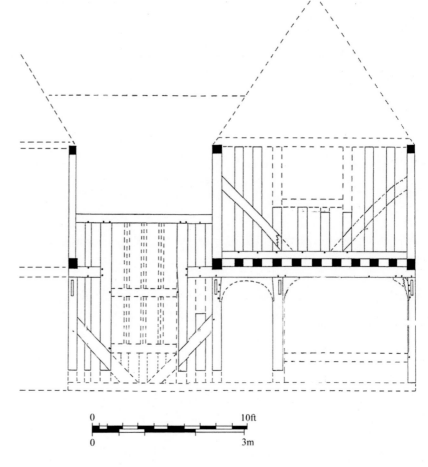

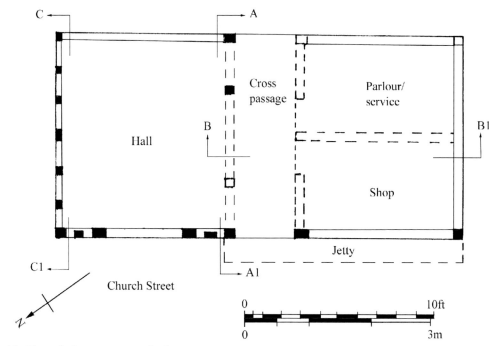

40 Church Street, ground plan

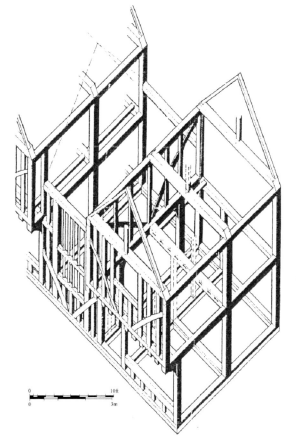

40 Church Street, axonometric reconstruction of the timber frame

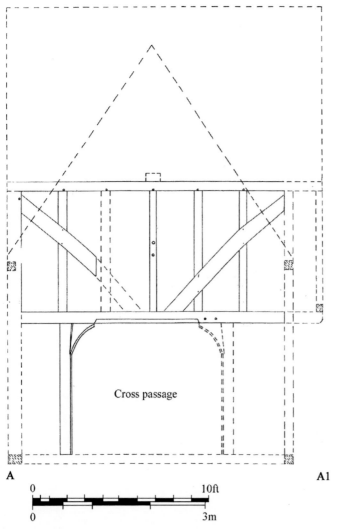

Cross passage

0   10ft

0   3m

40 Church Street, section A-A1

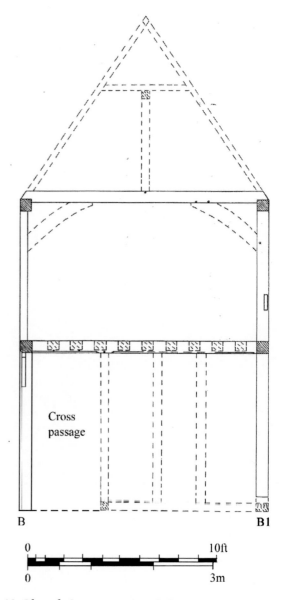

Cross
passage

0   10ft

0   3m

40 Church Street, section B-B1

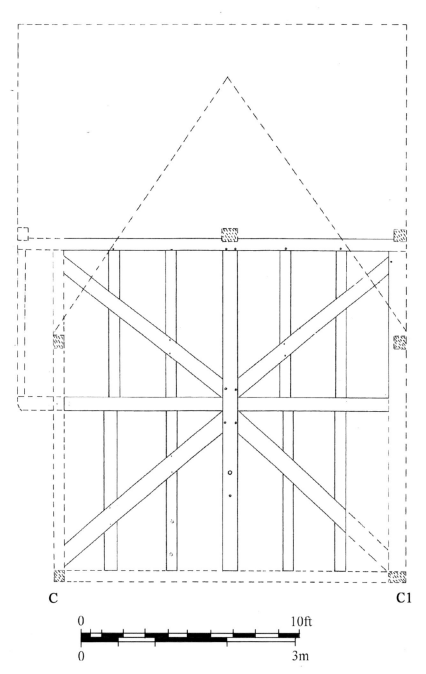

C   C1

40 Church Street, section C- C1

2-4 East Street

Brenda Watkin and Elphin Watkin

Introduction

Originally built in the 17th century as a two-storey lobby-entry house approximately 19ft (5.8m) wide by 33ft (10.05m) long, this building was not jettied to the front. There was a one-and-a-half storey rear wing to the east and possibly a central stair tower. In the 19th century the property was modified to two semi-detached properties. A central passage, to the rear gardens, was created through the central stack, and the rear elevations were clad in brick with a rear extension in brick to no. 2 and a cellar constructed under the extension and the frontage range. The front elevation has symmetrically placed 19th-century tripartite sashes with contemporary geometric patterned pargetting. Two gabled dormers sit either side of the slightly offset central stack in a tiled gabled roof aligned with the street. Most of the framing is now covered in no. 2 so evidence for openings and framing comes from no. 4.

Description

The original structure is timber-framed and incorporates reused oak timbers with elm used mainly for the structural frame. The ground floor would have originally contained two rooms, one either side of the entry lobby and both heated by the central stack. 4 East Street, the eastern half of the property, had a rear wing as evidenced by the four pegged but now empty mortices for joists in the external face of the rear midrail.

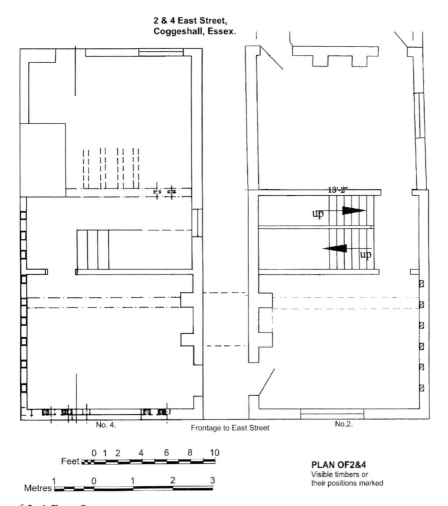

2 & 4 East Street,
Coggeshall, Essex.

13'-2"

up

up

No. 4.

Frontage to East Street

No.2.

0 1 2   4   6   8   10
Feet

1   0   1   2   3
Metres

PLAN OF 2&4
Visible timbers or
their positions marked

Ground plan of 2-4 East Street

In the main range of the building the joists rest on the midrail. The configuration of joists would have left a gap against the later passage wall and there is also an incomplete joist mortice against the brick stack, which forms part of the division wall, and would have heated the rear space. The midrail also has evidence for two studs against the later passage wall and below the opening in the joists. There are no further mortices along the soffit of the midrail leaving a gap of 7ft 6ins (2.2m) between the last stud and stack. The ground floor wall framing appears to consist of close studding set at approximately 1ft 6ins (0.45m) centres. The framing to the front wall is rebuilt but the pattern of pegging shows an original window opening 6ft (1.82m) wide. The elm axial beams are heavily chamfered with lamb's tongue stops and all the common joists are covered. The common joists sit on a deep midrail and are jointed into the axial beam. The profile of the empty mortices is for a soffit tenon with diminished haunch joint and it is assumed that this is the floor joist joint used throughout the building.

The cellar under no. 2 is built of brick with diagonal pressure marks indicating an age before 1800. Typical to such a storage use are the niches with arched heads. There is an arched brick support to the ground floor hearth and stack. Reused timbers have been incorporated into the floor structure although in the front half, under the original build, most of the joists have been replaced.

115

4 East Street, Coggeshall, Esse

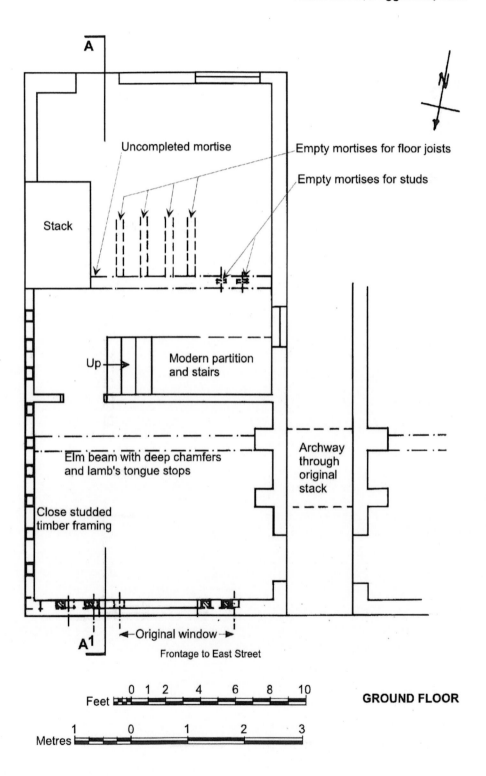

Ground floor plan of 4 East Street

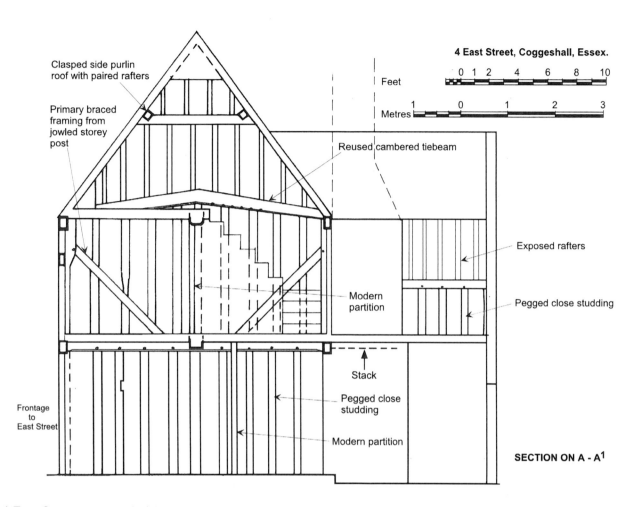

4 East Street, section A-A1

The first floor walls are of primary-braced construction with braces falling from the jowled storey posts. The rear wall plate is of elm and has been worked to size by both axe and saw conversion. At first floor there are two further rooms in the frontage range, one either side of the stack. There appears to be no direct access between these rooms other than from a rear stair or stair tower. There is a later blocked door opening between the front and rear range of no. 4 with the evidence for the original door opening being a gap in the pegging of the rear wall against the central storey post. No primary brace has been used in this position as it would have blocked the opening. A section of wall plate and studding, which is part of the rear wall of the medieval shop/store set behind 6 East Street, is exposed south of the stack in the rear room of the one-and-a-half storey wing to no. 4. Also visible in the rear wall is the upper section of a jowled storey post with the jowl facing to the west and evidence for infill on the east edge of the post. The position of this storey post lines up with the east side of a two-storey central gable that could have originally functioned as a stair tower. (There are a number of lobby entry houses in Essex that have a stair tower in this position.) The original door opening at first floor level in the rear wall would also have been contained within this structure. The lack of pegging in the front wall plate gives the position of a window 6ft (1.82m) wide above that found on the ground floor. A deep cut-out in a stud for the cill gives a depth of 4ft (1.2m) but no evidence was visible to confirm if it was for an oriel window or to indicate any defined mullion profile. Only the front wall plate is exposed in 2 East Street but the pattern of pegholes echoes that to no. 4. Ceiling joists are covered and housed into a heavy chamfered elm axial beam. It is suggested that, given the cambered tie-beam reused in the end frame, the attic floor was a slightly later 17th-century insertion.

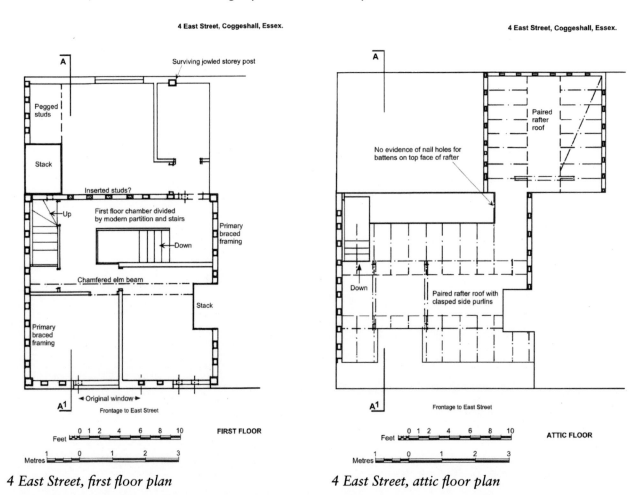

4 East Street, first floor plan   4 East Street, attic floor plan

A 19th-century winder stair gives access from the first floor to the attic space against the end frame to the east. This wall is of primary-braced construction with a 15th-century reused cambered tie-beam. This has come from a former open truss as evidenced by the six visible pegs and mortices under that would have been for heavy arched braces. The paired rafter roof is of gabled form with clasped side purlins. The collars have been raised to allow sufficient head height and a dormer inserted into the front roof slope. Both purlins are joined by a short nailed splayed scarf. A rafter has been removed to allow access into the space of the central rear gable and it is interesting to note that the external face of the adjacent rafter has no nails for tile battens,suggesting that it has always been covered by a building to the rear that may have been the stair tower. The rear attic room has a reused tie-beam to the south frame. The reused rafters on the west roof have a nailed diagonal brace, 9 x 1ins (0.23 x 0.3m). Below the wall plate on the west side are pegged studs of average size 4½ x 4ins (0.11 x 0.10m) at 1ft 8ins (0.51m) centres, those to the east are more uneven in spacing and pegging. From the existing framing evidence it would appear alterations and repairs were made in the 19th century.

Discussion

The original lobby entrance house has undergone considerable alteration and much of the frame is covered making the original form and function of the individual rooms difficult to define. It is suggested that the room to the west of the lobby was the parlour with the hall to the east. It is unusual to have such a wide opening from the hall into a rear room. The configuration of the floor joists and the opening suggest that there was a draft screen separating the two spaces with an opening for stairs to the chamber or store above. The rear room was heated and could have been used as a kitchen or was it for a more specific use? It is interesting to note that there would have been a difference in floor level between the main frontage range and that to the rear. Was this an attempt to increase the head height in the one-and-a-half storey rear wing? The lack of access between the two first floor rooms, parlour and hall chamber, through the central partition, points to the presence of rear stairs or a stair tower with separate entrances to the first-floor chambers by doorways through the rear wall of the frontage range. Originally there was minimal studding to the first floor rear wall of no. 4. This would have been blocked by the stack and partly by the lower roof structure. Given the gap in the floor joist mortices it appears that there was a separate stair trap so allowing separate access to the possible storage area of the upper rear wing from that to the hall chamber via the stair tower.

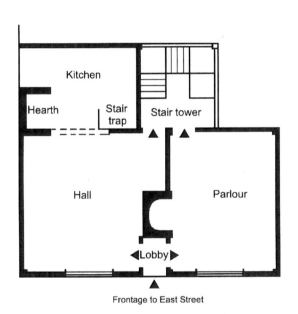

GROUND FLOOR PLAN

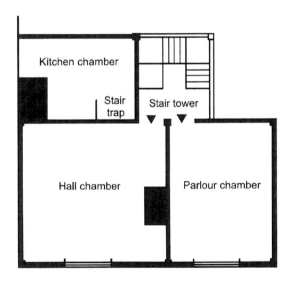

FIRST FLOOR PLAN

2-4 East Street, conjectural original layout

History

At the time of the 1575 survey, the site of the eastern half of the house (no. 4) formed part of a lane belonging to Mr Longe and thus part of the Coggeshall Hall manor, whilst the western half (no. 2) was part of a freehold plot with a tenement and orchard owned by Christopher Wade. The construction of the house in the 17th century seems to have represented a re-arrangement of the landholdings in this area.

6 East Street

Brenda Watkin, Elphin Watkin and David Stenning

Outline description

6 East Street is a remarkably complete and extensive late medieval tenement plot which by the 1600s had become occupied by long ranges of buildings extending 45m back from the south side of the street.

On the frontage there is a 15th century cross-wing and a rebuilt hall with a compact urban plan. The undershot cross-passage of the cross-wing gave access to a yard where there is a range of two 15th-century jettied workshops or commercial buildings continuing the line of the cross-wing. The more northerly has been dated successfully to 1441. A single bay rear extension, provided parlour accommodation, probably replacing an earlier parlour which was originally single storey. The hall was remodelled in the 16th century, a floor being inserted into it and its roof raised.

To the south of the commercial ranges, there are a further three adjoining outbuildings datable to the 17th century, 6C and 6D, and a further building which has been interpreted as a stable.[1]

Today the complex is divided into multiple ownership. The frontage buildings, a beauty parlour with flats above, have proved particularly difficult to interpret. The other buildings are separate dwellings.

---

1   Shackle 2001.

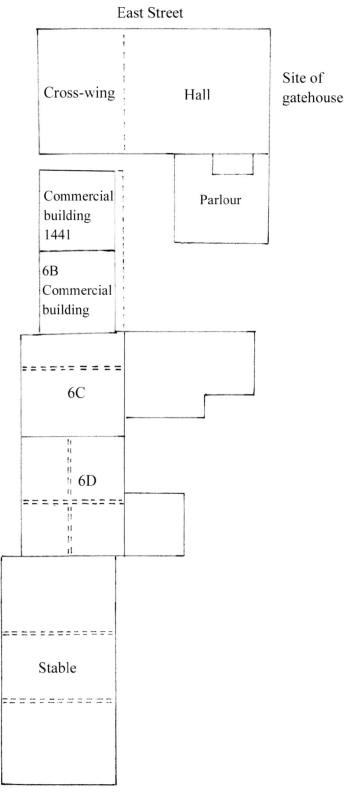

Sketch plan of the layout of the buildings at 6 East Street

Only the first floor of the parlour wing behind the hall, and the more northerly of the units in the commercial range, were tree-ring dated. The hall and cross-wing, and the two commercial buildings, were probably built over a short space of time in the 15th century, but there is insufficient evidence to be confident of the chronological relationship between them. The subsequent development of the hall and cross-wing units is also problematic. The sequence proposed below is the best interpretation that can be advanced on the available evidence. Three main periods are identified:

1. Two commercial buildings or workshops (mid 15th century)

2. Hall and cross-wing built on the street frontage (later 15th century)

3. Gatehouse or carriage arch built to the east, floor inserted in hall, and rear parlour with brick chimney, stable building to the south (16th century)

4. ranges of outbuildings to the south (17th century)

Period 1A. The more southerly workshop or commercial building (6B East Street)

Since the adjacent workshop to the north dated to 1441 was built with an open frame against this building, it is concluded that this is the older of the two adjacent commercial buildings. The timber is fast grown oak, well converted, and whilst the sections are substantial, the timber has been used to its limit and the building was not considered suitable for tree-ring dating.

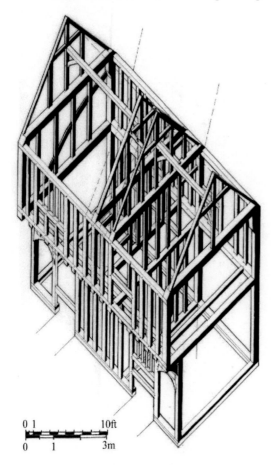

0 1   10ft
0   1   3m

Reconstructions of the more southerly of the two commercial buildings

The building is of 2½ bays, with an almost central smoke bay, with timbers for a louvre, dividing it into two units. Its overall length is 26ft (7.92m) with the width at ground floor 12ft (3.65m) and a 2 ft (0.6m) jetty overhang to the front. The average size of the common joists, housed with soffit tenons into the rear midrail, is 7½ x 5½ inches (0.19 x 0.14m). The timber-frame is of typical close studded style without any tension braces except for an unusually long tension brace extending almost across the full width of the southern end frame at first floor where there is an open frame beneath. Three of the main storey posts in the rear wall are jowled, the exception being that forming the rear wall of the smoke bay. None of the front posts are jowled and here the joint between the unjowled posts of the smoke bay and the tie-beams has been strengthened with a vertical peg. On the south mid rail an edge-halved bridled scarf with under-squinted abutments has been used to extend to the end of the jetty.

There are two arch headed doorways positioned at the north and south ends of the eastern elevation. The southern section, the larger of the two, was heated by the smoke bay. There was evidence for only one stair trap, placed against the rear wall in the southern half that gave access to the first floor. A new stair trap was created immediately to the inside of the south door and the solid tread stairs relocated. This feature was retained in the modern residential conversion. Diamond mullioned windows survive to both the ground and first floors but that to the side of the south door has been raised in height as evidenced by the inserted head below the jetty plate that contains pegged mortices for studs.

Beneath each of the ground floor windows, there is a lower head or lintel that could have marked openings into the sub-basement which runs under the building. This is built of well fired bricks of an average size of 9¼ x 4½ x 2 inches (0.23 x 0.11 x 0.05m). It is undivided and 3ft 9ins (1.14m) deep. The openings in the front elevation are only 2ft 2ins (0.66m) high and would have lit the sub-basement, whilst access to it is assumed to have been made through an opening with a low head in the north smoke bay wall against the west wall. Unfortunately the evidence for studs in this wall only survives as mortices to the underside of the first floor transverse beam. The door has been interpreted from the evidence of a pegged mortice in the storey post. Depending on the direction of the solid tread stairs access to the sub-basement could have been from either the south or the north workshops.

The first floor is lit by two diamond mullioned windows with shutter rebates in the wall plate. A rare survival is a section of shutter board nailed over the rebate and a shaped shutter rail to the cill. Access between the first floor rooms appears to have been to the side of the smoke bay. A now mutilated ogee door head has been inserted, closer to the centre, in the rear wall of the smoke bay, presumably when this went out of use. The roof is of paired rafters and collars with a collar purlin and axial braced crown posts. In the north gable the crown post runs through to the apex with the collar mortised and pegged into it. In the roof remnants of soot blackened plaster delineated the smoke bay and the side frame for the louver survived.

There appears to be no doubt that this building was commercial, with a working area in the left hand side, whilst the part to the right of the smoke bay could have been domestic. Medieval commercial buildings are rare survivals. It is possible that this was the dyehouse which gave its name to this or the adjoining property (see below), though how it might have functioned is unclear. The dyeing process has been described thus: 'The dye bath was usually prepared in a cauldron over a direct flame. The cloth might be dipped straight into this, or the liquor might be transferred to a separate vat.'[2] An excavation at Beverley uncovered a wooden tub set into the ground with shuttering around its edge and fed by a wooden channel. Madder root was found nearby, and a small keyhole shaped hearth which was probably used to heat the dye solution.

2   Blair and Ramsay 1991, *English Medieval Industries*.

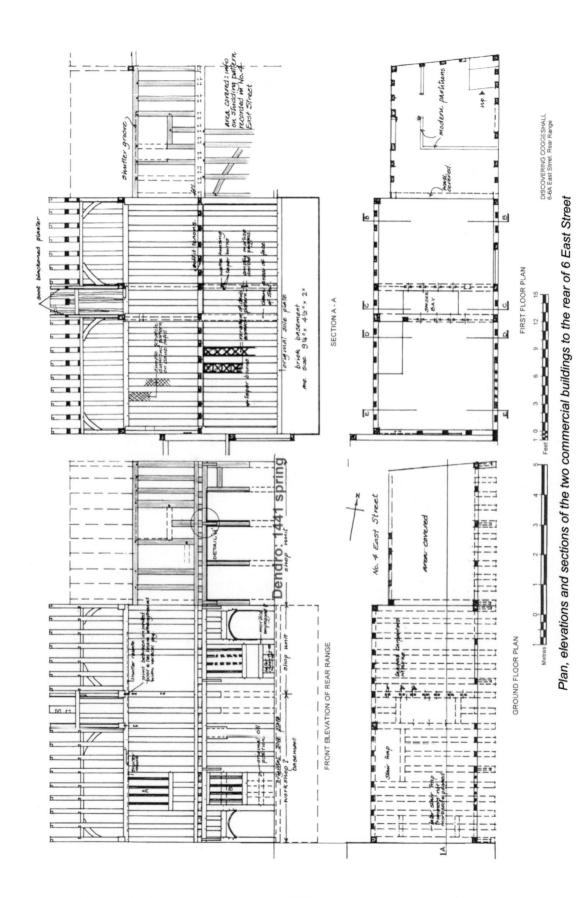

Plan, elevations and sections of the two commercial buildings to the rear of 6 East Street

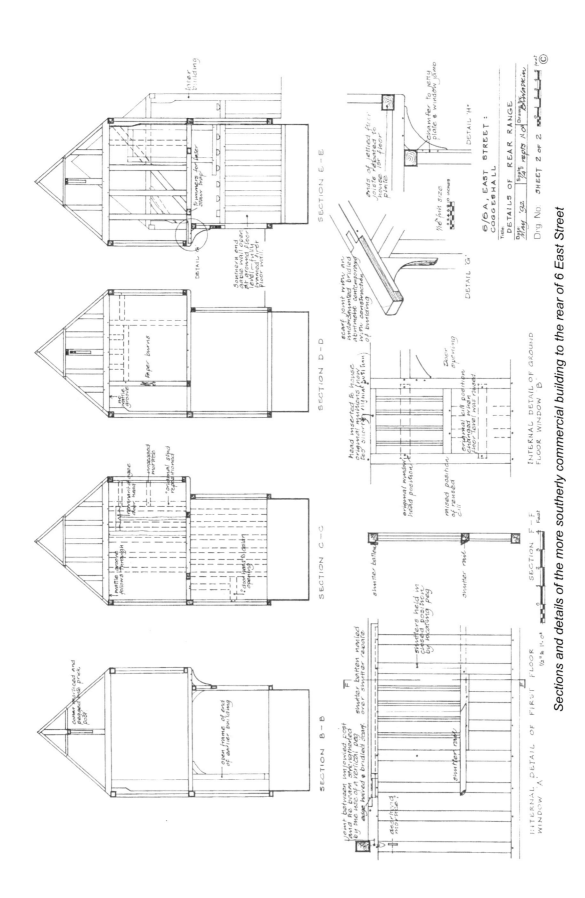

Sections and details of the more southerly commercial building to the rear of 6 East Street

Similar keyhole shaped hearths have been found in London and a medieval dyehouse excavated in Norwich had a single hearth and well. A good supply of water was essential to the dyers craft, as was also a place to dump the waste from the dye-vat. Here in this building there was a source of heat, the smoke bay, but no evidence for the exact position of the hearth at sub-basement height or ground floor. Whilst the low height of the sub-basement would have been acceptable for storage, could it have been used for the dye-vats or was this process only taking place at ground floor level in the heated south workshop? That there was a good water supply is evidenced by the pump which was retained in place against the front elevation when conversion took place. The site slopes to the south and before the later buildings were erected was the waste just allowed to seep away?

Period 1B. The 1441 commercial building

Although in line with the frontage cross-wing, this building is separated from it by a gap of 6ft (1.82m) and does not quite share the same orientation, being trapezoidal in plan. It is of 10ft 6ins (3.2m) overall width at ground floor with the rear wall 14ft (4.26m) and the front wall 15ft 9ins (4.8m), and a jetty of 2ft (0.6m) to the front eastern elevation. It is built of typical close studded timber-framing spaced at 1ft 6ins (0.45m) centres, with unjowled corner storey posts. It is suggested that this building was longer to the north, and was truncated when the cross-wing on the frontage was constructed.

At ground floor the workshop is lit by three square headed windows chamfered to the external face. The entrance is through a door positioned at the north end of the range. As the joists are covered from below and above, it cannot be determined if there was any access via a stair trap to the first floor. The spacing of the studs to the north wall widens to 3ft (0.91m) against the west corner post leaving adequate space for a door into the area between the workshop and cross-wing. There is also an external door opening at first floor level in the east elevation with evidence for a low pegged rail. As there is no evidence of the joists being extended to make a landing for an external stair, this was probably a loading door (a modern pulley still survives above the blocked doorway). To the north of the door, there is a window with diamond mullions and internal shutter grooves. There is a similar window in the west elevation. The roof is of the simple paired rafter and collared type often found in narrow buildings.

Two cores were taken from the building, from a joist and from the front top plate, the latter giving the precise date of 1441.

Period 1C. A single storey outbuilding

To the rear of the hall on the street there is a two storey parlour that is a later addition to it. This building is difficult to interpret satisfactorily, but it is concluded that in origin it was single storey. At ground floor the frame and floor joists are covered and the only evidence for original features are pressure marks to the soffit of the west mid rail. These clearly show the profile of moulded mullions at 14 inch (0.36m) centres that were originally glazed with ¾ inch (0.02m) stanchions diagonally set for securing the leaded casements. A sophisticated window of this sort could be seen as fitting better with a later rather than mid 15th century date. The southern tie-beam at first floor has an unusual pegging pattern of alternating double and single pegging that appears to represent studs of wide and narrow widths. It is suggested that it was reused from the north wall of the original single storey building where dimensionally it would also be a better fit.

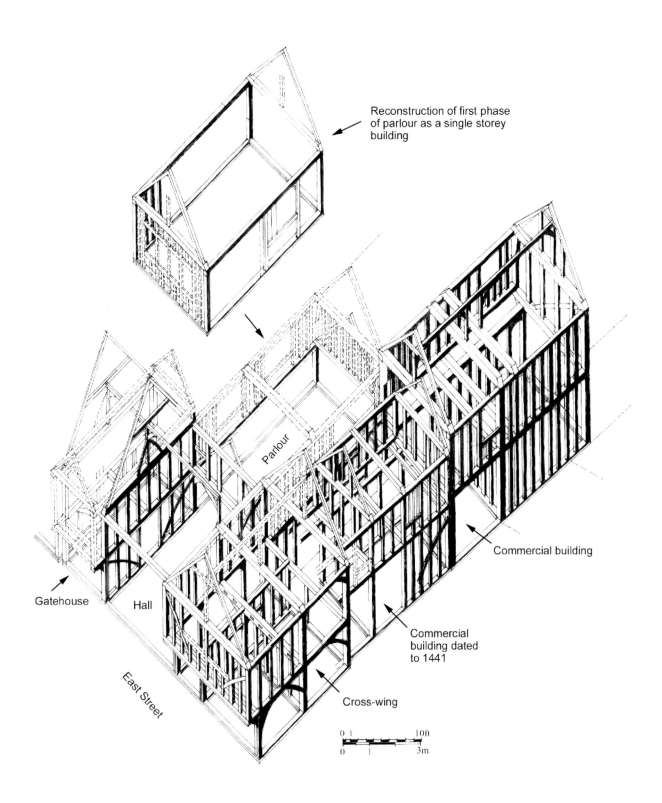

Reconstruction of first phase
of parlour as a single storey
building

Parlour

Commercial building

Commercial
building dated
to 1441

Gatehouse   Hall

Cross-wing

East Street

0 1   10ft
0   1   3m

*Axonometric drawing of the frontage buildings and the 1441 commercial building
behind them at 6 East Street*

127

Period 2. The cross-wing and hall

The front elevation to the street range of this complex gives little indication of the original built form of a two bay cross-wing and a single bay open hall. When this had a first floor inserted in it, the front wall was rebuilt as two full storeys with a jetty at first floor to line through with that of the cross-wing, and at a yet later date the double height bay window was inserted. The cross-wing roof was then replaced to run in line with the street and now encompasses the former open hall.

The cross-wing

The two bay cross-wing, 16ft wide x 18ft 6ins (4.87 x 5.48m) deep, has an undershot cross-passage that is separated from the hall by a spere truss. Two separate doors, with three centred arched heads and hollow mouldings, led from the passage into separate rooms. The door heads are set square into mortises instead of having the more usual shouldered profile. A bracket with hollow moulding is set between the doors and housed into the central bridging joist to support the spere opening. There is a Colchester style brace rising from the jamb of the door in the front bay to the stud in the front wall. Remnants of the arched head to the front door of the cross-passage remain, although no evidence could be found for a door head for an opposing opening at the rear of the wing.

As the room to the front appears to have been a shop, on the evidence of the typical deep mortises for window heads in the jetty posts, the rear room would have had a service function. The west wall of the cross-wing is constructed as an open frame with heavy arched braces at ground floor level and close studding to the front bay at first floor level (section G-G[1]). It is assumed that there was an earlier adjoining building but on the 1575 rental the plot is noted as a lane. The timbers are all of substantial scantling with the floor joists of average 7½ x 6ins (0.19 x 0.15m) deep at 1ft 8ins (0.45m) centres. The common joists are housed into the chamfered bridging beam, 10 x 9ins (0.25 x 0.23m) deep, with bare faced soffit tenons. The side girts are tenoned into the bressumer with an unusual mitred joint. The joists are also tenoned into the bressumer which has a moulded soffit and is supported on brackets flowing into attached round shafts with moulded capitals on the posts. There is no evidence for a stair trap that would give access to the first floor. With the loss of framing to the rear wall any evidence for a door has been lost. It is interesting to note that although the holes for the pintle hinges to the front door to the cross passage are clearly visible none were found for a rear door. There is a gap between the rear of the cross-wing and the first of the buildings of the commercial range behind it, tree-ring dated to 1441, which could have accommodated stairs. At first floor level there is evidence for a central window, unjowled storey posts and close studding to the east wall and front bay of the west wall. The rear bay of the west wall has an open frame with evidence for a brace against the rear storey post. The roof has been completely rebuilt to provide attic accommodation but traces of painting survive on the west wall plate.

The spere sides to the one bay open hall were originally infilled either side of a central stud with vertical boards as evidenced by the board slot in the soffit of the mid rail and the side of the *in situ* spere post. The boards appear to have been held in place by a horizontal timber housed into mortises in the front and rear posts and cogs cut into the spere posts. There is no board slot to the rear storey post or front jetty post. The spere opening has brackets to either end with the moulding continuing along the soffit of the midrail.

*Ground floor plan
of the hall and
cross-wing*

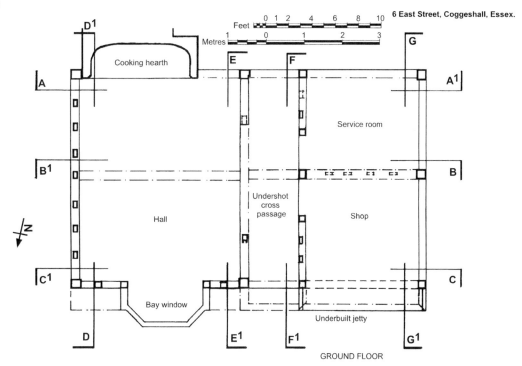

*First floor plan
of the hall and
cross-wing*

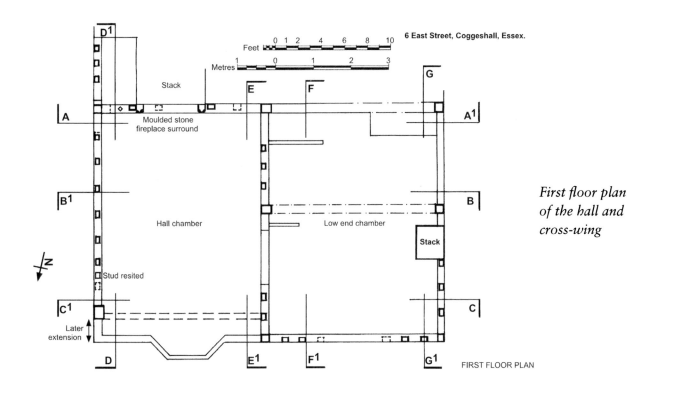

Section through hall and cross-wing at A-A¹

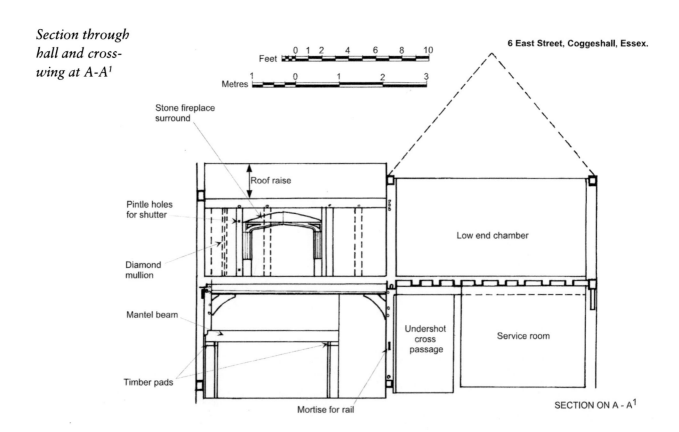

6 East Street, Coggeshall, Essex.

Stone fireplace surround

Roof raise

Pintle holes for shutter

Diamond mullion

Mantel beam

Timber pads

Mortise for rail

Low end chamber

Undershot cross passage

Service room

SECTION ON A - A¹

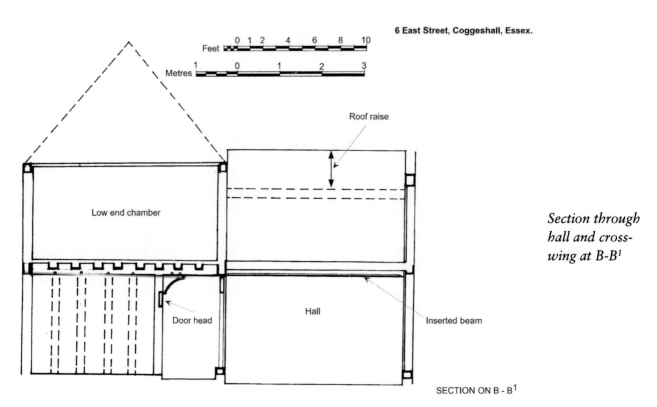

6 East Street, Coggeshall, Essex.

Roof raise

Low end chamber

Door head

Hall

Inserted beam

Section through hall and cross-wing at B-B¹

SECTION ON B - B¹

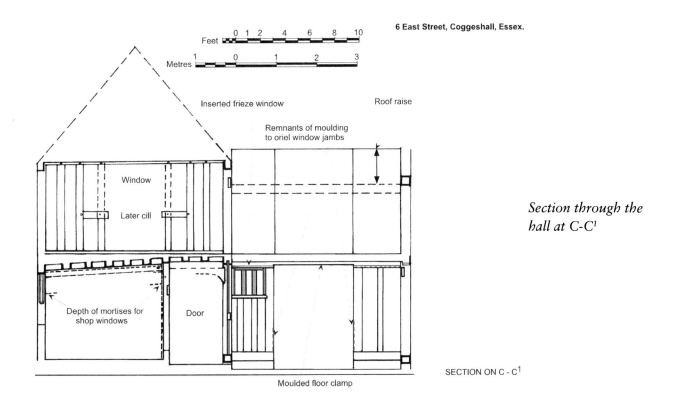

6 East Street, Coggeshall, Essex.

Inserted frieze window

Roof raise

Remnants of moulding
to oriel window jambs

Window

Later cill

*Section through the
hall at C-C¹*

Depth of mortises for
shop windows

Door

SECTION ON C - C¹

Moulded floor clamp

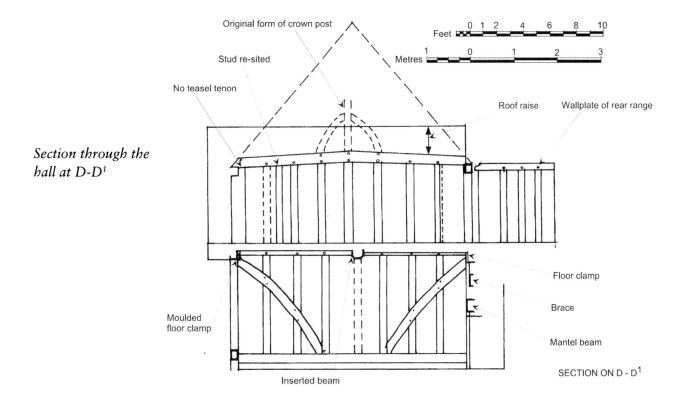

Original form of crown post

Stud re-sited

No teasel tenon

Roof raise   Wallplate of rear range

*Section through the
hall at D-D¹*

Floor clamp

Brace

Moulded
floor clamp

Mantel beam

SECTION ON D - D¹

Inserted beam

*Section through
the hall at E-E1*

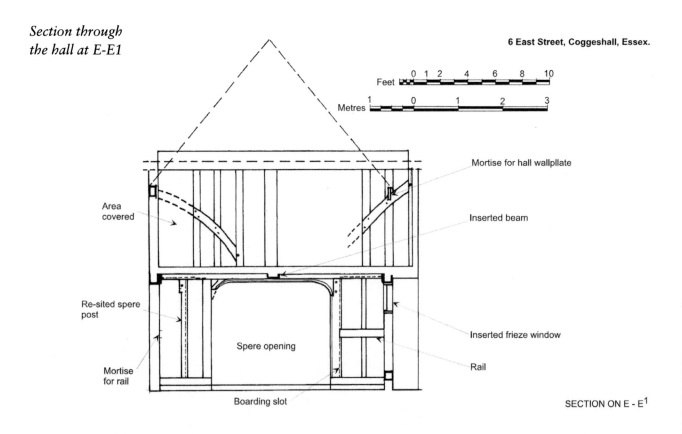

6 East Street, Coggeshall, Essex.

Feet 0 1 2 4 6 8 10

Metres 1 0 1 2 3

Mortise for hall wallpllate

Area
covered

Inserted beam

Re-sited spere
post

Spere opening

Inserted frieze window

Mortise
for rail

Rail

Boarding slot

SECTION ON E - E¹

6 East Street, Coggeshall, Essex.

Feet 0 1 2 4 6 8 10

Metres 1 0 1 2 3

Low end chamber

*Section through
the cross-passage
at F-F¹*

Door   Door

Door head

SECTION ON F - F¹

*Section through
the cross-passage
at G-G¹*

6 East Street, Coggeshall, Essex.

— · — · — Underside of collar in replaced roof

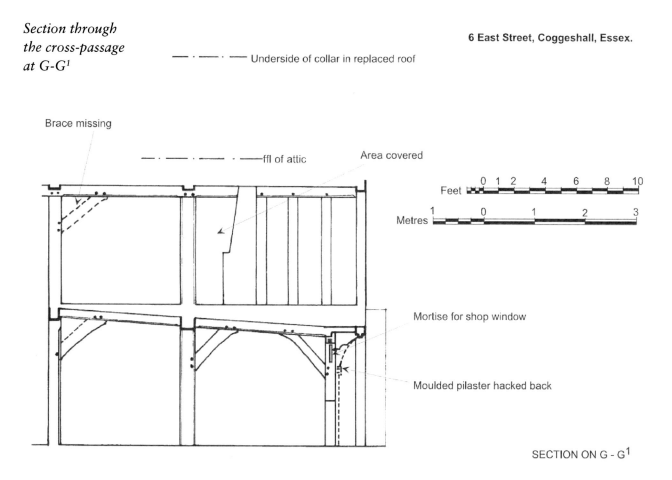

Brace missing

— · — · — · — ffl of attic   Area covered

Feet 0 1 2 4 6 8 10

Metres 1 0 1 2 3

Mortise for shop window

Moulded pilaster hacked back

SECTION ON G - G¹

The hall

The open hall, 16ft x 18ft 6ins (4.87 x 5.63m) deep, has been much altered with the front wall being completely replaced. The east wall is completely close studded with Colchester style bracing and shows no evidence of a door opening. A carpenter's mark survives against the brace mortise on the south storey post consisting of circle with a line through it. The south wall is open framed below the mid rail and appears to be contemporary with the cross-wing.

At first floor level, an open mortise in the east face of a stud in the cross-wing frame denotes the position of the original front wall plate (section E-E¹). This is cut partly through a trenched brace where it passes the stud. Matching trenched Colchester style bracing survives in the wall above the spere opening. Peg holes in the top of the tie-beam show that the roof was originally of crown post type with foot braces as found in other Coggeshall buildings. Against the south-east storey post is evidence for a single diamond mullioned window running from wall plate to mid rail with evidence of two pintles holes for a hinged shutter. The stone fireplace surround dates from the insertion of a floor into the hall, but a gap in the peg holes of the rear wall plate suggests that there was an earlier stack.

Discussion

The timbers of the hall and cross-wing were not suitable for tree-ring dating. It is probable that they were later than the 1441 range to the south which it is suggested was truncated when the cross-wing was built. A date in the third quarter of the 15th century is proposed on stylistic grounds and timber characteristics.

The lack of a defined stair trap in the low end cross-wing is unusual. Was there an extension to the rear of the cross-wing effectively filling in the gap to the 1441 building and thus precluding the need for a door to the rear of the cross-passage? It must be noted that no arched door head, as found elsewhere, was used in this position.

The house on the frontage lacked clear evidence for a parlour to complement the cross-wing and hall. There seem to be two possibilities. There may have been an in-line parlour east of the hall, where later there was a carriage arch or gatehouse. A possible gap in the frame of the east ground floor wall of the hall suggests the existence of a door which led into it. Alternatively, the open frame under the mid rail of the rear wall of the hall, as well as containing a chimney, provided sufficient space to access a rear parlour which could have been accommodated in the single storey outbuilding of the previous phase.

Period 3. 16th century improvements

Period 3A

By 1532 there is documentary evidence for a gatehouse with a chamber over it which gave access to the rear of 6 and 8 East Street, down what is now Pettitt's Lane. Vehicle damage to 6 briefly revealed a jetty bracket for this gatehouse. If the possibility is accepted that the hall had an in-line parlour, it is also possible that the parlour was remodelled as a cross-wing which then had a carriage arch opened in it at the ground floor.

Period 3B. The parlour wing to the rear of the hall

A two-bay two-storey structure behind the hall on the frontage forms a typical urban plan-form with a parlour to the rear of the hall. It has been argued above that in origin this was a single storey free-standing building, which could later have been used as a parlour to the hall. The parlour wing covers a first-floor window in the wall of the hall, evidence that as an enlarged two-storey structure it was later than the construction of the hall.

At first floor the frame is exposed with evidence for large windows to both the east and west walls, but with the soffit of the wall plates covered, the mullion profile cannot be confirmed. The two bays are divided by what appears to be a reused tie-beam with mortises for a fully studded partition. If there was a partition in this position it would have been prior to the introduction of a stack as limited space to the front of the fireplace would have made its use impossible. Edge-halved and bridled scarf joints are positioned in the top plates under the tie-beam. The south end tie-beam has a completely different pegging pattern of alternating double and single pegging that appears to represent studs of wide and narrow widths. It has been argued that this was reused from the single storey building when it was raised in height. It is unfortunate that the roof space is sealed as it could shed further light on this complicated building.

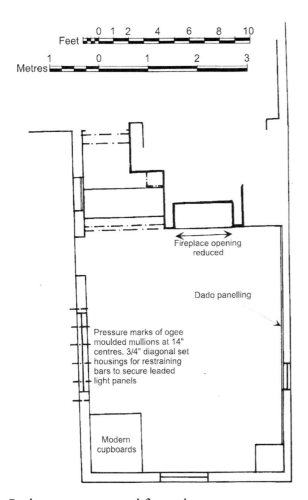

Parlour range, ground floor plan

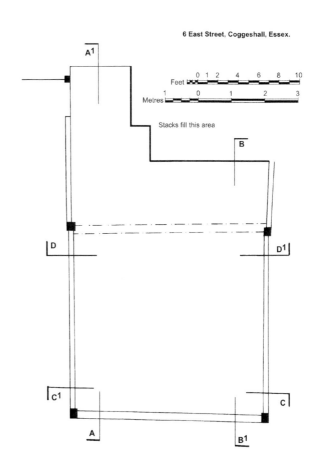

Parlour range, first floor

Tree–ring dates were obtained from cored timbers at first floor level. The timbers that dated were the west wall plate with shutter groove from the north bay, 1464-97; and a window stud from the west wall of the south bay, 1484-1520, yielding a combined date of 1484-97. Since the two storey parlour seems to have been integral with the insertion of a floor into the hall, which is thought to have occurred in the 16th century (see below), it seems likely that these timbers, like others at first floor level, were reused.

Phase 3C. The remodelled hall

A floor was inserted in the hall and its roof raised to provide attic accommodation, the remodelling extending the new roof across the cross-wing range and creating a long-wall jetty to unify the appearance of the house. These changes are most visible at first floor, where the surviving rear wall plate and upper part of the east wall and tie-beam have been left in position and cripple pieces added to achieve the roof raise.

The inserted floor has a central beam with a hollow and ogee moulding and the common joists are covered. The ends of the southern common joists are held in place by a clamp. To the west of the bay window is a frieze window with ovolo moulded mullions. The wall to the east of the bay could have also have housed a frieze light that flanked an earlier oriel window.

A brick chimney built in the parlour against the south side of the rebuilt hall must belong to this phase as it provided a hearth at first floor in the hall, as well as a large cooking hearth to the ground floor of the hall, and a smaller one at that level to the parlour. The fireplace at first floor is made of stone, an exceptional feature indicative of wealth and high status.

A date in the second half of the 16th century is suggested for these alterations.

Discussion

The insertion of the floor into the hall, and the erection of an upper floor to the single storey outbuilding to form a rear parlour, with the brick chimney between the two, would seem to be linked events, inasmuch as they would have been communication between them, and hence approximately contemporary. The tree-ring date of 1484-97 for the first floor of the parlour seems early for these changes to have been made, and the timbers therefore are probably reused. These improvements would have provided high class accommodation in the frontage buildings

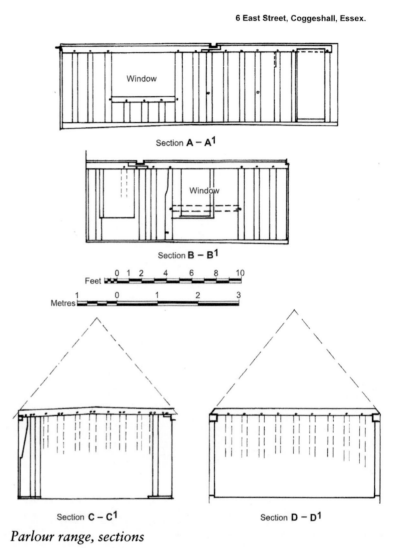

6 East Street, Coggeshall, Essex.

Section **A – A**[1]

Section **B – B**[1]

Section **C – C**[1]   Section **D – D**[1]

Parlour range, sections

Phase 3B. The southern stable

Of the row of three buildings to the south of the 15th century commercial buildings, the southernmost is the earliest and has been interpreted as a stable.[3] It is a three bay single storey building enclosing an undivided space, measuring about 22 x 40ft (6.70 x 12.19m). The building has narrow studding, with tension braces. There was wattle and daub between the studs. All the studs, except those in the south wall, have been removed, so windows and doors are difficult to identify. There was a door 2ft 5ins (0.75m) wide at the north end of the east side, and apparently an opposing one in the west wall. There is a crown-post roof, and an edge-halved scarf in the top plate. The drawings suggest that some of the timber was reused. These features point to a date in the later 15th or 16th centuries, but before 1600, probably in the second half of the 16th century. The building was later weatherboarded, and a large chimney inserted against the end of 6D.

---

3   Shackle 2001.

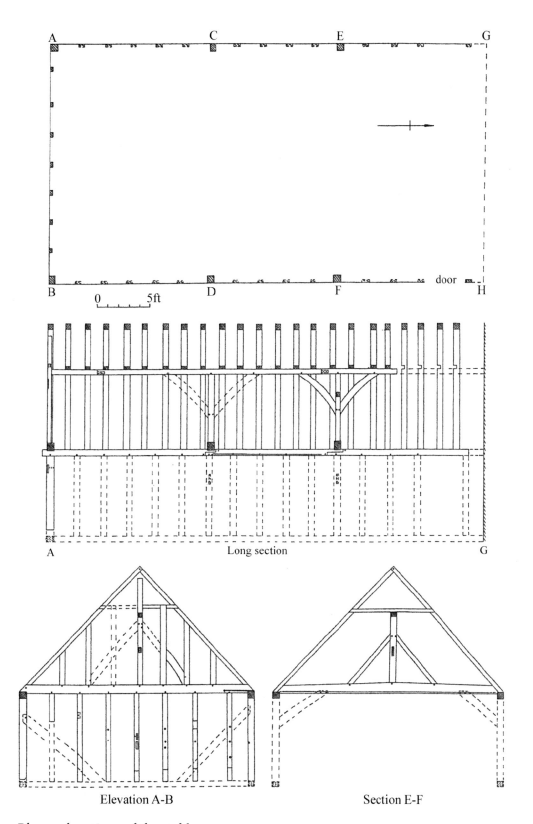

Plan and sections of the stable

Period 4. The 17th-century outbuildings

The stable and the southern commercial building are linked by two structures (now nos 6C and 6D) made almost entirely of reused timber, which look like older buildings moved here to function as workshops or similar. Unsuitable for dendrochronology, their characteristics suggest a 17th-century date.

6C East Street

This in-line two storey range of two unequal bays incorporates much reused timber and therefore was unsuitable for tree-ring dating. The extent of reuse suggests a 17th century date. It was a commercial building or workshop. The floor joists are moulded. Interesting is a reused window with a carved cove to the head rail. The roof is probably clasped purlin, being ceiled above the collars. The rear wall had a diamond mullion window at first floor. In the north wall at first floor, the tie-beam and braces were cut through to form a door into the commercial building at 6B. Although this looks like an alteration, the timbers are fully framed and pegged, and so they were probably built like this. On the east side, at right angles to it, there is a 19th-century extension with primary bracing.

6D East Street (Brook Cottage)

This is another former commercial building, a similar two storey in-line range aligned north-south. It too was unsuitable for tree-ring dating since it is probably built entirely of reused timber of 15th-century character, something that again suggests a 17th-century date, as does the fact that the studs are not pegged. It is presumed to be slightly later in date than 6C. There are axial spine beams either side of the binding joist which divides it into two bays, one moulded, the other plain. The common joists are flat section. Face-halved and edge-halved scarf joints occur in the top plate. At first floor there is a reused cambered tie-beam. Here there were four four-light diamond mullion windows, one either side in each bay. This fenestration pattern was probably repeated at ground floor, indicating that good light levels were important to whatever was done in the building. The roof was not seen.

History

6 East Street was adjacent to a property called the Dyehouse. There has been confusion over whether it too was part of this property. This seems not to have been the case, as the Dyehouse was part of Coggeshall Hall manor, whereas 6 was of Great Coggeshall. The documents do make it clear that there was a gatehouse and carriage way between 6 and 8 East Street.

By the time of the 1575 rental, 6 belonged to the clothier Robert Litherland. Although the property was clearly a commercial premises suited to the needs of a clothier, it is uncertain whether Litherland lived there. The court rolls apparently indicate he lived in Little Coggeshall. The two commercial buildings behind the hall and cross-wing clearly seem designed to have been rented out, comparable to the pair of 15th-century shops at no. 1 Church Street. The possibility has been considered that 6B, the more southerly of the two commercial buildings, was a dyehouse, but the evidence is not entirely convincing. Whilst clearly having been built to have a specific function, the precise use remains unclear. Litherland, and the relationship between 6 and 8 East Street, are discussed in more detail in the account of no. 8. The probable stable is the only one of its age identified in the town.

Until the 1980s, no. 6 was a butcher's shop. 6D and the stable are said to have been used as a slaughterhouse.

8 East Street (Durdens)

John Walker and David Andrews

This property was a two cell medieval house consisting of a medieval two bay service cross-wing to the west with a low open hall to the east, facing north onto East Street. The cross-wing was rejected for dating because the timbers were fast grown with insufficient rings. Its crown-post roof with thin 2in (51mm) thick braces probably indicates the late 15th or early 16th century, but this is not an infallible guide to the date as some late 14th century crown posts have relatively thin braces. Since no. 10 to the east was dated to 1386, it is concluded that there was no high end parlour, which suggests it may originally have had an urban plan with a parlour to the rear.

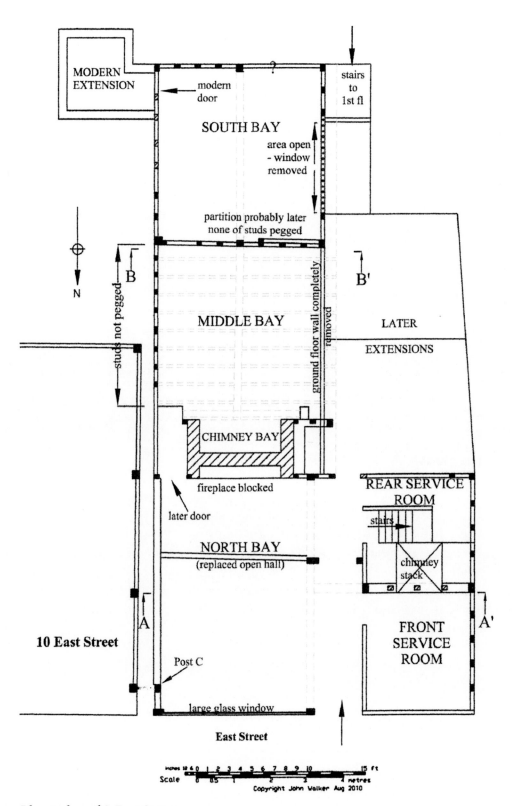

Plan today of 8 East Street

Gables removed in the
18th or 19th century

8 East Street today, showing how its roof has been changed

The 1618 tree-ring date obtained for the rear wing of the property has shown that the open hall was replaced by a long cross-wing of three bays, plus a chimney bay between the north and middle bays. This was built parallel to the medieval cross-wing, with the north bay on the site of the medieval open hall and the chimney bay and middle and south bays extending out behind the rear of the line of the old medieval open hall. The north bay of the cross-wing occupied the site of the old medieval open hall and was two storeys high with an upper floor, while the two southern bays behind the chimney stack had three floors, the top floor set 1ft 9in (0.5m) below the wall plate. At this stage the house had two gables facing onto East Street. At a later stage both gables were removed and replaced on the front by a hipped roof parallel to East Street. The house when examined in 2010 had been damaged by a fire located in an airing cupboard in the area of the stack, the damage being limited mainly to smoke blackening and charring of the timbers.

There is no evidence surviving to conclusively show if the hall was heated by an open hearth, or by a chimney on the rear wall like 6 East Street. If the latter, this may explain why the low open hall survived until 1618. If not built with a chimney, then one is likely to have been inserted during the 16th century but the hall could have been left open to the roof until the 17th century as happened with a number of houses in East Anglia.

To the west of the property there is a large gap, Pettitt's Lane, between this house and 6 East Street, wide enough for a carriage way. There is also a small gap on the east side between 8 and 10 East Street. This is only 19½ inches (0.495m) at the north end between the north-east corner post (post C on the plan of the house today) and the north-west jetty post of 10 East Street, and gets steadily narrower still towards the south.

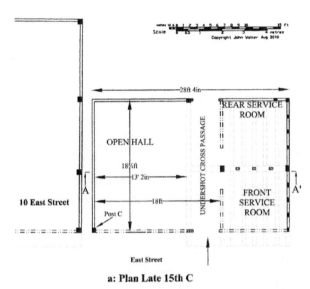

a: Plan Late 15th C

Phase plans showing the property in the late 15th century, and as enlarged in 1618

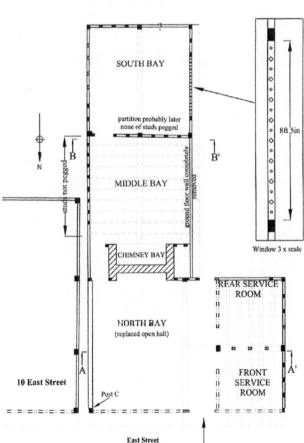

Phase 1. The late medieval cross-wing and hall

The cross-wing to the west of the former open hall was of two bays with an undershot cross passage and was jettied north to the street. It had two rooms on the ground floor, and a single room on the first floor. The first floor room was lit by windows in the centre of the front and rear walls. That in the rear wall has diamond mullions The cross-wing had heavy jowled posts, tension braces halved across the exterior of the studs, floor joists with central tenons and a plain crown-post roof with 2 inch (50mm) thick braces. Interestingly the collar purlin is a piece of reused timber indicated by redundant mortices in its soffit. On the first floor, its east side wall preserves its wattle and daub infill made with oak staves. The front (north) ground floor service room facing East Street may have been a shop or a room open to the public as all the studs in the west wall are 6½ to 7 inches (152-165mm) wide, while those in the rear service room are 5 to 5½ inches (127-140mm).

A partially truncated and cut back post with an arched head at the rear of the cross passage shows that there was a wide 'spere' opening between the passage and the hall. Most of the mid rail over the passage has been removed, but there would have been another such post with an arched head towards the front, framing the opening. To judge from a groove in the soffit of the rail where the damaged post survives, there was boarded infill between these posts and the front and back walls of the cross-wing.

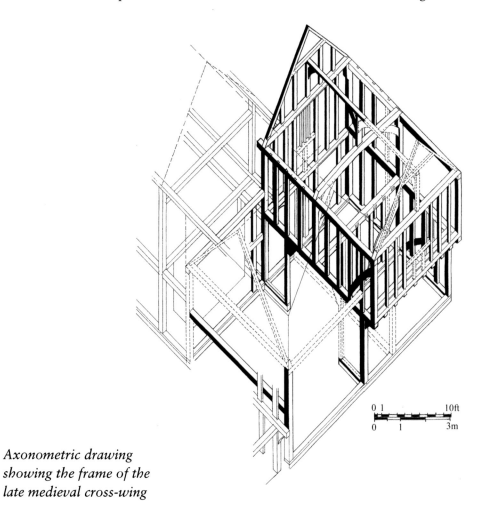

Axonometric drawing
showing the frame of the
late medieval cross-wing

The timber frame of the cross-wing has over time twisted and subsided in places, with the result that the front of the wing is lower than at the rear. The front jetty has been underbuilt, possibly done when the open hall was replaced as suggested below. Also the height of the ground floor in the hall and the front north half of the cross-wing has been raised so that it is about the same level as the external pavement. It is 10in (254mm) above the floor in the rear of the cross-wing, which is probably about the original level as this is 10in (254mm) below the ground sill in the west wall (though it is estimated that there is an extra 6in. void below the boards, which could of course have been dug out rather than representing an earlier floor level). The ground floor of the rear two bays of the 1618 wing is 1ft 8in (0.5m) below the level in the rear of the cross-wing.

All that survives of the open hall is the north-east corner post (post C on the ground plan) and the mid-rail in the east wall tenoned into it, plus mortices in the east wall of the medieval cross-wing for the wall plates for the hall. In the south-east corner post of the medieval cross-wing is an 8in (20cm) long mortice for the rear wall plate. There is another one in the east wall of the cross-wing for the front wall plate set 2ft (0.6m) back from the front of the jetty. The top of these lost plates would have been around 11ft (3.35m) above the floor level in the rear of the medieval cross-wing. The north-east post (post C) is complete, including a tenon at the top where it was morticed in to the soffit of the lost medieval wall plate, and can be seen in the narrow gap between 8 and 10 East Street. It cannot be seen if the post was jowled at the top. This post has a mortice on its west for a mid-rail in the north front wall of the hall at about the height of the inner bressumer of the cross-wing, suggesting the bressumer continued as the mid-rail of the open hall. It is possible that a mortice on the east side of the post indicates that the building continued with a third unit to the east which was replaced by the cross-wing of 10 East Street, but the early date of the latter makes this seem improbable. The rafters of 10 East Street continue down over the small gap between 8 and 10 East Street, not inconsistent with no. 10 being earlier. In addition, there are no indents on the east side of the post to indicate wattle and daub infill to the east of the post.

It is not possible to see if the surviving timbers of the open hall are smoke blackened from an open hearth because all are either painted black or blackened from the recent fire in the building. There are smoke blackened timbers in the later roof.

Phase 2. The 1618 remodelling and east wing

The east wing is of three bays plus a chimney bay between the north and middle bays. The north front bay replaced the open hall. It seems to be all of one build as the east wall plate of the rear two bays appears to continue as the east wall plate of the north bay. The rear two south bays and the chimney bay are jettied on the west side. It is not known if the wing was jettied to the north to the street, but probably not as there is no evidence on the surviving north-east medieval post C to suggest it supported a later jetty. If so the jetty to the front of the medieval west cross-wing will have been underbuilt at this time.

Very little is visible of the north bay on either floor. The roof over the rear southern half of this north bay, running north to south, is very crude with side purlins supported by collars and is probably not original, but it reuses bits from a medieval coupled rafter roof. Most of the rafters are two timbers scarfed together, some pieces with seatings for medieval collars. At a later date in the 18th or 19th century the front half of the roof was realigned parallel with the street.

The chimney bay contains a much altered brick stack which had fireplaces on both sides on the ground floor heating the room in the north bay which replaced the open hall, and to the south the middle bay of the wing. The bricks measure 230 x 100-110 x 45-50mm (9 x 4 x 2ins), and are well made with fairly square arrises. The front of the north ground floor fireplace has been cut back while that in the middle bay has been reworked and the mantel beam replaced by a deeply carved decorated beam, probably done around 1900 by the Coggeshall carpenter Beckwith. Opening up of the ground floor fireplace to the north showed it to have been a parlour hearth with a brick arch and canted sides. On the first floor the stack has been drastically cut back on the north side and a later fireplace inserted on the south side. Also reused on the ground floor as studs and posts, mainly in the middle bay, are a number of moulded 16th century floor joists. Two of these joists form the jambs of a later door frame with an arched head in the north bay on the east side of the north ground floor fireplace.

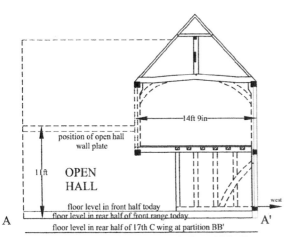

a: Cross-section of front range in late 15th Century

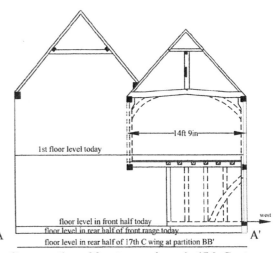

b: Cross-section of front range in early 17th Century

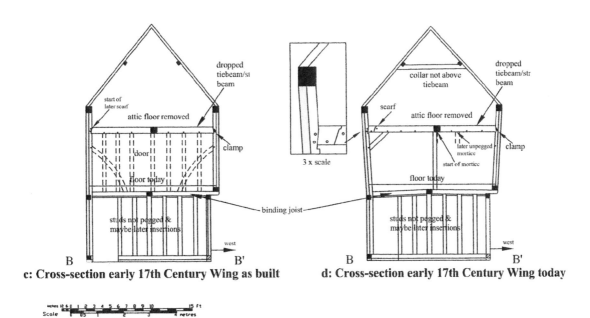

c: Cross-section early 17th Century Wing as built

d: Cross-section early 17th Century Wing today

Sections through the building at different phases in its development

In the two rear southern bays of the 1618 cross-wing, the height of the ground floor is 1ft 8in (0.5m) below the level in the rear of the medieval crosswing and the first floor is lower than in the north bay over the site of the open hall. These two rear bays were constructed with an attic, the floor of which was 1ft 9in (0.53m) below the hall plates (truss BB'). All the common joists for this attic have been removed; all that remains of this floor is the dropped tie-beam/strainer beam in the truss BB' between the rear two bays, part of the dropped tie-beam/strainer beam in the truss on the south side of the chimney bay, and the axial beams with their mortices for the common joists.

This whole wing has experienced considerable structural problems, and the frame of the two south bays has sunk on both their east and west sides. The binding joists on the ground floor on the south side of the chimney bay and in truss BB' have sagged and deflected, and are now of a cambered profile. A new floor has been built at a higher level at the first storey to address this unevenness. In truss BB' between the two rear bays the dropped tie-beam/strainer beam failed (that directly in front of the chimney has been cut) and a new piece of timber scarfed in, increasing the length of the beam by 10½inches (266mm) and leaving the side walls leaning outwards. The east post in truss BB' has dropped 3½in (89mm) more than the west post, but the dropped tie-beam/strainer beam has been put back level, leaving it 3½in (89mm) above the bottom of the notched mortice which originally carried the beam. The extent of the movement in the building is evident on the ends of the single tie-beam where a type of filler has been used to make good the gaps on each side where the dovetail joint has moved away from the top plate. The tie-beam is now secured with iron straps. It is not located above the strainer beam and must have been inconvenient in the attic, but the filler shows it to be an original feature. This deflection in the side walls may in part be the result of deflection caused by the roof which is inadequately supplied with collars. The roof has been reinforced with numerous bird-mouthed collars and struts from the axial beams to the purlins and rafters, and a tie-beam has been added just to the north of truss BB' to stabilise the leaning side walls.

The rear two bays were divided into two rooms on the first floor with a narrow door to the east of the centre of truss BB'. This partition no longer survives. The attic above was a single two bay room. The ground floor today is divided into two rooms with a partition on truss BB', but the studwork of the partition wall is unconvincing as the studs are unpegged; it is probably a later insertion. Probably the east wall of the middle bay has also been rebuilt on the ground floor as its studs are also unpegged and more closely spaced than in the east wall of the south bay. There is no evidence of any pegs in the mid-rail of the this east wall of the middle bay, though elsewhere in the wing most of the studs are pegged, including the ground floor studs in the south bay. It is therefore possible that this wall was originally left open because when built there was another low building immediately to the east of the middle bay, something suggested also by the absence of windows in this side.

On the ground floor there is no evidence of doors or windows in the east wall of the 1618 wing. The only surviving evidence for a window on the ground floor is in the west wall of the rear south bay. This was a very large 8ft 5in (2.57m) long glazed window consisting of 8 diamond mullions 1¾in (44mm) square with mortices for small ¾in (19mm) diameter glazing bars between the mullions. Nothing survives on the ground floor of the west wall of the middle bay to indicate if it had any windows or doors. On the ground floor the south rear wall of the south bay had no door or window in its east half, and nothing is visible of the original structure in the western half.

On the first floor of the two south bays there is no evidence for windows in the east and south walls. The west wall, in contrast, had large windows. The room in the middle bay had a single window flanked by frieze or clearstorey windows, and the south room two windows. These windows were both wide and full height, apparently lacking evidence of any pegged cills above the level of the jetty plate. Possibly they were oriels, further evidence being obscured by the external weatherboarding, or else portable window frames were fitted in them, but it is also possible that these large openings had some industrial function and were first floor loading doors.

The attic storey of the rear two bays lacked any windows unless they were in the south gable, where a window was later inserted. It is unclear today how access was achieved to this attic as all the common joists have been removed.

The carpentry of the 1618 wing

The two principal corner posts in the south wall are not jowled. The walls of the two south bays have secondary internal straight braces halved across the inside of the studs. On the first floor of the rear two bays the studs are at about 2 ft (0.6m) centres, or 19 inches (0.48m) apart, in the exterior walls and between 1ft 8in (0.51m) and 1ft 11in (0.58m) centres in the lost partition in truss BB'. On the ground floor they are at around 1ft 6in (0.46m) centres in the east wall of the middle bay, at about 1ft 10in (0.56m) centres in the inserted ground floor partition in truss BB', while in the south end bay the spacing varies between 1ft 3in and 2ft 1in (0.38 & 0.63m) centres with most at around 1ft 10in (0.56m) centres. The common floor joists in the ground floor ceiling and those in the attic storey, now missing, were narrow section, 2¾ x 5 inches (70x127mm), laid on their narrowest edge with soffit tenons, set at 18in (0.46m) centres. On the first floor these were supported on the west wall by the lintels of the windows or on clamps where there were no windows. Empty peg holes indicate there were clamps on the east wall. In the wall plates there are edge-halved and bridled scarf joints, one of the latest dated instances of the use of this joint in Essex.

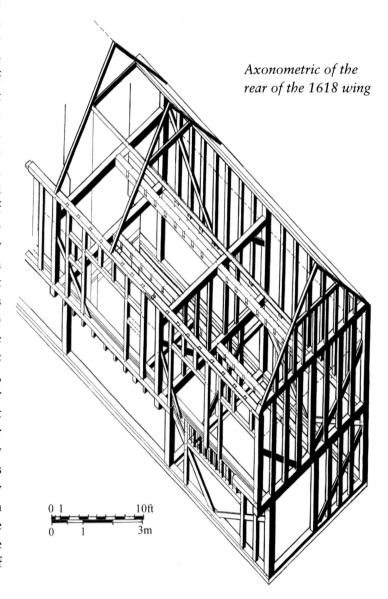

Axonometric of the rear of the 1618 wing

0 1   10ft

0   1   3m

Summary of phasing

Phase 1. Cross-wing at right angles to the street, and on the east side a low building, probably an open hall. Probably built in the late 15th or early 16th century, with a maximum date range of *c.*1450-1575.

Phase 1a. There should have been a modification to the original phase 1 house with the insertion of a chimney in to the open hall, most likely in the first half of the 16th century, unless the open hall was built with a chimney, like 6 East Street. No evidence survives for this phase.

Phase 3. Three bay east cross-wing replaced open hall, extending behind the original building line by two bays plus a chimney bay, built 1618.

Phase 4. In the late 18th or early 19th century, the two front gables were removed and the northern parts of the roof facing East Street were realigned parallel with the street.

Phase 4a. In the early 20th century, the carpenter Ernest Beckwith carried out restoration and alterations. The external weatherboarding may have been added by him. The ceiling in the rear range may have been removed at this time, and the strengthening to the roof with tie bars and struts may also have been done, together with the use of filler for cosmetic repairs to the timbers.

View looking south down the rear of the 1618 wing after the fire in 2010

History

This property was known as Durdens. There is a bundle of deeds for it under that name in the Essex Record Office, and the present owners have a similar collection of deeds.[1] At the time of the 1575 Rental, it was held of the Coggeshall Hall manor and so there is no entry for it. The Rental does record a garden held by Thomas Paycocke which seems to have been in the backlands behind Durdens, enclosed by Coggeshall Hall land. The oldest part of 8 East Street, the cross-wing, pre-dates 1575 and must have been a frontage building forming part of the Dyehouse tenement.

---

1   Essex Record Office D/DO/T337.

Durdens was part of a plot or tenement called the Dyehouse which has a complicated history. It was always held of Coggeshall Hall. The first known reference to the Dyehouse is of 1498 when it was divided into two, the larger by value belonging to Robert Paycock and the other to Andrew Curby.[2] In a 1532 survey of Coggeshall Hall manor, Clement Wiborowe was tenant at will of a tenement called the *Dihouse*, 'lyinge voide .. and he to support the reparacon', and Richard Peverell held 'by coppie one parcel of land with a great gate called a cart gate with a chamber parcell of the tenement called Dyehouse otherwise Browninge with garden parcel of the same teniment.' By the time of a 1605 survey of Coggeshall Hall, the tenement was held by John Browninge, whilst the gatehouse had passed through the hands of Thomas Paycock (who might have found it useful for access to his garden?) to Robert Litherland.

When Litherland made his will in 1610, he left the houses where he lived to his wife, who was also assigned the rent from a piece of land with a gatehouse and garden, parcel of the Dyehouse, and held of Coggeshall Hall.[3] The 1575 Rental shows Litherland to have held property of Great Coggeshall which seems identifiable with no. 6, and possibly with his dwelling-houses referred to in his will. The two parts of the Dyehouse gatehouse and associated land seem thus to have become attached to land held of a different manor.

The Durdens deeds show that in 1688 the property belonged to Thomas Stafford, glover, one of at least four in the town. He was the son or grandson of the Thomas Stafford, glover, who made his will in 1626.[4] This refers to his *new dwelling house* held of Coggeshall Hall, where his *stocke* was and where his sons were to continue in business to support his wife and children. This suggests that Stafford could have been responsible for the 1618 remodelling of no. 8, and that the rear wing with its large windows and attic storage was adapted to carrying on a glover's business.

In 1691, Thomas Stafford died in possession of a messuage or tenement divided into two tenements 'called Durdens alias Durdes parcel of a tenement called the Dyehouse *cum una area et gardino eidem pertinente in Gallows Street*'(an old name for East Street). The property was occupied by William Carnell and William Davyes. This implies the house was divided into two, as the gatehouse seems to have been separate from both nos 6 and 8, being sold by Stafford's son Thomas in 1708. When the same Thomas, described as fellmonger of London, sold Durdens in 1718, it was still divided into two, being occupied by William Davyes and Peter Lorrence.

A 1789 rental for Coggeshall Hall records James Whitaker as owning and living at Durdens in East Street, divided into several tenements.[5] Adjacent to it was the Dyehouse owned and occupied by Thomas Whitaker, part of which had been pulled down to make a gateway to his house.

Ernest Beckwith, the well known carpenter and joiner, who restored Paycockes House and Thaxted Guildhall, acquired the house in 1899 and used the rear range as a first-floor workshop and the front as a shop.[6] Before the fire in 2010, the house preserved some interesting Arts and Crafts features made by him.

---

2   National Archives SC11/182.
3   Essex Record Office D/ABW 24/99.
4   Essex Record Office D/ACW 10/197.
5   Beaumont 1899, 152.
6   Riley and Beckwith 2000.

10-18 East Street

These properties have the appearance of a pair of large H-plan houses with two cross-wings each which have evolved through a process of alternate rebuilding over a period of almost 300 years, though whether their development was quite as straightforward as this is a matter of debate. Their individual phases are described separately below, but the following plan is offered to help clarify the sequence of development.

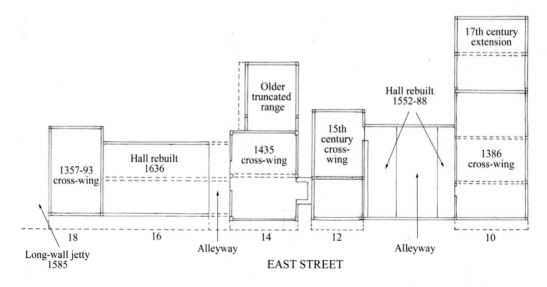

Plan to explain the development of the component parts of 14-18 East Street

10-12 East Street

David Andrews, Richard Shackle, Brenda Watkin and Elphin Watkin

10 and 12 each comprise a cross-wing and approximately half of a hall of what looks like a large H-plan house. These elements are all of different dates. No. 10, the low end cross-wing, was built in 1386, no. 12 probably in the 15th century, whilst the hall was rebuilt in the second half of the 16th century. A two bay extension was added to the rear of the cross-wing at no. 10 in the 17th century. A wide ground floor passageway from the street to the rear has been opened through the hall against the side of no. 12.

No. 10

The cross-wing at no. 10 is large, about 16½ ft (5m) wide, and of three bays, undivided at both ground and first floors. The framing in the front wall is lost or invisible, but there was probably a door and a shop front at the ground floor. There is a door in the east flank wall communicating with the hall, and a stair trap in the floor of the middle bay. There are diamond mullion windows off centre in the rear wall at both floors. There are traces of ruddle or red paint on this wall. The building has Colchester style carpentry, the storey posts being without jowls. Short braces connect the posts to the binding joists and tie-beams. Studs are at intervals of about 2ft (600mm). The joists have centre tenons. The roof has a plain crown post with down braces to the tie-beam. At first floor, there are dowel holes in the east wall for a warp frame. Cores taken from two rafters gave a felling date of 1386.

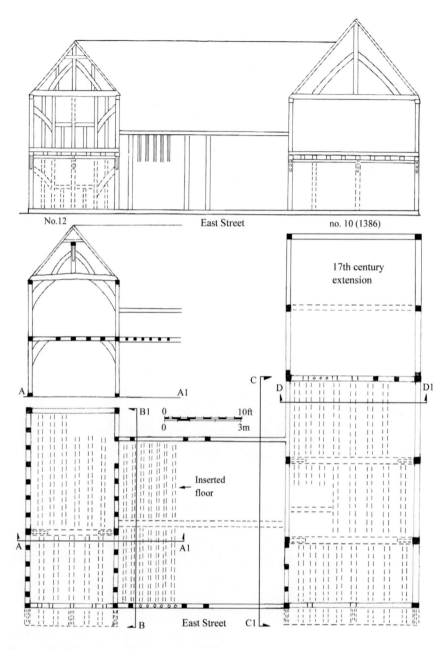

Plan and elevation of 10-12 East Street

No. 12

The cross-wing here was the high or parlour end. At about 12ft (3.65m) wide, it is narrower than the other cross-wing, and being of two unequal bays is also shorter. The first floor was undivided. There were central windows at both floors in the front elevation, and also windows at the rear of the west flank wall one above the other, probably to light a stair. A door in this wall gave access from the hall. As in no. 10, the crown posts in the roof have down braces. The general character of this cross-wing and its carpentry suggests a 15th century date.

The hall

Of the original hall, apparently contemporary with no. 12, there survive some full height posts and a top plate, in the soffit of which the position of a large hall window can be identified. This was presumably of two bays, measuring about 14ft (4.26m) to the street and 20ft (5.94m) deep. The west elevation of the parlour wing at no. 12 presents a dramatic pattern of saltire bracing which must have been an impressive feature of the interior of the hall. Dowel holes in this wall were for a high end bench.

The hall was rebuilt and a floor inserted, one joist giving a date range of 1552-1588. The joists are moulded, with a hollow and an ogee, and over them are 16 inch oak boards. There is a face halved scarf in the top plate. The roof is of clasped purlin construction with wind braces. A building of this quality must have had a stair and chimney; in the absence of evidence for them, it can be suggested that they were located against the rear wall.

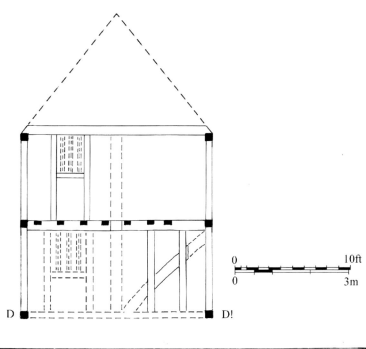

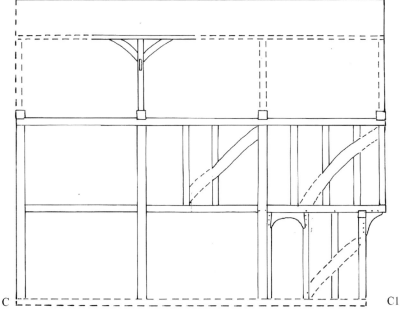

Elevation of the north wall of the cross-wing at 10 East Street seen from the inside (top), and of the west wall seen from the outside

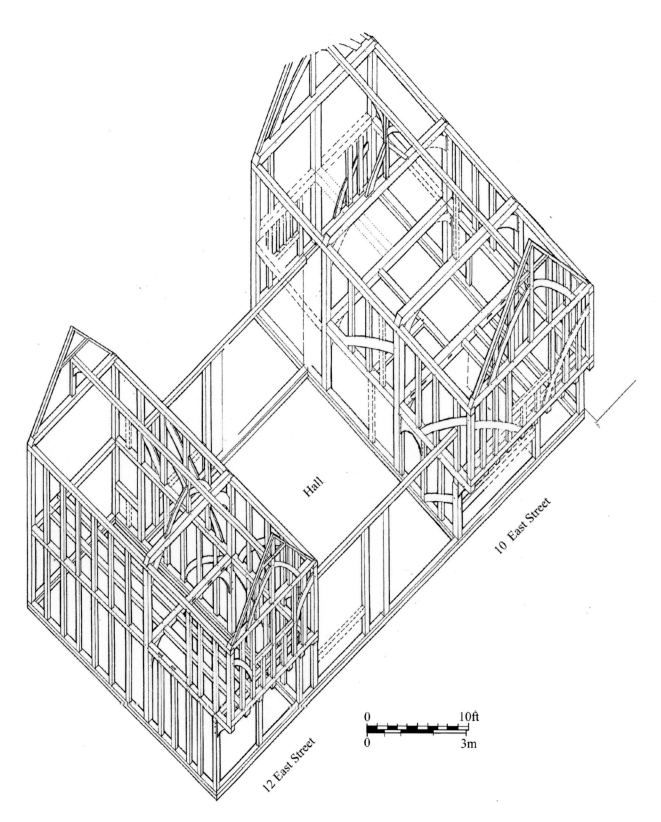

Hall

10 East Street

12 East Street

0 ────────── 10ft
0 ────────── 3m

Axonometric reconstruction of 10-12 East Street

The extension to the rear of no. 10

At the rear of the service cross-wing is a two-bay extension with the ground floor lower than that of the cross wing taking account of the land sloping down to the river. The extension measures internally 15ft 9ins x 17ft (4.8 x 5.18m) wide. The main frame is a mix of oak and elm with the infill in the typical close studding style of the area with evidence for internal trenched braces. The storey posts are jowled and the open frame against the earlier rear wall has arched braces at first floor level. The central truss is open at both ground and first floor creating a single

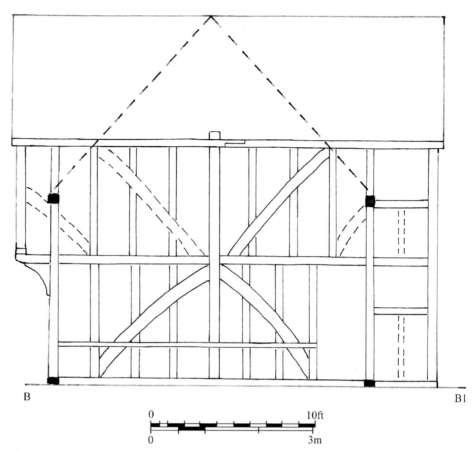

The west wall of the cross-wing at 12 East Street seen from inside the hall

room to each floor. There are no braces at first floor level to the central tie-beam which has a carpenter's face mark (which identifies the fair/working face of the timber) on the north side. The floor has been made up from reused shortened moulded oak joists housed into two axial beams supported by a central transverse beam which is housed into the storey posts of the central truss. Three joists have been replaced and a late 18th or early 19th century stack inserted against the rear wall of the earlier cross wing. No evidence was found for a trimmed stair opening giving access to the first floor.

The south and west walls were covered at ground floor, but there was evidence for a small window in the south bay of the east wall. In the north bay of this wall there was no evidence for either studs or a window.

At first floor level there is a window opening extant in the north bay of the east wall. In the south bay there is part of an internal trenched arch brace crossing the studs. The gabled south wall is covered below the tie beam but the intermittent spacing of pegs along this timber suggests an interesting pattern of windows and possibly a door. As there was no evidence for a stair trap access could have been by a first-floor door, as at the rear range of 6 East Street. Some reused moulded timbers are used as infill studs above the tie beam.

The roof is of clasped side purlin type with principal rafters, pegged collars and wind braces. The wind braces are paired in the northern bay but only one in the south bay against the gable wall.

155

T

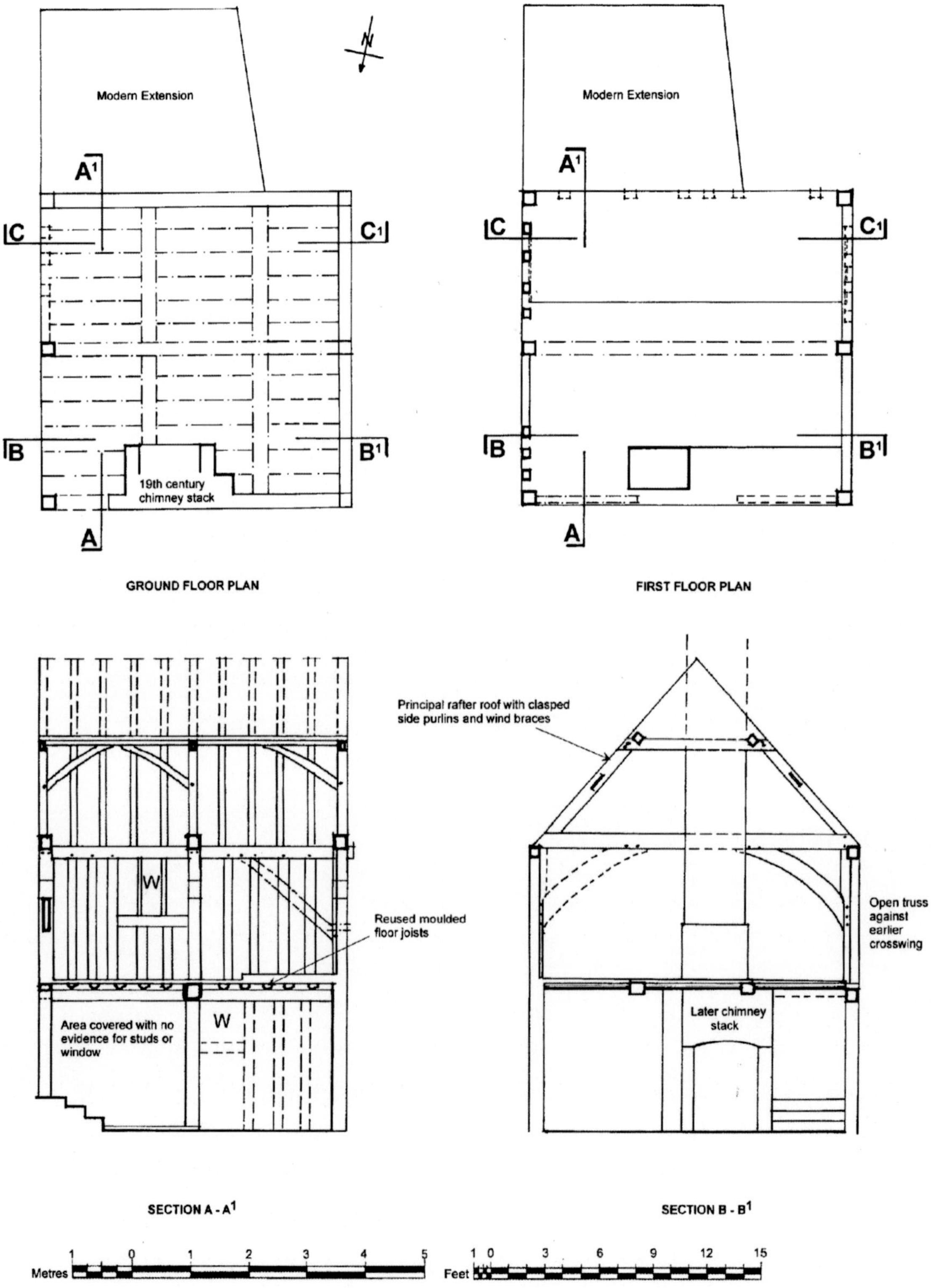

Modern Extension

A¹

|C   C¹|

|B   B¹|

19th century
chimney stack

A

GROUND FLOOR PLAN

Modern Extension

A¹

|C   C¹|

|B   B¹|

A

FIRST FLOOR PLAN

W

Area covered with no
evidence for studs or
window

W

Reused moulded
floor joists

SECTION A - A¹

Principal rafter roof with clasped
side purlins and wind braces

Open truss
against
earlier
crosswing

Later chimney
stack

SECTION B - B¹

1   0   1   2   3   4   5
Metres

1 0   3   6   9   12   15
Feet

Plans, elevation and section of the rear extension to 10 East Street

When originally built the two bay extension appears to have been independent from the cross-wing as the door openings connecting the two builds are later features. Much of the frame is now covered and access to the ground floor could not be found, although the absence of studs or window to the north bay of the east wall is puzzling. Access to the first floor could have been by a door in the south gable wall. Although the reused moulded timbers now give the building a grand feel, this appears to have been a utilitarian building, possibly a workshop, built at the end of the medieval cross wing in the 17th century. The reused joists with the hollow/ogee mouldings are 16th century.

The extension was rejected for tree-ring dating due to the presence of elm and insufficient rings in the oak timbers.

Discussion

The service cross-wing at no. 10 is very large. Its undivided spaces suggest it was essentially a commercial building such as a wool hall. If so, the resemblance of these buildings to a typical H-plan house is somewhat misleading. The 15th century cross wing at no. 12 and the probably contemporary hall seem to have been built as a self-contained unit against the earlier commercial building, though there seems to have been communication between them. The span of the hall at about 20ft (6m) was unusually wide, raising the possibility that it had a rear aisle which might have accommodated service functions.

History

Robert Revy is given as the owner in the 1575 rental survey.

14 East Street

Brenda Watkin, Elphin Watkin and David Andrews

The large gable of this cross-wing is a dominant feature on this side of East Street. The interior does not disappoint, comprising two bays of imposing dimensions 24ft 9ins x 15ft 6ins (7.54 x 4.72m) internally, with a ceiling height of over 10ft (3.04m) at ground floor and 9ft 6ins (2.89m) at first floor. This cross-wing has been tree-ring dated to 1435. To the rear is another range, now of two and a half bays, the half bay truncated by the cross-wing, indicating that this building is the earlier. Cores from this rear range, however, failed to date.

The older rear range

The rear range is built of substantial timbers, and was jettied on the east side, the jetty now underbuilt. A carpenter's mark, IIII, on the south-east corner post, indicates that the building was never more than three bays long. Its ground floor is 2ft 5ins (0.74m) below the level in the cross-wing, and the first floor 5ft 5ins (1.65m) lower. The drop in level seems to correspond to the line of an old terrace of the river Blackwater. The carpentry is Colchester style, lacking jowls to the posts. Studs are at 18ins (0.45m) centres. The two intact bays are of slightly different dimensions, the southern one being the larger, 10ft 10ins x 11ft 5ins (3.30 x 3.48m), with the central bay 8ft 10ins x 11ft 5ins (2.68 x 3.48m) wide internally. It is uncertain whether the ground floor was divided; the binding joist between the two bays is a replacement timber. The first floor was undivided and open to the crown-post roof. The crown post is plain with thick braces. The collar purlin has a splayed scarf joint with under-squinted butts suggestive of a 14th century date. There was a window, indicated by a gap in the pegging and a shutter groove in the east side of the southern bay at first floor, and probably another in the same side of the truncated northern bay. As the pegging along the wall plate is at regular spacing, it can only be suggested that the window is formed by a central mullion between the studs as in the reused wall plate at 33 East Street.

The 1435 cross-wing

The cross-wing was built to impress. It was undivided at both floors. At ground floor the bays are divided by a truss with a beam with an ogee and two hollow mouldings rising from slender shafts with Perpendicular capitals. Similar shafts occurred on the jettied front, now underbuilt, which was divided by three equally spaced posts. Against the west wall there is a chimney stack built of flint, tile and brick, with a stone fireplace, with foliate carving in the

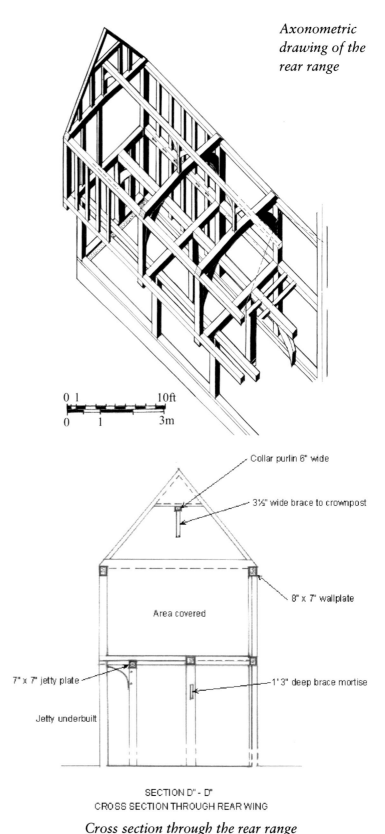

Axonometric drawing of the rear range

0 1   10ft

0   1   3m

Collar purlin 6" wide

3½" wide brace to crownpost

Area covered

8" x 7" wallplate

7" x 7" jetty plate

1'3" deep brace mortise

Jetty underbuilt

SECTION D" - D"
CROSS SECTION THROUGH REAR WING

Cross section through the rear range

spandrels of the Tudor arch. This was thought to be made of clunch, but conservation in 2012, which saw the removal of disfiguring brown paint, showed it to be of a harder stone, possibly a type of Kentish Rag. Graffiti on the lintel of the fireplace include the name 'Paycok'. In the east wall there is a pair of service doors 43ins (1.1m) wide with dropped heads and moulded surrounds. A big Colchester style brace descends to the side of the jamb of the northern door; there is a similar brace at first floor. No window or stair position was identified but much of the frame is concealed. The first floor, originally an undivided two-bay chamber, was designed to show off the roof, which has an octagonal crown post with moulded capitals and base and four-way bracing. The rafters have soulaces and ashlar pieces to the moulded wallplate. A door in the back wall with a four-centred arched head communicates with the rear range. As with the rear range the carpentry follows the Colchester style with no jowls to the storey posts and braces running from vertical to vertical. Studs are at 18ins centres (0.45m).

There is a cellar about 15ft (4.57m) square under the rear of the cross-wing. Like the chimney, it is built of irregularly coursed tile and brick, which was originally plastered. A scar in the north wall marks the former position of a wall which must have flanked a passage leading down into it from the garden or yard to the rear. The drop in level of over 2 feet (0.6m) to the back of the house meant that relatively few steps would have been required to access it. Today there is still a light well, possibly once a coal chute, in this position. In the north and east walls, there are niches 16ins (0.41m) wide and high with pointed heads. A chamfered beam 14ins (0.36m) wide spans the cellar from north to south. The floor construction is covered, but there are probably joists tenoned into this beam. The floor is boarded, possibly because damp is a problem.

The hall to the west, now occupied by no. 16, was rebuilt in 1636 with an upper floor. The position of the cross-passage is now a covered alleyway 31ins (0.79m) wide between the two properties.

On one of the crown post braces is chalked 'H. Ruffle 1873', and what appears to be T. Ruffle and possibly the same date occur on another brace, a record of repairs to the roof at that time.

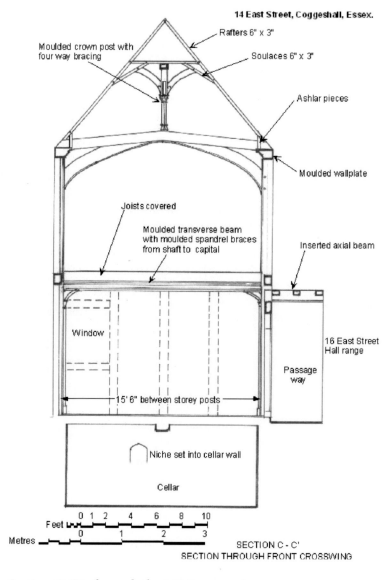

Section C-C1 through the 1435 cross-wing

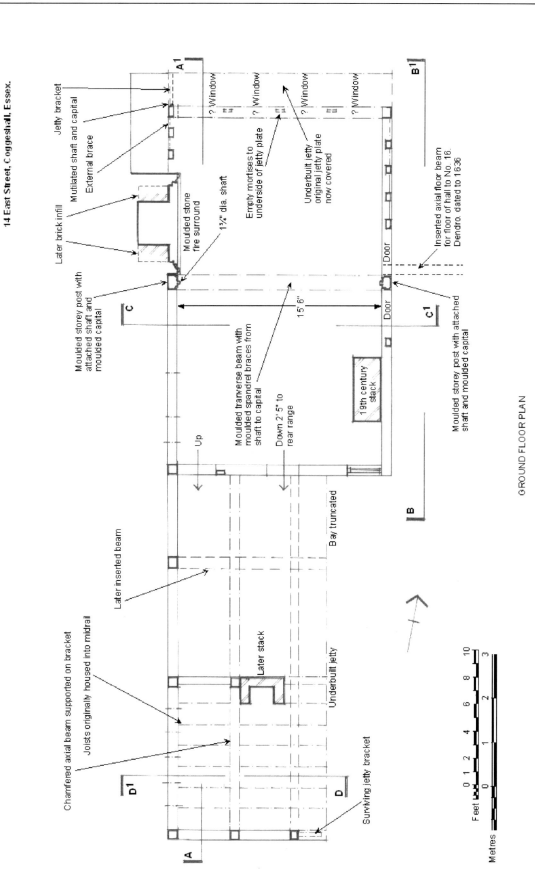

14 East Street, Coggeshall. Essex.

Jetty bracket

Mutilated shaft and capital

External brace

Later brick infill

Moulded stone fire surround

1¾" dia. shaft

Empty mortises to underside of jetty plate

Underbuilt jetty original jetty plate now covered

Inserted axial floor beam for floor of hall to No. 16. Dendro. dated to 1636

Moulded storey post with attached shaft and moulded capital

Moulded tranverse beam with moulded spandrel braces from shaft to capital

Down 2' 5" to rear range

Up

15' 6"

19th century stack

Door

Door

Moulded storey post with attached shaft and moulded capital

GROUND FLOOR PLAN

Later inserted beam

Chamfered axial beam supported on bracket

Joists originally housed into midrail

Later stack

Underbuilt jetty

Bay truncated

Surviving jetty bracket

Feet 0 1 2 4 6 8 10

Metres 0 1 2 3

14 East Street, ground floor plan

161

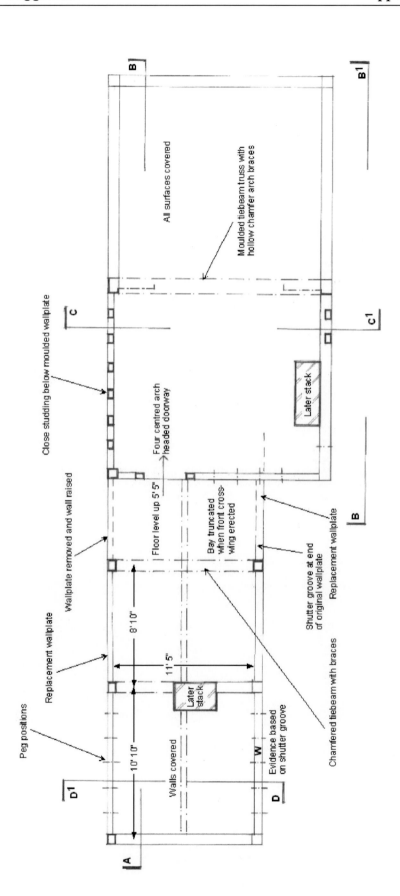

14 East Street, Coggeshall, Essex.

All surfaces covered

Moulded tiebeam truss with hollow chamfer arch braces

Close studding below moulded wallplate

Four centred arch headed doorway

Later stack

Floor level up 5' 5"

Bay truncated when front cross-wing erected

Shutter groove at end of original wallplate

Replacement wallplate

Chamfered tiebeam with braces

Wallplate removed and wall raised

Replacement wallplate

8' 10"

11' 5"

10' 10"

Later stack

Peg positions

Walls covered

Evidence based on shutter groove

FIRST FLOOR PLAN

Feet   0 1 2   4   6   8   10

Metres 0   1   2   3

14 East Street, first floor plan

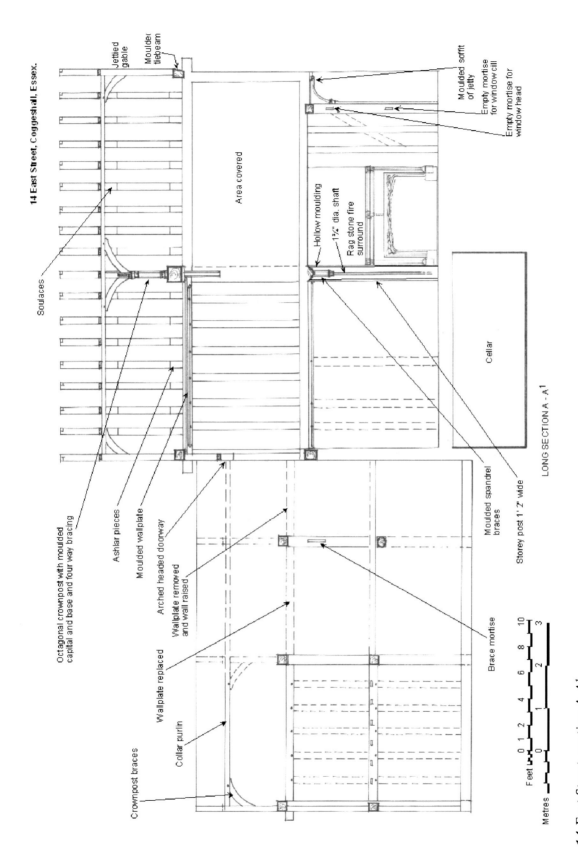

14 East Street, Coggeshall, Essex.

Jettied gable

Moulded tiebeam

Moulded soffit of jetty

Empty mortise for window cill

Empty mortise for window head

Area covered

Hollow moulding

1¾" dia. shaft

Rag stone fire surround

Cellar

LONG SECTION A - A¹

Soulaces

Octagonal crownpost with moulded capital and base and four way bracing

Ashlar pieces

Moulded wallplate

Arched headed doorway

Wallplate removed and wall raised

Wallplate replaced

Collar purlin

Crownpost braces

Moulded spandrel braces

Storey post 1' 2" wide

Brace mortise

Feet 0 2 4 6 8 10

Metres 0 1 2 3

14 East Street, section A-A¹

163

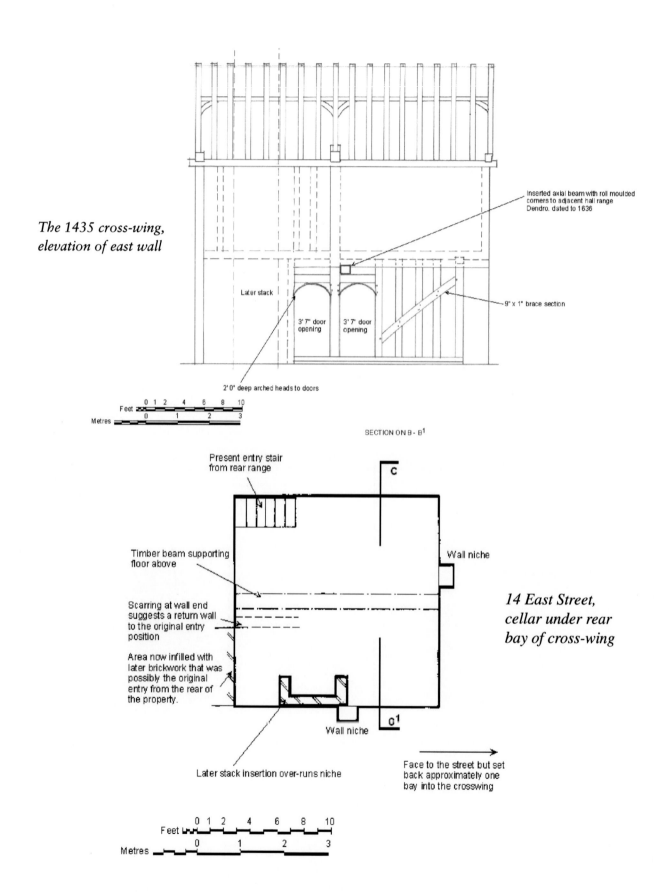

The 1435 cross-wing,
elevation of east wall

Inserted axial beam with roll moulded
corners to adjacent hall range
Dendro. dated to 1636

Later stack

9" x 1" brace section

3' 7" door
opening

3' 7" door
opening

2' 0" deep arched heads to doors

Feet   0 1 2   4   6   8   10
Metres   0   1   2   3

SECTION ON B - B¹

Present entry stair
from rear range

C

Timber beam supporting
floor above

Wall niche

Scarring at wall end
suggests a return wall
to the original entry
position

14 East Street,
cellar under rear
bay of cross-wing

Area now infilled with
later brickwork that was
possibly the original
entry from the rear of
the property.

Wall niche

c¹

Later stack insertion over-runs niche

Face to the street but set
back approximately one
bay into the crosswing

Feet   0 1 2   4   6   8   10
Metres   0   1   2   3

164

Discussion

The rear range resembles the two 15th century buildings behind 6 East Street and like them must have had a commercial use, possibly with a shop front at ground floor. That this range was truncated when the cross-wing was built suggests that there was initially an in-line house on the frontage which was not as deep as the cross-wing.

The existence of the rear range probably explains why the cross-wing is shorter than most in Coggeshall, only two bays rather than three, again as at 6 East Street. However impressive it might be, the cross-wing was a functional building, presumably with a shop to the street, and linked to the range to the rear. The division of the ground floor front wall into four units by three posts is similar to the cross-wing at 29 East Street. Part of the traditional storage function of the service wing was accommodated in the cellar which had an entrance to the rear. The access is similar to the arrangement at the Old House, Spring Road, St. Osyth, except that there it was entered from the street. Remarkably, the cross-wing was heated at the ground floor with what is the earliest known surviving masonry stack in Essex (though chimneys of similar construction exist at Earls Colne and elsewhere). The slender shafts and capitals of the central truss, and front elevation posts, also found at 6 East Street, are a feature of north Essex and Suffolk.

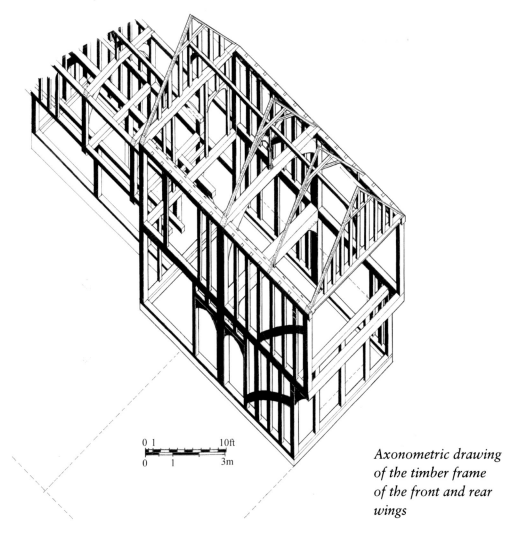

0 1   10ft

0   1   3m

Axonometric drawing
of the timber frame
of the front and rear
wings

Whilst the cross-wing appears to be at the low end of the original hall and has the traditional feature of two service doors, the lack of a defining division or partition between them presents numerous questions. With a possible shop front, imposing stone fireplace in a county of virtually no free stone, and intricate mouldings to the structural timbers, did it really have a service function or serve as a display area for a prosperous merchant? This would then equate to the suggested use of the Ancient House (Olde Hall) at Thetford, Norfolk, where it is thought that the shop went with a very elaborate hall that could be used by a merchant as a display area.[1] If this was the case then the rear range and the cellar could have provided the service space.

History

At the time of the 1575 rental, no. 14 and 16 and 18 to the east were in the ownership of Richard Warner. In view of the graffito on the fireplace, it is probable that at one stage it belonged to the Paycock family.

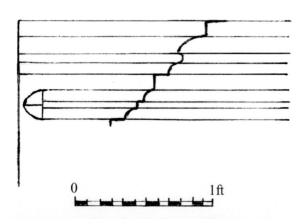

0   1 ft

Left: Moulding of top plate at first floor of the cross-wing

Right: Capital on the central truss at ground floor of the cross-wing

Above: The name Paycok incised on the fireplace

Right: Coursed flint and tile rubble masonry in the cellar. The chimney is built of similar masonry.

---

1   Smith, R. 2001 and 2002.

16 East Street

Brenda Watkin, Elphin Watkin and David Andrews

This house is a former hall located between two tall cross-wings at 14 and 18 East Street, with which it once formed one house. It was rebuilt as a single bay structure measuring about 23ft 6ins x 21ft wide (7.16 x 6.40m), with a jetty and upper floor, in 1636, four cores taken from principal rafters having been successfully dated.

Like the adjacent cross-wings, the rebuilt hall was of high quality, of excellent oak timber, with substantial bridging joists with deep chamfers with lamb's tongue stops at the first floor, and with principal and common joists at ground floor all with quarter round mouldings to the arrises of the soffits. The joists have housed soffit tenons.

At ground floor, the jetty has been underbuilt. The jetty plate is covered or cut back, and so the front wall cannot be reconstructed. A timber with a simple scroll moulding has been fixed to the inside face of the jetty place, forming a groove or slot where they meet. This is not an original feature; it is probably the fascia from the front of the jetty which was removed and placed here when the jetty was underbuilt. Similarly no features of the rear elevation at ground floor can be reconstructed. It is improbable that this rebuilt part of the house was not heated; the most likely position for a chimney is against the rear wall between two storey posts.

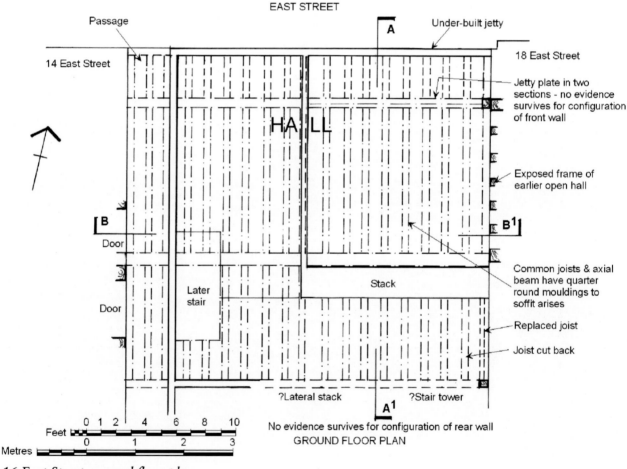

16 East Street, ground floor plan

At first floor, where there was a single chamber, much of the frame is also covered. However a photograph of the front of the house with the render removed at first floor shows that there was a six-light transomed window with stanchions for attaching the glazing, and two frieze lights either side. Access to the first floor was probably via a stair tower, the best evidence for which is a gap in the rafters in the easternmost bay of the rear roof pitch where, curiously, there are two purlins set close together.

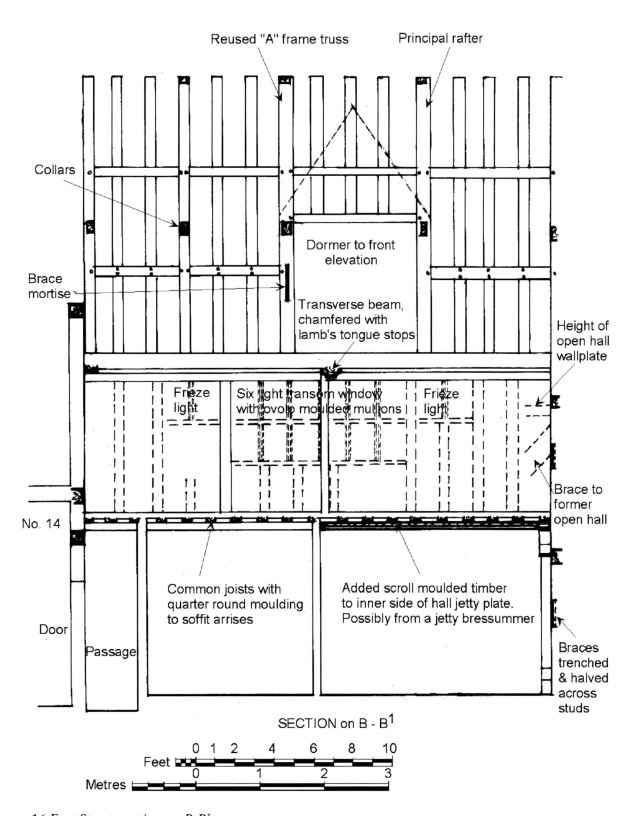

Reused "A" frame truss   Principal rafter

Collars

Brace mortise

Dormer to front elevation

Transverse beam, chamfered with lamb's tongue stops

Height of open hall wallplate

Freize light   Six light transom window with ovolo moulded mullions   Frieze light

Brace to former open hall

No. 14

Common joists with quarter round moulding to soffit arrises

Added scroll moulded timber to inner side of hall jetty plate. Possibly from a jetty bressummer

Door

Passage

Braces trenched & halved across studs

SECTION on B - B^1

Feet   0 1 2   4   6   8   10

Metres   0   1   2   3

16 East Street, section on B-B^1

The roof is of butt purlin construction in four bays with two levels of purlins, the rafters passing over the upper level and tenoned into the lower one. The common rafters are reused from the old roof, being sooted with empty mortices for collars. There are reused timbers of other types, a purlin for instance having mortices for moulded joists. The studs in the east gable wall at the junction with no. 18 next door are nailed and splay jointed into the collar; if original to the construction of the house, this is an early dated instance of this technique of framing. In the second bay from the east of the front roof pitch, there was a gap in the rafters which must have been for an off-centre gable forming a dormer window. The roof was used as an attic, floored with oak boards with rebated edges. There were large braces between the collars and the principal rafters located either side of the former gable on the front elevation. These are an unusual feature in a roof of this sort as they formed obstacles to movement within it. It may be that they were intended to strengthen the roof structure around the dormer, something which raises the possibility that it actually functioned as a lucam, with a pulley for lifting objects up from the street. This seems likely as the roof was clearly designed for storage.

At both floors the east wall has large tension bracing 1ft (0.3m) wide which is trenched into and halved over the face of the studs, and which descends from the central storey post in a fan pattern. It is clearly much older than 1636, and must be the flank wall of the hall before it was rebuilt. At first floor, modifications were made to this wall when the hall was changed to a floored long-wall jetty form. The original tie-beam was removed, the top of the north jowled post recut and a new rail, extending forward to the jetty, fitted over the stud tenons. The jowled storey post was double pegged, but both the studs and the new studs or cripple pieces set into the top of the rail to raise the height of the wall were not pegged. The front storey post has a cut-out for the wall plate of the former open hall and a large mortice in it at first floor for a tension brace that would have been visible in the front elevation of the hall. At the ground floor, this storey post is largely concealed, a post having been applied against it to support the jetty plate. This post is reused and has a curious moulded top forming a sort of bulbous capital. It may have come from an earlier phase of the hall.

The flank wall raises questions about the development of the hall and its relationship to the cross-wings. The cross-wing at no. 18, which has been dated to 1361-97, is open-framed against no. 16. The flank wall of the hall could therefore be earlier than this, but it could equally survive from a hall which was a replacement of one against which no. 18 had been built, an alternate rebuild scenario. The latter seems more probable, which suggests the hall may be contemporary with no. 14 which was dated to 1435. However, there is no structural evidence available to support or disprove this. At about 20ft (6.1m), the hall was unusually wide for Essex, though that at 19 East Street was wider still.

Later alterations were typical of the fashionable improvements made to houses in the town in the 18th and 19th centuries, as well as being linked to the division of the property into three dwellings. It was given a flat façade with sash windows and the dormer gable was removed from the roof. Inside the timber frame was covered up, timbers being cut back as necessary to achieve flush wall surfaces, and the chimney stack and stair tower to the rear were demolished. With the sub-division of the property, the cross passage position between no. 16 and no. 14 became an alleyway.

History

Together with 14 and 18 East Street, this building was in the ownership of Richard Warner at the time of the 1575 rental.

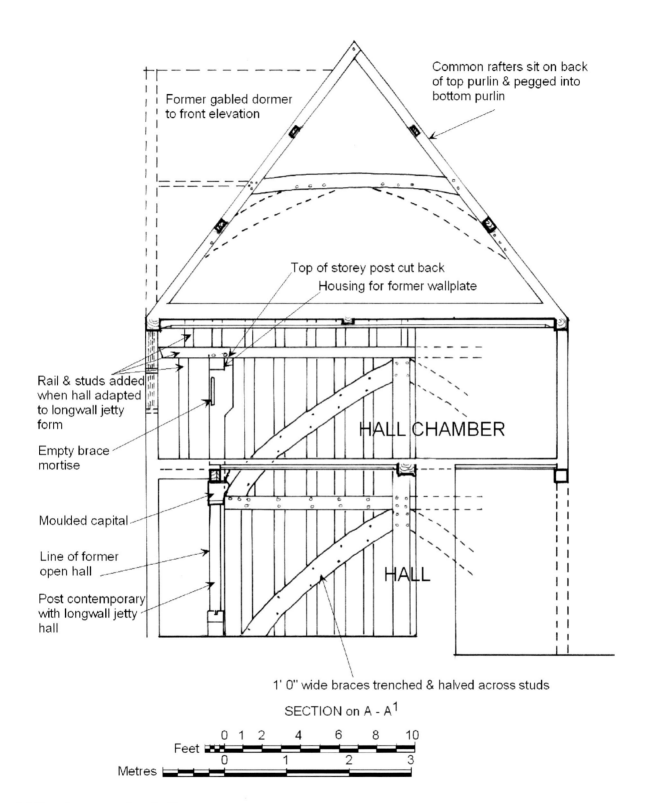

Former gabled dormer
to front elevation

Common rafters sit on back
of top purlin & pegged into
bottom purlin

Top of storey post cut back
Housing for former wallplate

HALL CHAMBER

Rail & studs added
when hall adapted
to longwall jetty
form

Empty brace
mortise

Moulded capital

Line of former
open hall

HALL

Post contemporary
with longwall jetty
hall

1' 0" wide braces trenched & halved across studs

SECTION on A - A¹

Feet

Metres

16 East Street, section A-A¹

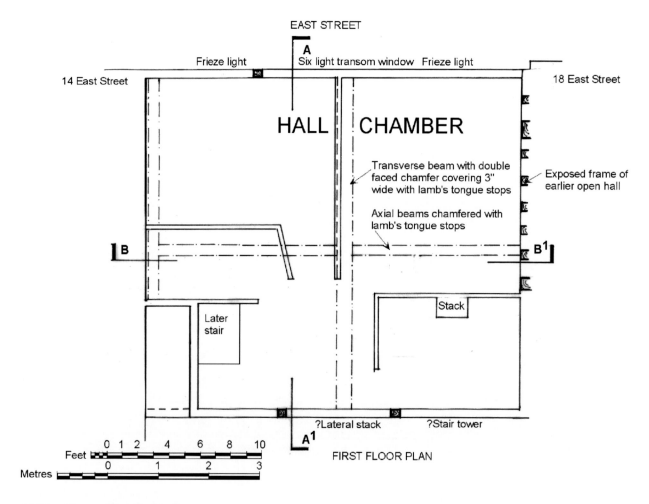

16 East Street, first floor plan

18 EAST STREET, COGGESHALL

Brenda Watkin

Introduction

This is a multi-phase building with a tree-ring date of 1357-1393 obtained for the western section, which is the surviving front bay of a jettied cross-wing the original length of which cannot be determined. To the east is one bay of a long-wall jetty range that was truncated to give access to land at the rear. This range has a carved bressumer with a date of 1585. To the rear are extensions of various dates.

Description

The truncated cross-wing now only consists of one bay, 10ft 6½ins (3.21m) wide by 15ft 2ins (4.63m), with the front jetty underbuilt. The evidence for the jetty is the cut-out for the jetty plate in the soffit of each of the common joists and an empty peg hole showing that the jetty plate was not only housed but pegged. This is usually a sign of early high quality carpentry. The joists are of substantial section, 8 x 4ins (200 x

100mm) at 1ft 9ins (540mm) centres, and of well converted oak which for Essex is unusual in that it is from large trees, as evidenced from the sawn side and bottom faces, rather than from single trees. They are un-chamfered and housed into the plain transverse beam with central tenons. A later stair trap has been formed and then in-filled in the south-east corner of the bay against a former open frame with evidence for braces. The trimmer for this stair trap cuts through an original trimmed opening for a first floor fireplace. At ground floor level the framing of the east wall has been removed and very little framing is visible apart from the south-west storey post and evidence for braces to mid rail and transverse beam.

The existing ceiling height at the ground floor is 8ft 3ins (2.52m) with the first floor originally having the impressive height of nearly 10ft (3.05m) to the underside of the cambered tie-beam. Little evidence of decoration survives at ground floor but the cambered tie-beam has a moulded soffit comprising 1¾ins (44mm) and 1in (25mm) hollow chamfers. The latter continue down the arch braces of the open truss. A short additional moulded section has been pegged to the soffit of the tie-beam continuing the moulding to the west brace. Was this to cover a carpenter's mistake or a poor piece of timber?

A section of the east wall framing is visible at first floor with heavy internal braces either side of a framed opening for a stack. They are trenched into the studs and double nailed to each. Some of the stud faces have also been cut back to accommodate the braces. The conversion of the studs is similar to the floor joists in that they are quartered from larger trees as evidenced by the sawn faces. The position of the south brace is marked by a scribed line across both brace and stud whereas a circular carpenter's mark on the north brace is matched by a circle on the stud. Cores were taken for tree-ring dating from each of the heavier studs forming the opening, in which were rectangular mortises cut at a suitable height, 4ft 6ins to 5ft 1in (1.37m to 1.55m), for a projecting fire hood. Below the north mortise were two peg holes above which were a cluster of taper burns. Viewed from the adjacent roof it can be seen that the heavier framing timbers were double pegged into the wall plate which terminated close to the framed opening. The wall plate and the common rafters, trimmed back for the stack, appear to have been pieced in when the stack was removed. There was no visible evidence that confirmed whether the stack was timber-framed or built from masonry, though the former is the more probable. The insertion of an attic room has reduced the ceiling height and destroyed all evidence of roof construction other than the coupled rafters. Evidence survives in the form of a central peg hole in the tie-beam of the open truss where the wing has been truncated showing that the original roof had a crown post.

The ground floor bay of the truncated long-wall jettied range has also had the jetty plate moved but the carved bressumer of the same design to the rest of the long wall jetty range remains exposed. The former line of the front wall now shows as a pressure mark emphasised by the end of the lamb's tongue stop to the chamfered common joists against the removed jetty plate. The common joists are housed into the axial beam with soffit tenons with diminished haunches. The original gap between the two builds has been in-filled by a scarfed addition to the axial beam and un-chamfered joists of smaller scantling. Reused studs in the typical close studded pattern and pegged top and bottom form the infill of the ground floor eastern wall of the truncated range. No door position was noted although there is a section of the wall to the south corner that is hidden.

At first floor the rear south-east jowled storey post is visible together with close studding with a trenched internal brace of reverse arch form from the tie-beam to the north-east corner post. This type of brace is more common in north Suffolk and Norfolk than Essex. A core taken from the south-east storey post could not be tree-ring dated.

The roof was of simple clasped side purlin form without wind braces. It appears that changes were made to the roof when the gap between the two phases was closed; these and the additional strengthening over the years made analysis difficult.

Discussion

As with many properties in Coggeshall the house comprises numerous builds. The frontage range is made up of one bay of a 14th century cross-wing and another bay of a 16th century long-wall jetty house, originally separated by the stack. It has then been extended in depth to give additional accommodation as the original property comprising 14-18 East Street became sub-divided. The cross-wing may have been associated with an aisled hall to the west[1] but no firm evidence was noted. It could have been a low open hall which was then replaced by a higher open hall in the 15th century. The east frame of this hall is still visible in 16 East Street where with modifications to height and width it was incorporated into the 1636 floored hall. It has not been possible to prove conclusively that the early cross-wing also formed part of the continuous alternate rebuilding of a double cross-wing house comprising no. 14 East Street, a 15th century cross-wing, and nos 16 and 18 East Street. However by the time of the 1575 survey the complete plot was owned by Richard Warner. His property extended to the east where he also owned a narrow plot that encompassed the present 16th century bay of 18 East Street and the adjacent lane. Beyond to the east and behind to the south of this plot was land owned by Richard Sammes. Ten years after the 1575 survey, the long wall jetty range, dated 1585, extended across what had been two separate ownerships. Presumably Sammes, or his successor, had acquired the narrow plot from Warner. At a later stage the lane was recreated by the demolition of one bay of the 1585 range.

As with the other elements of this range the original use of the cross-wing is obscure. However it would appear from the plain nature of decoration to the ground floor that it performed a function of a utilitarian nature. This was in direct contrast to the first floor where the impressive first floor chamber of at least two bays was heated and decorated. It could also be said that the unusual early use of internal braces also contributed to the internal decoration and grandeur.

---

1   The original building at 16 East Street, pre-dating the 1636 rebuild, has been interpreted by David Stenning as having been an aisled hall.

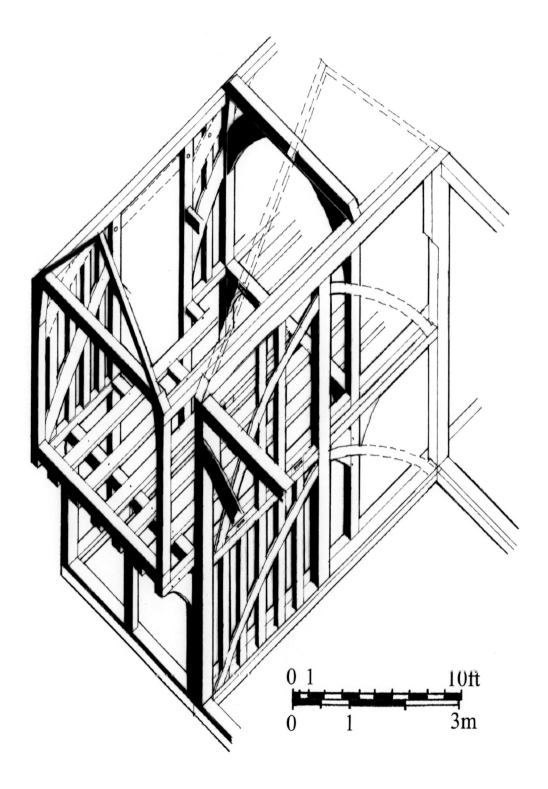

Axonometric reconstruction of the 14th century cross-wing at 18 East Street

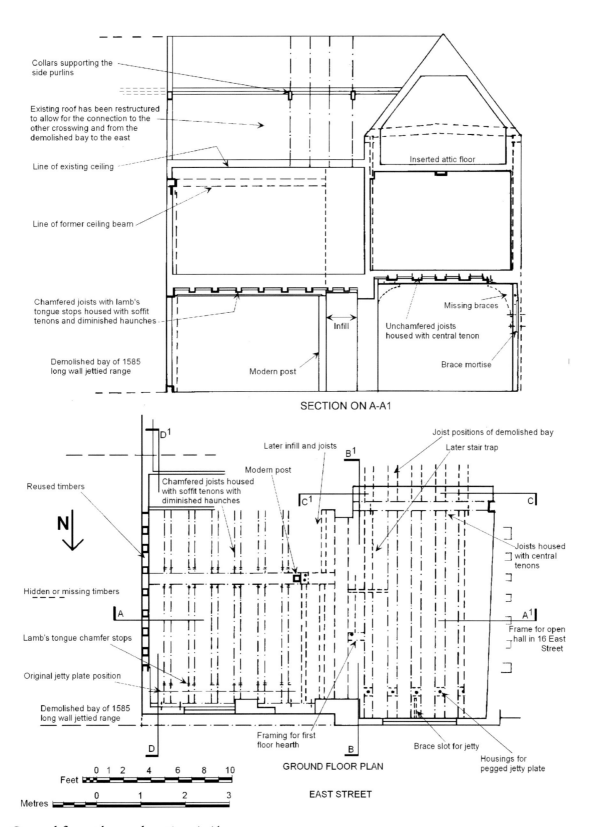

Collars supporting the side purlins

Existing roof has been restructured to allow for the connection to the other crosswing and from the demolished bay to the east

Line of existing ceiling

Inserted attic floor

Line of former ceiling beam

Chamfered joists with lamb's tongue stops housed with soffit tenons and diminished haunches

Missing braces

Infill

Unchamfered joists housed with central tenon

Demolished bay of 1585 long wall jettied range

Modern post

Brace mortise

SECTION ON A-A1

Joist positions of demolished bay

Later infill and joists

Later stair trap

Modern post

Chamfered joists housed with soffit tenons with diminished haunches

Reused timbers

Joists housed with central tenons

Hidden or missing timbers

Lamb's tongue chamfer stops

Frame for open hall in 16 East Street

Original jetty plate position

Demolished bay of 1585 long wall jettied range

Framing for first floor hearth

Brace slot for jetty

Housings for pegged jetty plate

GROUND FLOOR PLAN

Feet 0 1 2 4 6 8 10

Metres 0 1 2 3

EAST STREET

Ground floor plan and section A A¹

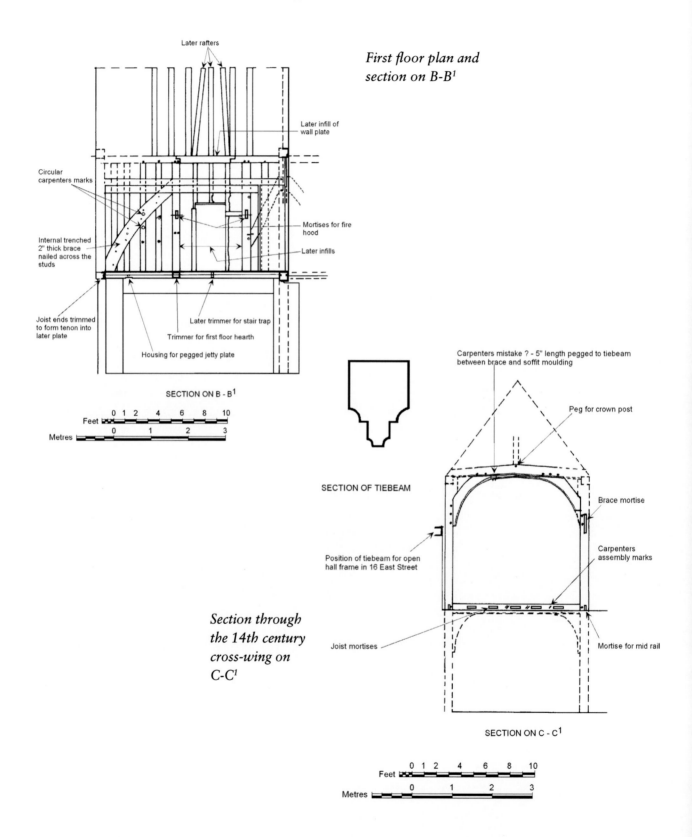

18 East Street, Coggeshall, Essex.

First floor plan and section on B-B¹

Later rafters

Later infill of wall plate

Circular carpenters marks

Mortises for fire hood

Internal trenched 2" thick brace nailed across the studs

Later infills

Joist ends trimmed to form tenon into later plate

Later trimmer for stair trap

Trimmer for first floor hearth

Housing for pegged jetty plate

SECTION ON B - B¹

Feet 0 1 2 4 6 8 10
Metres 0   1   2   3

SECTION OF TIEBEAM

Carpenters mistake ? - 5" length pegged to tiebeam between brace and soffit moulding

Peg for crown post

Brace mortise

Carpenters assembly marks

Position of tiebeam for open hall frame in 16 East Street

Joist mortises

Mortise for mid rail

Section through the 14th century cross-wing on C-C¹

SECTION ON C - C¹

Feet 0 1 2 4 6 8 10
Metres 0   1   2   3

178

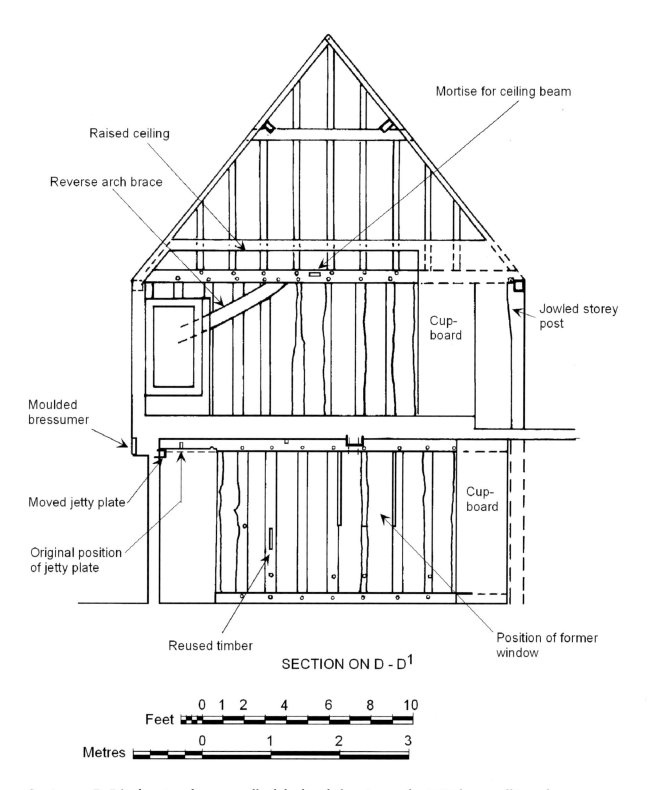

Section on D-D¹, showing the east wall of the bay belonging to the 1585 long-wall jetty house

9 East Street

Brenda Watkin and Elphin Watkin

9 East Street is a building that has been adapted to domestic use from a two bay unheated building. The original building measured 23ft 3ins x 18ft 5ins (7.08 x 5.63m) internally and was two storey, with one room on each floor and a jetty to the front, now underbuilt. The main frame is built of well converted oak with primary brace infill, some of which is reused. All of the studs and braces are pegged and the storey posts have deep 'gunstock' jowls. A bladed scarf is present in the rear wall plate. The axial beams are chamfered and have lamb's tongue stops with the common joists of vertical section 4½ x 3½ins (0.11 x 0.09m) housed with soffit tenons and diminished haunches. There is evidence that the ceiling was plastered which would have provided additional strength to the minimal section joists.

It is assumed that the roof was originally a simple clasped side purlin with principal rafters and collars that incorporated, as common rafters, some reused rafters from a crown post roof. However, as there have been changes in design and subsequent rebuilding it is now impossible to verify its original form.

The alterations made to change the unheated range to domestic use involved the provision of a brick stack on the rear wall and an extension to the north to provide a service function. The stack occupies most of the north wall of the west bay and part of the east bay which has resulted in the north storey post of the central truss being truncated. The mantel beam is chamfered and has lamb's tongue stops with the typical 17th century outer notch. This type of stop can also be found in the rear extension.

The later rear extension is of trapezoidal plan (possibly caused by an existing building to the west?) and appears to be of the same or similar date to the stack. The frame is of oak with unjowled storey posts and primary brace infill with more use of reused timber. The roof was changed in form to a hip at the east end when the extension was created. A subsequent rebuild is suggested by the presence of a ridge board, reused collars with nail fixings and another phase of repairs incorporating softwood.

Four cores for tree-ring dating were taken in the building at the points indicated but they did not date. This is unfortunate as they would have indicated when the first of the two main building phases was constructed. The carpentry of both phases suggests a date in the first half of the 17th century.

History

This property is identifiable with the site of a copyhold tenement in the 1575 rental owned by Thomas Felsted. The building is puzzling, as it does not, in its first phase, fit the pattern of a conventional house and at first probably had a commercial use.

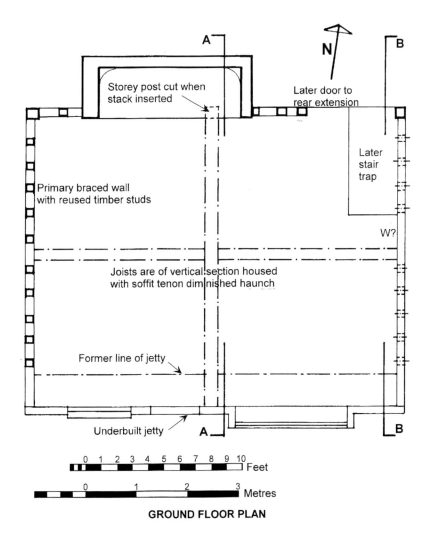

GROUND FLOOR PLAN

9 East Street, ground floor plan

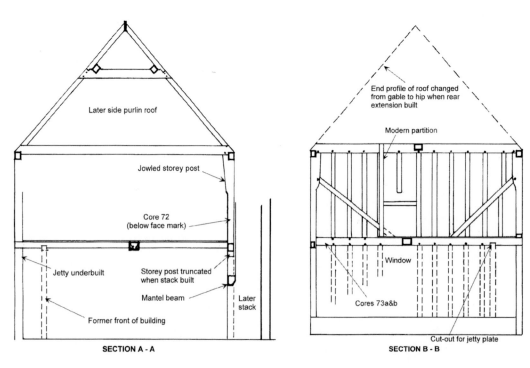

9 East Street, section A-A   *9 East Street, section B-B*

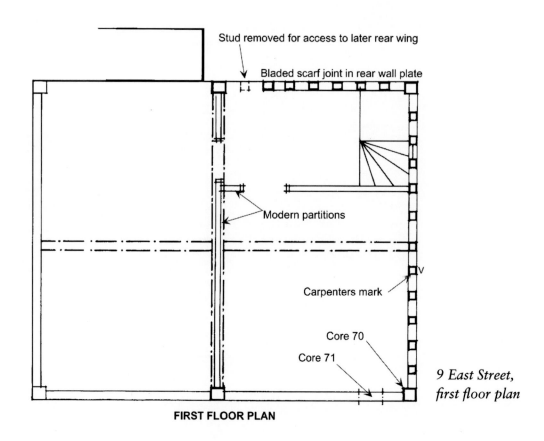

*9 East Street,
first floor plan*

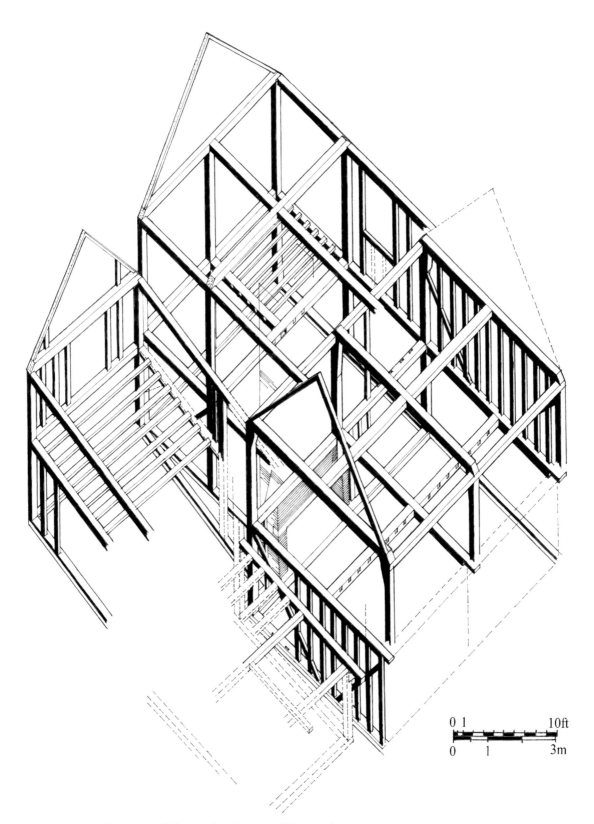

Axonometric drawing of the timber frame of 9 East Street

11-15 East Street

David Stenning, Richard Shackle and David Andrews

These houses were once a single property. They comprise a 15th-century cross-wing at no. 11, to the east of which on the site of nos 13-15, there was a hall. This hall was rebuilt with an upper floor and new roof in the 17th century, though some timbers of the earlier construction survive.

The 15th century cross-wing at 11 East Street

11 is a jettied cross-wing of three almost equal bays and 16ft 9ins (5.1m) wide with an undershot cross-passage. A timber offcut from repairs carried out to the building has been tree-ring dated to 1414-40. The front elevation is more or less non-existent as the jettied first floor has been cut back flush with the ground floor for road widening, as at no. 17 East Street. The crown-post roof is now hipped on the street front. All the ground floor partitions have been removed and now can only be reconstructed from the evidence of the mortices. Fortunately, the mortices above the dropped head doorways are unpegged, making it possible to locate the door positions.

At the ground floor, the front two bays form a pair of apparently conventional service rooms, though the front one was probably a shop. Beyond these two rooms, there is a four-centred arch in the cross-passage effectively forming a 'back door' to the rear of the building. The room in this rear third bay has a pair of narrow flat headed doors, one probably leading to a staircase. This room may have been a kitchen, and now has a fireplace, probably 17th century, in its rear wall. At the end of the cross-passage, in its eastern side, there is a wide four-centred arch or door. Some extended cross-passages in Essex buildings have an open arcade in this position.

The western flank elevation has three window openings and a probable door, demonstrating that there was no building abutting it. It may be that this building represents a stage in the infilling of the town's marketplace.

Whether the front two bays at first floor were divided is now unclear. Above the tie-beam of the front bay there are pegs for an open truss with a crown post and down braces. This kind of truss is unusual in north-east Essex, but can be paralleled in the north-west of the county in, for instance, Great Chesterford and Littlebury. Curiously there is no evidence for a collar purlin over the rear bay. In the eastern flank of this bay at first floor, there is a pair of openings which could possibly be interpreted as doors.

The cross-wing could well have formed part of a clothier's house. It probably had a commercial function, with a shop in the front as suggested, whilst the big first floor, together with the flank doors, suggest the potential for storage use.

The hall at 13-15 East Street

A short corridor-like space separates 11 from 13. To the east there is a pair of full height posts linked to the cross-wing by a pair of girts, and surmounted by a flat tie-beam. There are mortices in each post for arch braces which were slightly asymmetrically set. This truss relates to a former open hall which might possibly have had a Wealden type of roof. Inserted in this truss is an elaborately moulded beam and a partition of high quality studwork. This forms a party wall with 13. Inside 13 has a floor of impressive moulded timbers with folded leaf pattern which has been reused from elsewhere. This floor is reinforced by a Georgian timber column with a capital. The roof which covers 13 and 15 is of clasped purlin construction. Other features observed are a lamb's tongue chamfer and a top plate face-halved scarf joint in no. 13, and diamond mullion window seen in repairs in the rear of no. 15 where there is also evidence for a large first floor front window in the form of a rebate running the full length of the top plate. These elements all point to a date in the 17th for the rebuild of the hall.

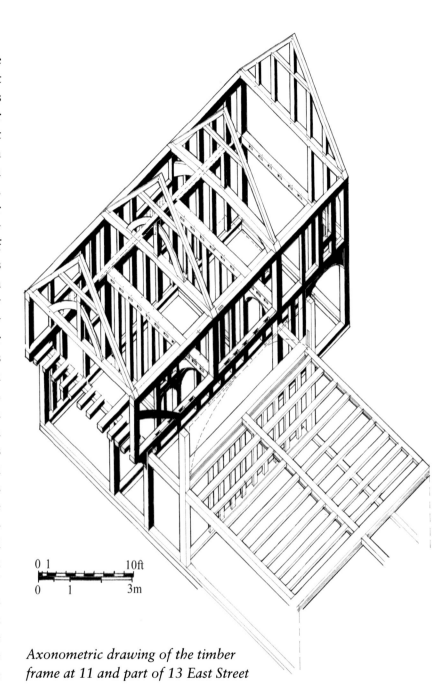

0 1   10ft

0   1   3m

Axonometric drawing of the timber frame at 11 and part of 13 East Street

The chimney in no. 15 has the remains of lined out or ashlared plasterwork within the hearth area, and three openings or 'nostrils' in the back of the hearth, a device thought to improve the draught. The bricks measure 8½ x 4 ¼ x 2 1/4ins (210 x 105 x 55mm). This is one of a small group of 'nostril' fireplaces known from central Essex, probably all much the same date and built by the same contractor or group of contractors. They all seem to date from around 1600. The chimney here is probably contemporary with the rebuild of the hall.

History

In 1575, 11-15 East Street belonged to the clothier Peter Ryce.

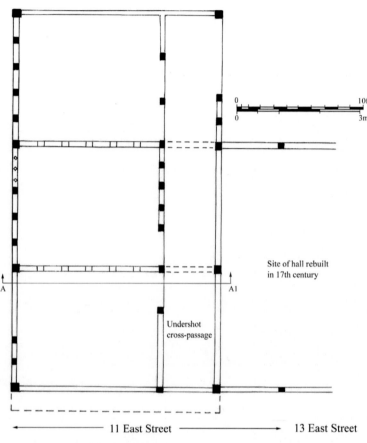

Site of hall rebuilt in 17th century

Undershot cross-passage

11 East Street ⟷ 13 East Street

Plan of the cross-wing at 11 East Street

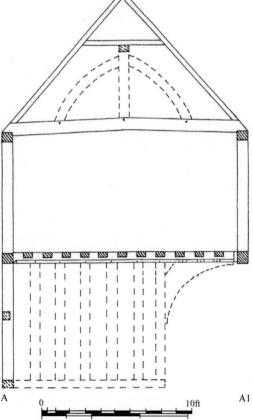

The cross-wing at 11 East Street, section A-A1

17-19 East Street. The Through Inn

Brenda Watkin and David Andrews

These houses are situated to the east of the medieval market place within the tight urban development that lines the north side of East Street. Seen today they constitute a building of uniform height with the roof parallel to the road. The formal Georgian front now disguises the fact that behind the façade is a medieval H-plan house comprising an open hall and two cross-wings. The cross-passage, 7ft (2.135m) wide, to the west of the hall is undershot into the cross-wing of 17 East Street and now gives access to the rear of both properties, forming an alleyway linking East Street to Church Street, and giving rise to the name of the Through Inn. The buildings have been recorded on a number of occasions and an account of no. 19 has been published.[1] This report attempts to tie this work together, linking it to the 1575 rental and a tree-ring date of 1397 obtained for a building to the rear of no. 19 interpreted as originally a detached kitchen, and now incorporated into the main house.

---
1   Watkin 2009.

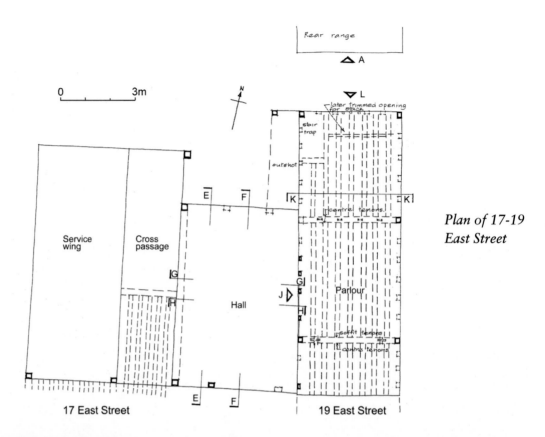

Plan of 17-19 East Street

The western cross-wing (no. 17)

The wing was formerly jettied, but the jettied first floor has now been cut off, leaving the floor joist ends exposed in the East Street façade. It is a large cross-wing, about 19ft (5.79m) wide, of three bays, two measuring about 10ft (3m), and a third to the rear which is about 6ft (1.82m) long. At this end, the building seems also to have been truncated, to judge from the tie-beam here which has no indication of having originally had any studs beneath it. At the ground floor, the front bay was divided off by a partition wall. The rear two bays and the first floor were undivided spaces.

The roof is of crown post construction. An attic floor has been inserted into it, probably at the same time as the roof was rebuilt with a ridge parallel to the street, rather than at right angles, and the whole house was Georgianised.

Studs are about 6ins (0.15m) wide and set about 14ins (0.35m) apart or at about 18ins (0.45m) centres. In the top plates there are edge-halved scarf joints. The crown post is plain; the braces are about 2ins (0.05m) thick. The crown posts were reinforced by down braces to the top of the tie-beams. There is a large brace in the east wall at first floor; a second brace opposed to this can be seen in no. 19, where it is also possible to see a first floor window in the rear bay. The heavy braces are trenched into the face of the studs and double nailed (as in the 14th-century hall at the now demolished Heybridge Hall). No other bracing was noted. The mid rail in the east side is cambered with a hollow moulding. Edge-halved scarf joints occur in the top plates. Like no. 19, the carpentry is in the so-called 'Colchester' style, the storey posts not having swellings or jowls at the top to make a three-way joint with the top plate and tie beam. Old floorboards 12-15ins (0.30-0.38m) wide survive at first floor.

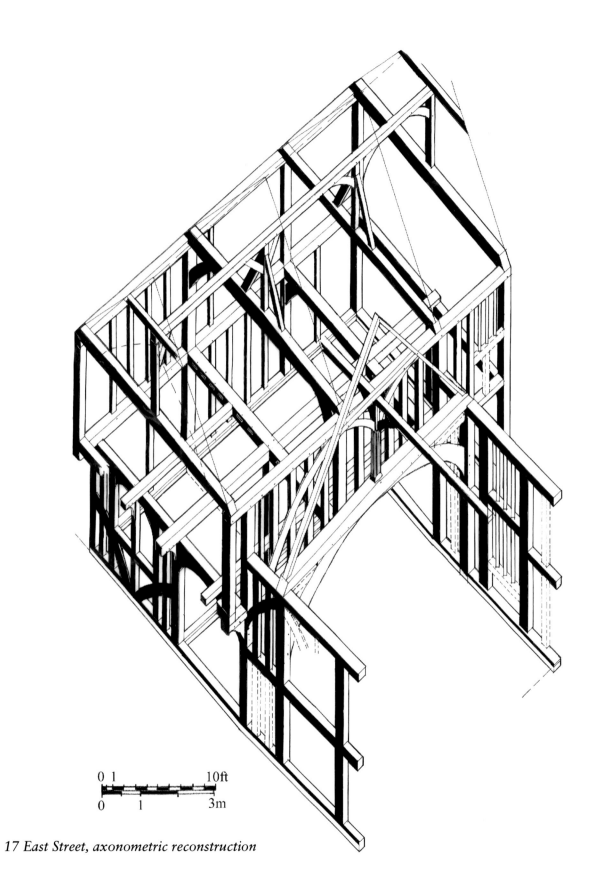

0 1   10ft
0   1   3m

17 East Street, axonometric reconstruction

The ground floor front wall is reconstructable from peg holes in the plate beneath the jetty and in the posts. These indicate a pair of closely set studs to either side of an opening which must have been a shop window, which was flanked by two tension braces.

Some framing is visible in the rear wall of the first floor bedroom, but none seems original apart from the storey posts and possibly a chamfered timber in the middle of the wall. The timbers are mostly 4 inch (0.1m), and seem to have once formed a window. Externally, the north-east corner post has a mortice for a bracket, a feature which with the lack of any traces of framing can be reconstructed as evidence for a garderobe in this position.

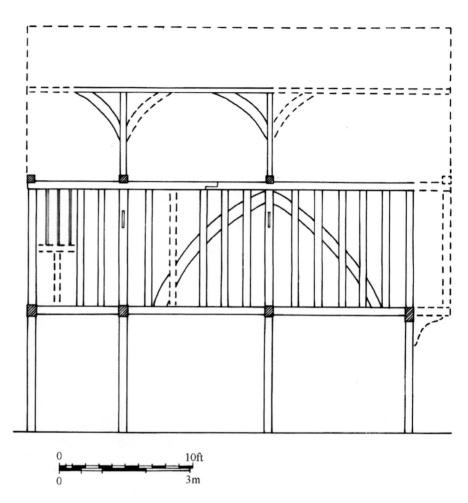

East wall of the cross-wing at no. 17

The open hall

The western cross-passage and hall were as far it is possible to tell of one build, the top plates of the hall being mortised into the storey posts of the wing. The hall showed had a very narrow bay against the undershot cross passage. As the midrail of the cross-wing had been under-built in brick, it was impossible to determine if speres framed the entrance into the hall. The width of the narrow low end bay was 4ft 8ins (1.42m) at the front of the building but tapered down to a mere 3ft (920mm) at the rear. Narrow bays adjacent to undershot cross passages have also been recorded at The Woolpack, Church Street, Coggeshall, Prouds, Thaxted and The Old Manor House, Chipping Hill, Witham. The high end bay is 10ft 8ins (3.25m) wide finished against the three-bay eastern cross-wing, the front bay of which, originally jettied, is now truncated to the street.

The central truss of the hall had a slightly cambered tie beam decorated with a hollow chamfer. The storey posts are unjowled in the style of Colchester carpentry. Empty mortices to the storey posts and the soffit of the tie beam denote the former pattern of heavy arch braces with spandrel struts, now all removed. The crown post is of cross-quadrate section with 2½ inch (64mm) four-way braces housed into the collar and collar purlin and heavily encrusted with soot.

The front hall wall plate had been cut for a later window when the roof was raised. However, enough evidence survived in the form of square mortices and a moulded edge to the window stud to show that the mullions to the hall window facing the street were moulded. The window in the rear wall has three surviving diamond mullions housed into the wall plate and transom.

The eastern cross-wing

The cross-wing to the east had similar features to the hall, i.e. a cross-quadrate crown post with four-way bracing and Colchester style carpentry. However the stud spacing was wider and there was evidence of reused timbers, and the question of its chronological relationship to the hall is unclear, though they cannot be widely separated in date.

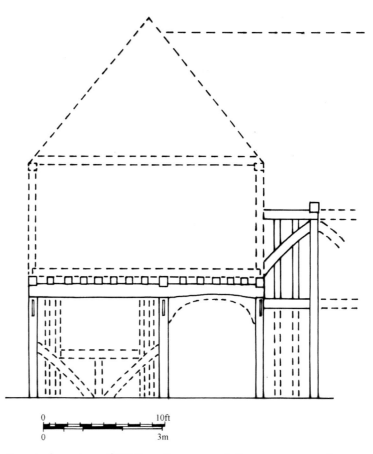

Front elevation of 17 East Street partially reconstructed

The wing is of three bays. The flat section floor joists were jointed into the transverse beams with central tenons. The central midrail to the hall had a dovetail joint and empty mortice consistent with a jettied end and the central common joist also had a mortice for a jetty brace. This shows that the front was jettied but has been truncated like the other wing. The front bay must have been shorter than the others, presumably reflecting problems in the layout of the house on a tight urban site.

A three-centred arch-headed doorway gave access from the hall to the front bay. There was a closed truss at ground floor between the centre and rear bays. In the north-west corner was a trimmed stair trap that would have given access to a three-bay chamber at first floor. As no evidence was found for another stair trap it is suggested that access to the rear bay was through a door with a dropped head in the missing partition wall. A narrow door was framed against the north-east storey post at first floor level in the rear wall. Evidence on the external face of the wall showed empty mortices in the midrail and in a stud adjacent to the diamond mullioned window in this wall, indicating the position of a gardrobe. Also present were V slots for wattle and daub infill for the structure of the latrine. The surviving crown post to the truss between the centre and rear bay was of cross-quadrate section with four-way bracing. Only the central bay of the cross-wing had evidence for narrow tension bracing to the high end hall wall. If the cross-wing and hall were contemporary, this would have given an unusual off-set pattern.

Remnants of an outshot survived to the rear of the hall and on the west side of the cross-wing.

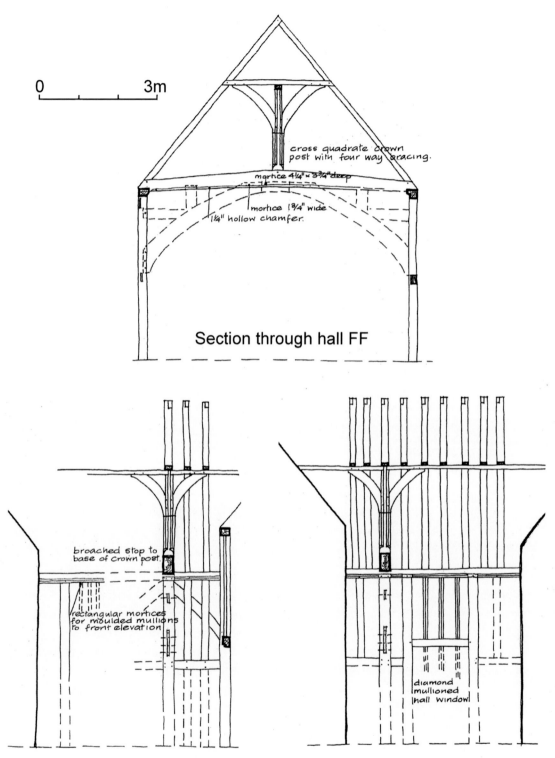

0 _____ 3m

cross quadrate crown
post with four way bracing.

mortice 4¼" x 3¾" deep

mortice 1¾" wide
¼" hollow chamfer.

Section through hall FF

broached stop to
base of crown post.

rectangular mortices
for moulded mullions
to front elevation

diamond
mullioned
hall window

North and south walls of hall, sections GG and HH

Details of the construction of the open hall

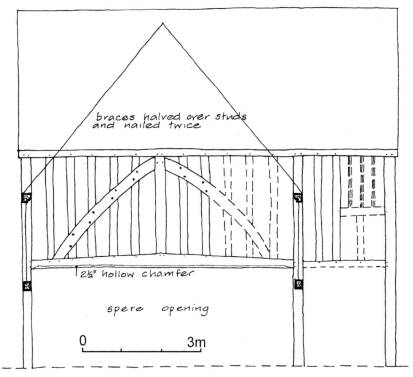

East side of west cross-wing, section EE

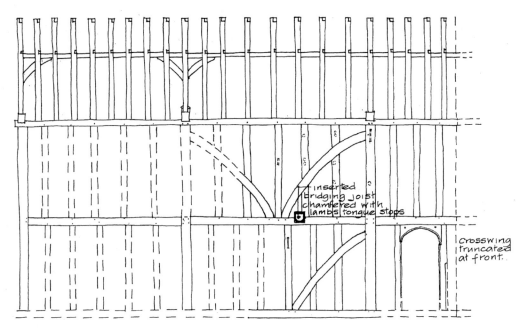

West side of east cross-wing, elevation J

Section EE through the hall, and east side of the cross-wing at 17 (top); and west side of the cross-wing at 19, elevation J (bottom)

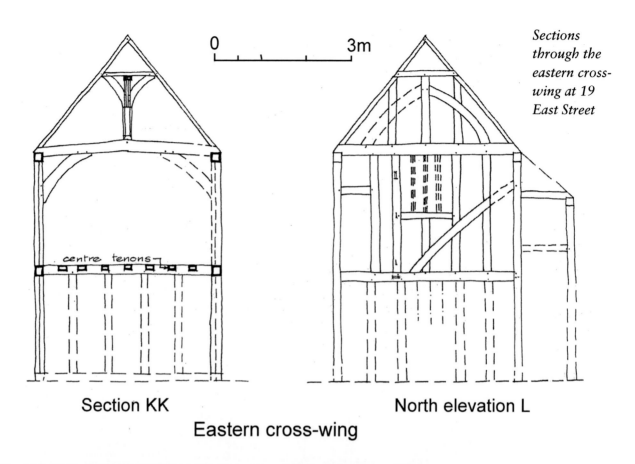

Sections through the eastern cross-wing at 19 East Street

Section KK   North elevation L

Eastern cross-wing

The probable detached kitchen to the rear of the east cross-wing

Only one bay of the outbuilding survived. This bay appeared to be floored as there was a midrail to the truncated bay consistent with the function of supporting lodged joists. Unfortunately no contemporary joists survived. A small diamond mullion window with shutter groove was evident at first floor level. No evidence was found for a window to the ground floor. An edge-halved and bridled scarf with sallied abutments and face key joined the wall plate near the window. The south gable had evidence for tension bracing and double collars. The pattern of double collars was also repeated on the next two rafter pairs. Although the internal timbers had been lime washed there was evidence of soot staining.

The position of the building to the rear of the house, what can be reconstructed of its form, and the soot staining, all point to it having been a kitchen. Three-bay detached kitchens have been identified that consist of floored ends flanking a kitchen space open to the roof so that they resemble an in-line hall house.[2] An interesting feature is the double collars to the last three rafter pairs. Leigh Alston has noted openings in vertical gables with double collars where the building may have had a possible kitchen use.[3] It is possible that the double collars provided the framework for a 'tunnel' taking away the worst of the smoke from the open kitchen from the floored end.

Three cores taken from the timbers of this building all preserved their sapwood, giving a felling date of summer 1397.

2   Martin 1997.
3   Alston 1998.

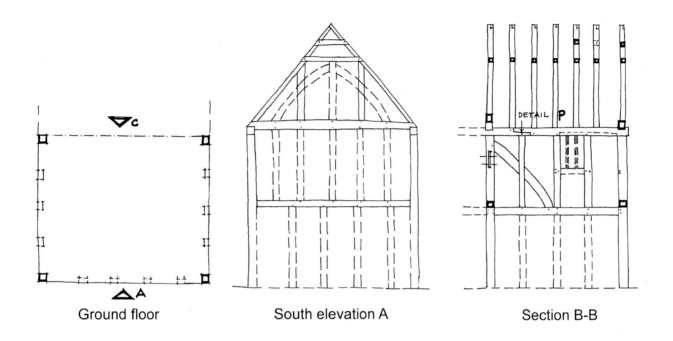

Ground floor   South elevation A   Section B-B

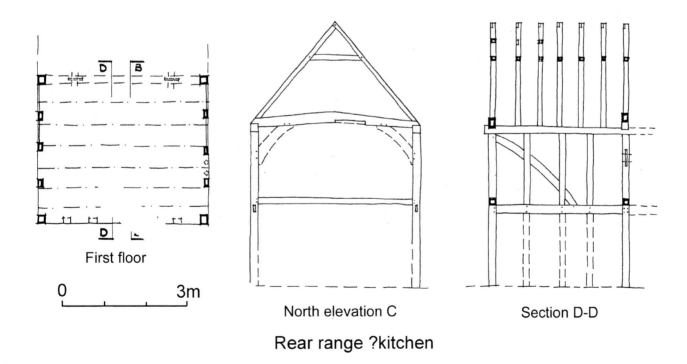

First floor

0 ———— 3m

North elevation C   Section D-D

Rear range ?kitchen

Details of the probable kitchen to the rear of 19 East Street

Discussion

This was a large house, incorporating a shop in the service wing and with a kitchen to the rear. The shop lacked a door from the street, and must therefore have been accessed from the cross-passage. The latter developed into an alleyway, something that happened elsewhere in Coggeshall.

The 1575 frontage is recorded as almost 3 perches, which corresponds to the existing 15m frontage. The plan of the property is interesting. It is generally compressed, no. 17 being quite wide, but the hall is short and the parlour cross-wing is narrow. The undershot cross-passage is an urban feature, appearing in many urban situations in Essex.[4] It is one way houses of a parallel plan coped with space restraints, avoiding the adoption of a plan at right angles to the road. The hall is askew. Its tapered narrow low end bay is clearly a response to the restrictions of an urban plot. It could be speculated that this was a rebuild of a more modest in-line house (i.e. one without cross-wings) and which might have been aisled, in view of the width (7m) of the existing hall.

As well as its layout, this building is important for the evidence for a kitchen, the early date obtained from that building, and the garderobes in the two wings. The kitchen and garderobes are the only ones so far identified in the town. It is frustrating that the tree-ring date of 1397 was obtained from the outbuilding. However, the spandrel struts of the central truss in the open hall are an early feature which one would not expect after *c*.1400, whilst cross-quadrate crown-posts seem to have been introduced about that time, so the tree-ring date can be regarded as broadly applicable to the complex as a whole, whatever the exact chronological relationship between the hall, eastern cross-wing and outbuilding.

It is a measure of how far the study of timber-framed buildings has moved on that the Royal Commission on Historical Monuments in 1911 dated no. 17 to the early 17th century.

History

In 1575 the property was held by George and John Ansell. It was already known as the Through Inn, which reflects the way that a screened undershot cross-passage in a cross-wing could become converted into an alleyway. It was later known as the Bird-in-Hand.

---

4   Stenning and Wadhams 1986.

21-23 East Street, Thaddeus (formerly Bucks)

David Andrews and Richard Shackle

Today this house has a lobby-entry plan with a central front door, with a Georgian exterior. Examination of the frame, and in particular the roof construction, reveals it to be of four bays with an off centre half bay for a chimney, and to have formerly had a jetty, now underbuilt. This indicates that it was a long wall jetty house, later remodelled with the chimney and door moved to a central position. It was built in 1599, six of the eight cores taken giving a tree-ring date in spring/summer of that year.

The initial remodelling of the house, with a central chimney, occurred in the 17th century. At the end of the 18th century or early in the 19th, the property was Georgianised, being given a four window bay symmetrical façade with sash windows, and a handsome central door case with a pediment, pulvinated frieze and rusticated jambs.

The westernmost bay has long been used as a separate dwelling, and today is no. 21 and known as The Cottage. No. 23 was known by its historic copyhold name Bucks until 1986 when it was changed to Thaddeus.[1]

---

1   This account of the building has benefited from a previous description of it, Hillman-Crouch 2008.

No. 21 The Cottage

The original frame is largely altered, rebuilt with timber of light scantling, or concealed. Some original principal timbers, such as storey posts, are evident. The house has a large central chimney with a wide cooking hearth, built of loam bonded Tudor-type bricks (8½ x 4½ x 2ins; 210-220 x 110 x 45-50mm). The floor joists are narrow section, contrasting with studs which from mortice evidence measured about 5½ x 4 inches (140 x 100mm).

The roof was of clasped purlin type but rebuilt with a ridge piece and softwood purlins. It includes some smoke blackened timbers. The outshot to the rear (now raised in height beneath a flat roof) may be original or added not long after construction.

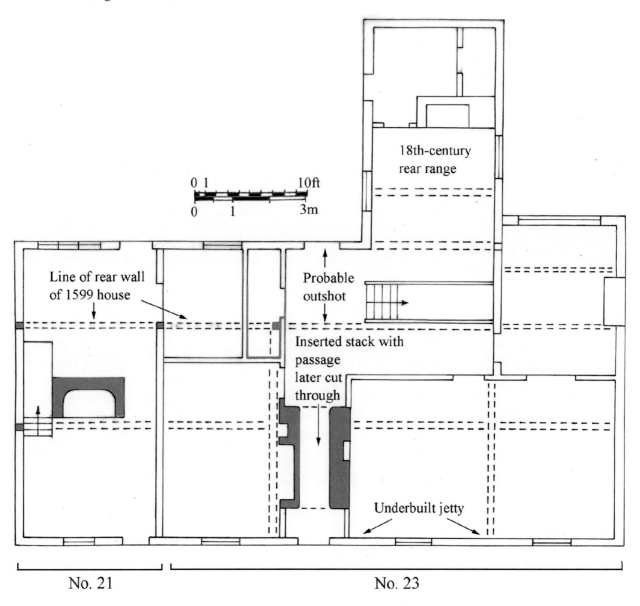

Plan of 21-23 East Street today

No. 23 Thaddeus/Bucks

At ground floor, the front wall was removed when the jetty was underbuilt, whilst the rear wall, apart from the storey posts, has been taken down to provide reorganised and enlarged accommodation. The original footprint of the house is, nevertheless, readily recognisable, with binding joists supported on jowls on the storey posts, and axial bridging joists running into them. The present central front door leads into an entrance passage cut through the brick chimney stack. This is not the original arrangement. The framing of the roof reveals the existence of a chimney bay for an earlier stack located to the east of the existing one. In addition, in the room to the west of the front door, there is an empty mortice in the binding joist for an axial beam removed when the stack was built.

The rear of the house has been much altered and rebuilt, but its layout suggests an outshot ran along the back of it. This may have been an original feature, or added not long after the house was built. It has been suggested that a small pent roof above the position of the existing stairs was for a stair tower.

The development of the house can be divided into three main phases.

Phase 1. The 1599 house

This was of four bays and a half bay. Empty mortices in the binding joist and mid rail of the western ground floor room indicate there was a jetty. Carpentry features include close studding, jowled posts, lamb's tongue chamfers (on the binding joist in the western room), and a clasped purlin roof with wind braces. There was a chimney in the half bay. It is probable that by 1599 any new substantial house would have had a brick chimney, but it is possible that initially it was timber framed. The location of the chimney in the bay is uncertain: it could have been against the front or back walls, or in the middle of the bay (as shown on the plan). There seems to have been a door in the wall that divides nos 21 and 23, whilst mortices in the rear wall mid rail (now in the kitchen of no. 21) suggest the position of a door in the back wall. At first floor, there would have been windows in the front wall, but the framing is insufficiently well preserved for a detailed reconstruction to be possible.

It is tempting to reconstruct the house with a lobby-entry plan, but as has been seen, the position of the chimney is not clear, and this would be a very early example of such a layout. Instead, the door identified in the rear wall in no. 21 suggests that there was a traditional cross-passage in this location. If so, then the probable internal arrangement would have been a service end in no. 21, a ground floor hall formed by the two bays west of the chimney, and a parlour in the easternmost bay. The service end may well have been a separate shop and possibly rented out.

Phase 2. 17th-century alterations

The chimney was moved to its existing position at some time in the 17th century on the evidence of its brickwork. The effects of this change were to divide the house into two equal-sized bays either side of the stack. Because the stack is too close to the front wall to allow space for a lobby until the jetty was removed, there could not have been a lobby-entry plan unless the jetty was already underbuilt, which is possible though this development might have been expected to have occurred rather later.

The history of the house (see below) indicates that it was routinely occupied by three tenants. This remodelling would have made its sub-division easier and may have been prompted by the need to accommodate several households.

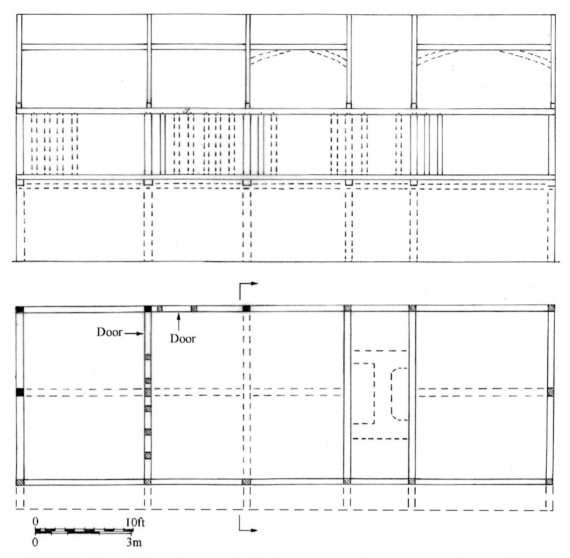

Door →   Door

0   10ft
0   3m

21-23 East Street, plan and front elevation, insofar as they can be reconstructed, of the house as built in 1599. The position of the stack in the chimney bay is speculative; it may well have been in the front or rear wall

The chimney in no. 21 is made of Tudor-type bricks and cannot date from later than the 17th century. It is probable that it is roughly contemporary with that in no. 23. Its construction was probably also connected with the sub-division of the house between several occupants. An outshot may have been added to the rear at this time if it did not already exist.

Phase 3. 18th- or early 19th-century Georgianisation and later

The jetty was underbuilt (if this had not already happened) and the house given a flat symmetrical façade with sash windows. Underbuilding the jetty created space in front of the stack for a lobby-entry plan. It would have been at this time or soon after that the passage was cut through the brick chimney, giving access to a spacious hall and staircase formed by partial removal of the rear wall. (The same expedient was adopted at 2-4 East Street, a lobby-entry house also with the chimney tunnelled through). The improved circulation created by the passage through the stack might equally well have facilitated the occupation of the house by several occupants or by a single household.

Cupboards were built into the corners of the western and eastern rooms of no. 23. The rear wing was probably built at this time if not before. It too would have provided more space for the various occupants of the property. The roof of the house has been remodelled such that the rear pitch has been raised to create first-floor headroom. The roof has a ridge piece which suggests this work took place *c.*1800 or later.

History

The 1575 rental records the property as two copyhold tenements and gardens belonging to Buck, hence the name by which it was known until the 1980s. Its frontage was 3 ¼ perches, the same width as today. In 1599, therefore, the two tenements were rebuilt as one.

A bundle of deeds for Bucks dating from 1698 is preserved in the Essex Record Office.[2] Bucks was copyhold, held of the manor of Great Coggeshall. Although this was copyhold by inheritance, which meant the property passed down a family line so long as manorial rights were observed and fines paid to the lord, there was in effect a free market in copyholds and they could be bought and sold. As family members moved away from their place of origin, so copyhold properties became merely another asset, and were often let and sub-tenanted. It is clear that most of the time Bucks was sub-let to several persons. In 1769, for instance, it was said to be 'made into Three Tenements'.

The documents for Bucks are mostly manorial. Ownership and occupation can be traced until 1906 when manorial rights were extinguished. The documents are not informative about the physical appearance of the house. Leases are more valuable for this, but only one survives, of 1788. This reveals that the house had outbuildings including a stable, and a pump. It was a repairing lease. The leaseholder was entitled to alter the property; these works would be assessed at the end of the fourteen year period and the owner, if he approved, could take them at a fair valuation, or else restore the house to its previous condition.

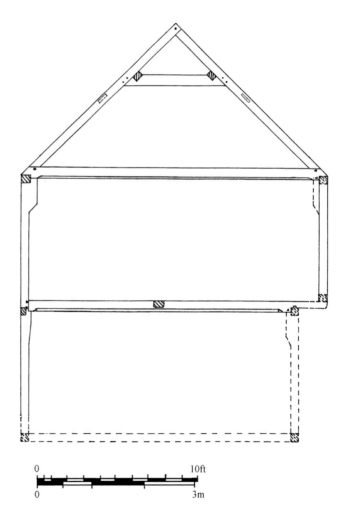

0   10ft

0   3m

21-23 East Street, reconstructed section through the 1599 house

2   Essex Record Office A12296.

The sequence of documents begins with the surrender in October 1698 by William Guyon into the hands of the lord of his copyhold messuages and tenements in Gallows Street, late in the occupation of Joan Hawes and now of John Taylor and an unnamed member of the Hawes family or their assigns, to the use of Robert Townsend. In the 1671 Hearth Tax, John Taylor paid for one hearth, and widow Hawes was exempt from payment for two hearths. If the latter is identifiable with Joan Hawes, it can be speculated that her two hearths were those in no. 21, and that this part of the property had already been divided off as separate accommodation for her.

The manorial records come to an end in 1906 when Charles Buckingham paid £4.11s.6d to have the property enfranchised, i.e. freed from manorial controls and made freehold, under the Copyhold Act of 1894.

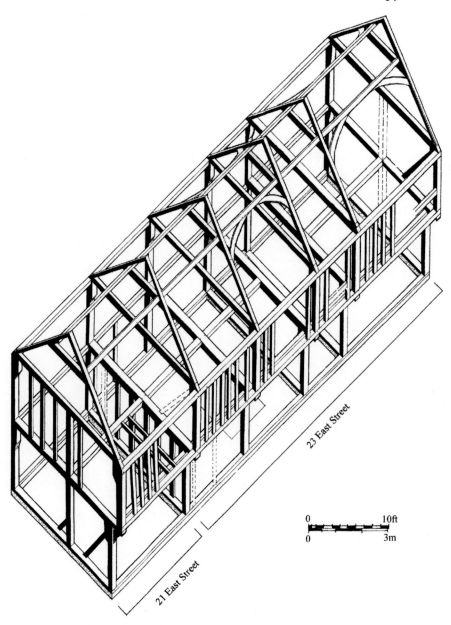

Axonometric frame drawing of 21-23 East Street

25-27 East Street

Brenda Watkin, Elphin Watkin and David Andrews

25-27 East Street were originally a jettied three-bay building which is now divided so that 25 occupies most of the western bay and 27 the eastern two bays. A narrow strip of the westernmost bay is split up to provide an entrance hall to 25 to the front, and to the rear a stairwell to 27.

The building was open-framed against no. 23 to the west. There are short straight braces between the corner posts and the top plate on this side. On its eastern side, 27 is built up against the wall of the 15th-century cross-wing of no. 29. The framing of this is visible at the first floor, where the top plate and studwork, including two curving down braces, of 29 are visible. Short thin studs or cripple pieces have been set on top of the top plate to support the tie-beam of 27 which is at a level about 2ft (0.6m) higher than the older next-door building. At ground floor, there is an enclosed passage between 27 and 29, reducing the floor area of 27 at this level. This looks like a cross-passage arrangement, but in fact seems to be an old access to the side of no. 29 which was apparently preserved when 25-27 was built.

Little of the timber frame of no. 27 is visible, except for the tie-beams, top plates and floor joists. More of the timber frame is visible in no. 25. The building is made of good quality well converted oak, the mortices being fully pegged. However, there is a certain amount of reused timber and the mid rail against no. 23 may be elm. The top plate in the rear wall in the easternmost bay in no. 27 has rows of blocked wide section mortices, suggestive of a reused floor joist. An old top-plate was reused as a binding joist in no. 27. This has a long central mortice for down braces and at its southern end mortices and dovetails. This is identified as being the top-plate removed when the hall of no. 29 next door was rebuilt on two storeys.

Studs occur in the rear wall of no. 25 at 16ins (400mm) centres at first floor, at 20ins (500mm) centres at ground floor. In the rear wall at first floor, there is a primary brace, set at a rather slack angle, with the studs aligned accurately above and below it. The jetty is now underbuilt, and no features of the front elevation can be made out at ground floor.

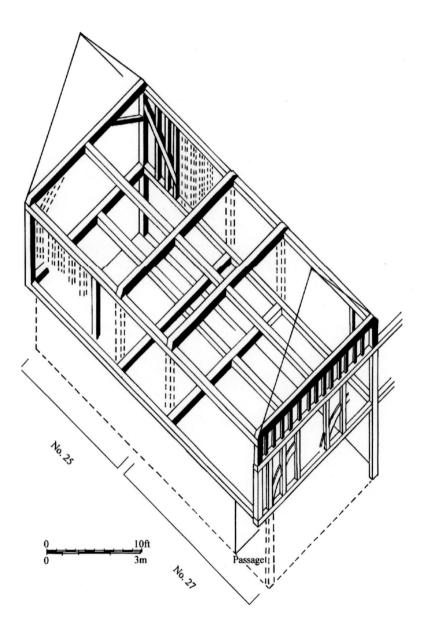

Axonometric illustration of the frame of 25-27 East Street

As far as it is possible to tell, the truss that effectively divides 25 and 27 was a closed truss. Thus that part of the building occupied by 27 comprised a two-bay ground-floor room and upstairs chamber. There is no clear evidence as to how the building functioned in terms of doors and access to the first floor.

Dating and discussion

The building seems to have been added to the side of no. 23 which has been dated to 1599 and thus provides a *terminus post quem*. Datable carpentry features include the primary brace, and possible evidence for an internal brace, seen in no. 25; and a face-halved scarf in the top plate of no. 27 where the floor is made of narrow section (4inch) joists. These would all be consistent with a 17th century date.

This is one of several buildings in Coggeshall which are not of obviously domestic character and which seem not to have been built primarily as a dwelling. In its initial phase of construction, it seems to have lacked chimneys. If dowel holes in the top plates in no. 25 have been correctly interpreted, to support a floor, then it seems to have been built with an attic for storage.

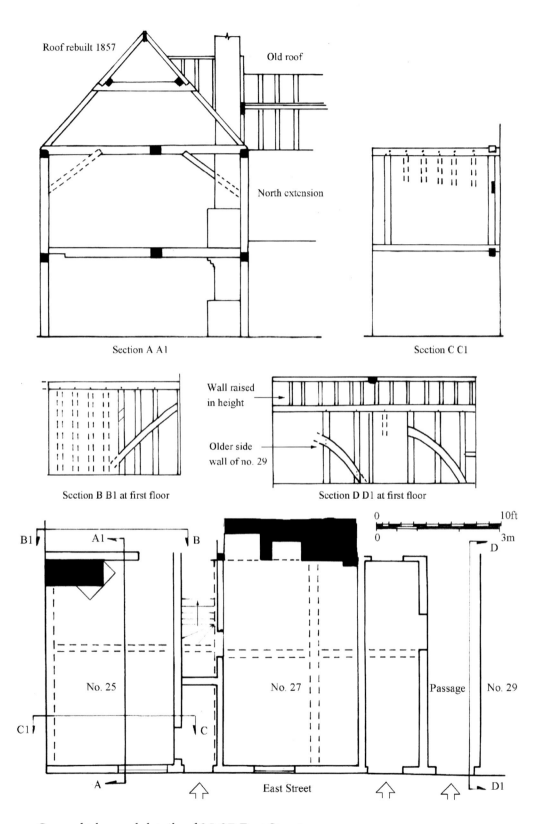

Ground plan and details of 25-27 East Street

Later phases

The western part of the building, corresponding to no. 25 and partially overlapping no. 27, was extended by about 5m to the rear. The frame includes reused timber and looks late 17th-century or 18th century in date. It is probably 18th century as it seems to be contemporary with the chimney which is built of 18th-century bricks (9 x 4½ x 2½ ins; 230 x 110 x 60-65mm) with diagonal pressure marks. This is apparent because the clasped purlin roof of the extension was later raised round the chimney, leaving the ghost of a chase mark from the original roof pitch on the side of the brickwork. This roof raise round the chimney dated from the rebuild of the roof in 1857, the date chalked on one of the collars in the void over no. 27. The roof fabric includes mechanically sawn elm collars nailed to the rafters, reused timbers, and softwood rafters with merchants' or trading marks.

In the rear wall of no. 27, there is a chimney built of Tudor bricks (9 x 4 ¼ x 2ins) datable to the 17th century. The fireplace, however, is rather small, more typical of the 18th century.

History

This property has been identified with a free tenement and garden belonging in 1575 to Edmund Hills.

29 East Street, the building to the right with a split roof line reflecting the two elements, cross-wing and hall. The left hand door belongs to 27 East Street. The right hand door leads into the passage between nos 27 and 29. The pair of early 20th century houses in the background beyond the entrance to Swan Yard occupy the site of the former Swan public house.

29 East Street

David Stenning, Richard Shackle and David Andrews

This house comprises a 15th-century cross-wing, its jetty now underbuilt, and a rebuilt hall to the east of it. There was a further wing to the east of the hall, but, apart from its side wall which forms the end or east wall of 29, this was pulled down when the Swan public house was demolished and Swan Lane was created early in the 20th century.

The cross-wing is of two bays. The rear one is truncated, and it is possible that there were more. It has massive floor joists, and widely spaced studding in its side walls. The ground-floor front bay was probably a shop, apparently without any access from the hall. The shop front had three relatively equally spaced posts interrupting a single shutter groove overhead. A stair at the back of the front bay, screened off from the shop, gave access to the chamber over the shop. This was accessed from a door in the west wall where there must have been a passageway, just as there is today separating this house from no. 27. The ground floor rear bay of the wing was entered by a door from the hall.

The timber framed partition wall between the two bays has a distinctive X-shaped pattern of bracing. The eastern flank wall of the front bay has a strong decorative pattern of bracing which probably continued in the side of the rear bay. Cores taken from two posts in this wall could not be tree-ring dated.

This bracing would have been a striking feature when seen from the open hall on this side. It is suggested that this hall was originally double-aisled, with a similar wing to the east. The evidence for this is to be found in 27 East Street where a binding joist is interpreted as part of a top plate from the former hall, the pair of curving braces that were once in its soffit indicating that it was from the open arcade of an aisled hall. The existing hall tie-beam was once located centrally spanning this presumed aisled hall. The western end was then demolished and replaced by the existing cross-wing. It was thought sufficient to only tenon-in some of the timbers. The bracing pattern was designed symmetrically to embellish the interior of the hall. The hall was later rebuilt, leaving only the tie-beam as a clue to this sequence of development.

The existing small hall only about 15ft (5m) long has narrow section floor joists and a clasped purlin roof, and must be a remodelling of the 17th century. Its east wall incorporates the surviving flank of the missing cross-wing. This has timber of excellent quality with carpenters' marks, close studwork and Colchester carpentry. At ground floor there are peg holes for a high end bench. A core from the centre post in this wall was tree-ring dated to 1418-54. Photographs of this missing wing before its demolition indicate that it was relatively narrow in width.

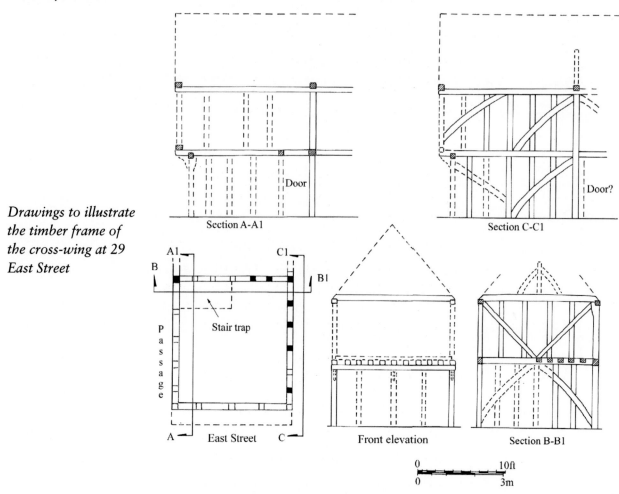

Drawings to illustrate the timber frame of the cross-wing at 29 East Street

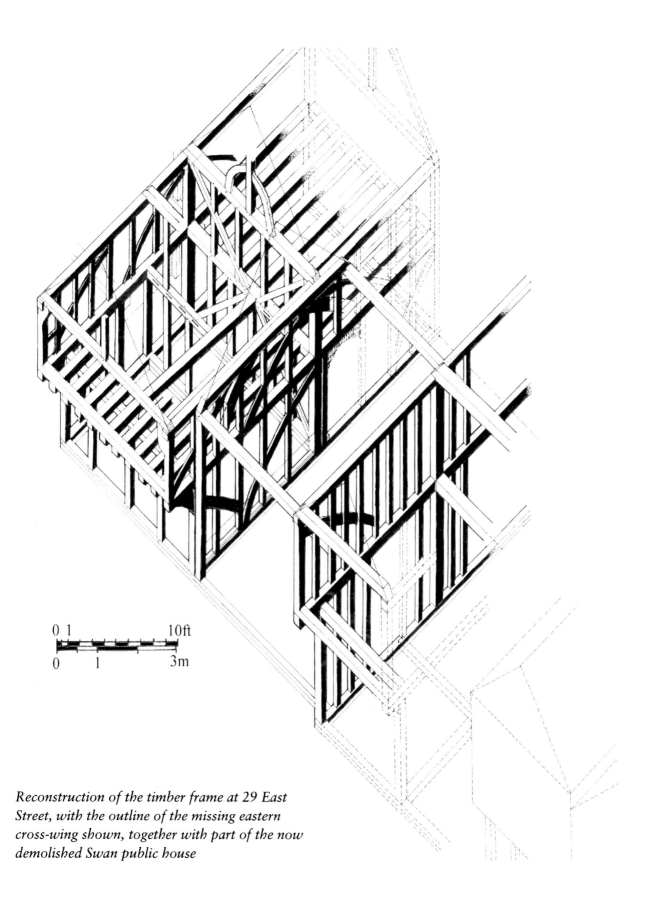

Reconstruction of the timber frame at 29 East Street, with the outline of the missing eastern cross-wing shown, together with part of the now demolished Swan public house

History and discussion

At the time of the 1575 rental, the house is identified as part belonging to Robert Webb whose property extended as far east as 39 East Street. In the 17th century, no. 27 was probably part of the same property as 29 in view of the apparent reuse of a timber from 27 in 29. The passageway between the two houses also implies probable joint ownership, especially as the east wall of 27 is built over the top of the west wall of 29.

The sequence here of an aisled hall being rebuilt with cross-wings to provide more accommodation, the hall becoming smaller and the appearance of the street frontage radically changing, is an interesting example of a process which seems to have been commonplace in Coggeshall.

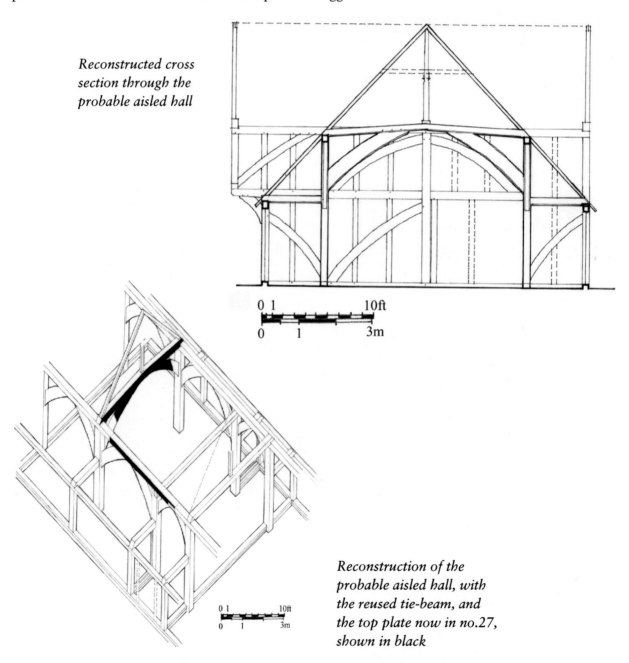

Reconstructed cross section through the probable aisled hall

Reconstruction of the probable aisled hall, with the reused tie-beam, and the top plate now in no.27, shown in black

33 East Street, looking north up Swan Lane towards Church Street

33 East Street

David Andrews

Located in Swan Yard, half way between East Street and Church Street, this is a rectangular building measuring about 52ft by 20ft (15.84 x 6.09m), aligned north-south. Now one house, the building was once several cottages according to sale particulars of 1968. An old photograph shows it with a roughly central door, and workshop or stable doors in the end bays. There have been further alterations to convert it to a single residence, and much of the frame is now concealed.

Four cores were taken for tree-ring dating, and two gave dates of 1428/29 and 1431/32. This looked promising, but closer examination of the house showed it to be made of reused timber.

The house is of four bays, the two southern ones of 11ft (3.35m), and the two northern ones of about 14ft (4.26m). The roof is of clasped purlin type. The two middle bays are built of substantial medieval timbers, which give the impression of being parts of a building, or several buildings, re-erected. The two posts of the central truss are a matching pair, but the tie-beam here (dated 1428/29) seems not to be original to them. The posts of the other two trusses are now largely concealed. All the tie-beams are from closed trusses. Nicks for laths for wattle and daub infill in the horizontal mid rail (dated to 1431/32) in the east (or front) wall show that this timber was once a vertical post. The top plate on the west side is made of two reused timbers joined together. There are mortices for diamond mullions for a window in the soffit on the top plate on the east side.

Whilst the two central bays of this house came from two or more 15th-century buildings, the northern and southern bays are different. Although there is reused timber, it is different in character and softwood is also present. There are late carpentry features in these two bays, such as a ridge piece in the roof of the southern one, something which normally occurs from the end of the 18th century in Essex. At the north-west corner in the northern bay, the top plate and tie-beam are butt-jointed, again a technique usually datable to the 18th century or later. Contemporary with these bays, or approximately so, are the two chimney stacks, the brickwork of which is late 18th or early 19th century. The house may therefore have been built of two bays (or more) of reused timber in the 17th or 18th century, and functioned probably as an outbuilding in view of its backland location. The end bays were built later, presumably as extensions, in the late 18th or early 19th century, and with the chimneys converted the building into a row of cottages. Alternatively it may have been built from the first as a row of cottages, incorporating a mixture of old and new timbers, making use of which gave rise to inconsistent carpentry features. It should be noted that throughout the building the joints at the tie-beams and top plates are strapped, a practice which became normal from the later 18th century, though such straps are often later reinforcements.

The 1575 rental shows Church Street properties having long boundaries to the south, whilst those on East Street north only had small plots, suggesting that the building was associated with 20 Church Street, known as Herrings, which belonged at that time to Ellen Scarlett. Access seems also originally to have been from Church Street, as old maps show there to have been none from East Street before the Swan was demolished. It is interesting that a tree-ring date of 1428 was also obtained for floor joists in 18 Church Street, but this may be no more than coincidence. The property was formerly part of a group of buildings which belonged to Browning Butchers who had premises in Church Street.

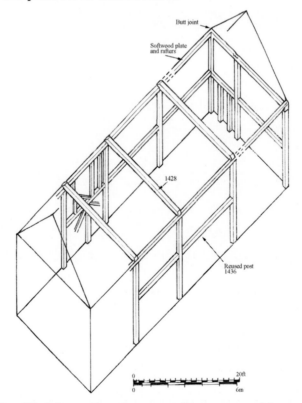

Simplified frame drawing to explain structural features

14 and 15 Market Hill

Brenda Watkin and Elphin Watkin

Introduction

This property is in multi-occupation with shops to the ground floor and flats at first and attic floors. Three cores were taken from the timbers but tree-ring dates could not be obtained. However the building has features which date it securely to the 17th century, with an earlier element to the rear. It represents infill to the east side of the northern market area. The north-west corner of the building has been cut back making it difficult to define the original length. This section has also been subject to a roof raise that created an additional storey under a slack pitch slate roof. The exterior was upgraded with vertical sliding sash windows and parapet in the late 18th century but since then windows have been changed and shop fronts inserted. This description is limited to the first floor and only the flats where access was available. There are few features preserved in the shops.

Flat 4

This forms a rear wing with the first floor chamber jettied with narrow section joists over the ground floor of an earlier building. The timber-framing, where visible, is of close studded construction with straight primary braces. An original brick fireplace intrudes into the chamber by 2ft 4ins (0.71m) with 9 inch (0.23m) side jambs and arch opening. The back of the hearth, 3ft 11ins (1.20m) wide by 2ft 1ins (0.64m) deep, is canted which is typical of first floor fireplaces. An original frieze window with ovolo moulded mullions survives in the south-east rear wall. This could have been flanked by an oriel and another matching frieze window but the evidence has either been covered or destroyed by the insertion of a later sash window. The chamber originally measured 16ft 4ins x 22ft 6ins (5.03 x 6.93m) internally but is now subdivided by modern partitions.

The stair tower

This is situated to the rear, adjacent to the rear wing. It now contains modern stairs and as all the timber frame is covered apart from the close studding under the frieze windows, no evidence is visible to be able to suggest the original layout. Fenestration to the south-east wall consists of a window with frieze lights and ovolo moulded mullions and saddle bars, showing that it was always glazed.

Flat 2

This formed another heated first floor chamber of 2½ bays with a width of 17ft 6ins (5.39m). The length is difficult to determine due to the cut back corner but appears to have been approximately 24ft 6ins (7.55m). Internally the features visible are the brick fireplace and transverse and axial beams as all the timber-frame is covered. The 10 inch (0.25m) wide transverse beam to the west of the stack is chamfered with lamb's tongue and notch stops typical of the 17th century. The chamfer is stopped on both sides to respect an axial beam although there is only one to the west. A pegged mortise survives for a brace close to the end where the axial beam was cut-back. No evidence was found for any other braces or studs. The brick fireplace has 9 inch (0.23m) wide chamfered jambs, and a canted back 1ft 10ins (0.56m) deep.

Discussion

On the 1575 survey this site formed part of a large plot of land owned by Thomas Hopper. It has been suggested by David Stenning that the ground floor room of the rear wing was originally a single storey building associated with the market. With the encroachment onto the market place by 14 and 15 Market Hill it would appear that rather than demolish the earlier structure it was incorporated as a rear wing with the addition of a first floor. This property, when built, would have made a significant statement in the street scene with the latest features such as the glazed windows. However, it is interesting to note that it not only incorporated an earlier building but also reused medieval sooted rafters for first floor joists. These would have been hidden by plaster ceilings but were seen when repair work was undertaken.

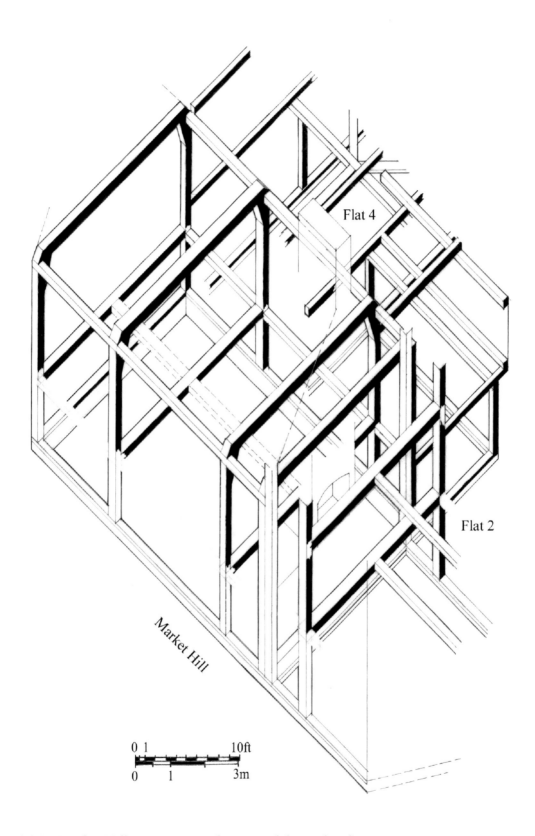

Flat 4

Flat 2

Market Hill

0 1   10ft

0   1   3m

14-15 Market Hill, axonometric drawing of the timber frame

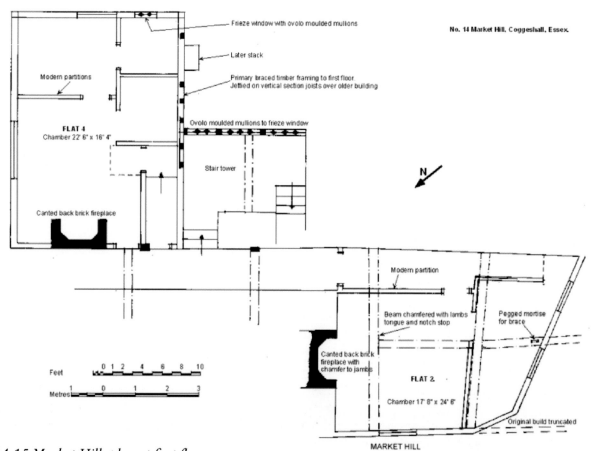

14-15 Market Hill, plan at first floor

*14-15 Market Hill,
the frieze window
at first floor of the
stair tower*

Cavendish House and the White Hart, Market End

David Andrews and David Stenning

This impressive building stands on a relatively small site in a key location in the town. It comprises a single-storey hall and three-storey service cross-wing that was jettied on each storey at both front and rear.

The hall and cross-wing are contemporary, but are distinct in character and now in separate ownership, the former being part of the White Hart, and the latter known as Cavendish House (a modern name). Only Cavendish House was sampled for tree-ring dating.

Cavendish House (the cross-wing)

Cores were taken from the front and rear jetty plates, the storey post on the west side, the crown post, and a joist on the east side in the front bay. They gave a date range of 1422-48 for the construction of the building.

The cross-wing is small, of two equal bays, and only about 23ft (7m) deep. It is made of over-sized timbers, whole trees with waney edges, the posts about 10ins (250mm) square, the central storey posts 14ins (360mm) square, and the floor joists 8-11ins (200-280mm) wide, equal to the gaps between them, and 9ins (220mm) deep. The floor joists have central tenons.

The ground floor was originally divided into two rooms by a partition wall, the mortices for which are evident in the soffit of the large binding joist. The spacing of these mortices, and the former existence of two

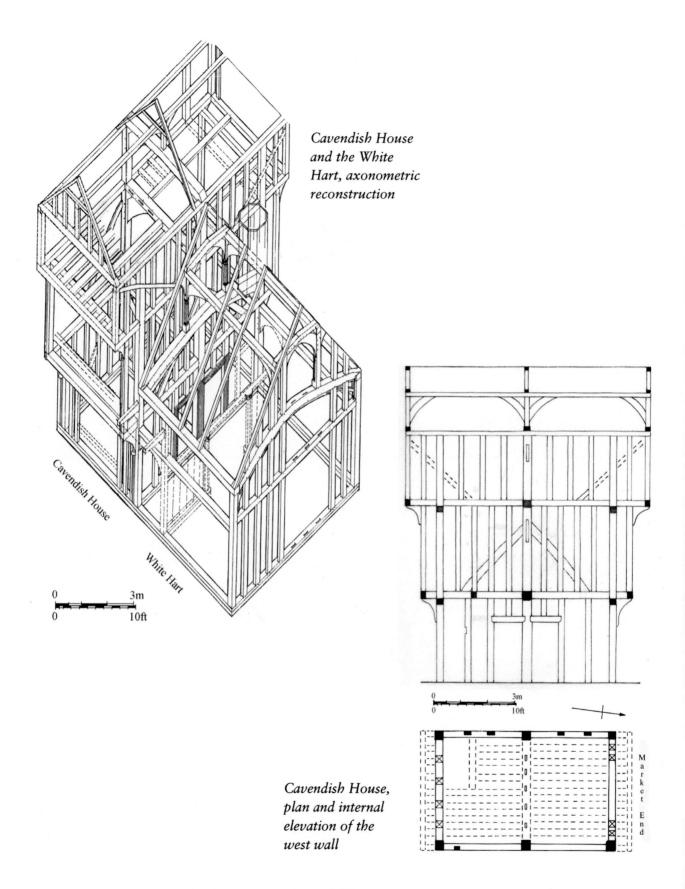

Cavendish House and the White Hart, axonometric reconstruction

Cavendish House

White Hart

0 _____ 3m

0 _____ 10ft

0 _____ 3m

0 _____ 10ft

Market End

Cavendish House, plan and internal elevation of the west wall

tension braces in the wall, suggests that there was no communication between the two rooms. In the flank wall on the west side, there are blocked doorways that linked the front and back rooms with the wing which is now the White Hart. On the White Hart side, these doors have applied surrounds with roll mouldings. There is evidence in this wall for a third lower doorway leading to a screened lobby beneath a stair trap for a ladder stair to the first floor.

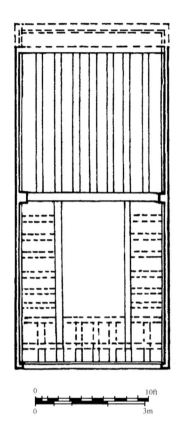

Plan of the joists at the second floor

The ground floor rooms would probably have been a parlour to the rear and a service room to the front. The front wall at this level had a pair of studs, each side of a wide opening. This looks like a shop window, but may not have been the case as there was no alternative location for a service room if it was not here. A jetty bracket survives on the front elevation, carved with a grimacing head with a protruding tongue, a not uncommon medieval motif with parallels in churches and elsewhere. The rear wall has been removed; in the jetty plate there are mortices for four studs. The floor joists are tenoned into the jetty bressumers.

Most of the timber frame is concealed at the first and second floors. The first floor was occupied by a chamber or solar. Two handsome braces are exposed between the central storey posts. At this level there is a suggestion in the east wall of a former window opening. The absence of peg holes for floor joists in the central binding joist at the level of the first floor ceiling suggest that there were no joists in the centre of the rear bay, in which case there seems to have been a large well surrounded by a gallery. This would be very unusual and difficult to explain in terms of its function. The roof is of crown post construction and well preserved. It was originally gabled to the front and not hipped as today.

The queen post truss in the White Hart

Apart from modern finishes and decorations, and a Georgian exterior, the building is surprisingly little altered, the result in part of the quality of its timbers. A corner fireplace was inserted in the rear bay in the 18th or 19th century, and there is a rear single storey extension.

The White Hart

The hall was about 320 sq. ft (29m²) in area, and had a boarded spere wall with octagonal posts and a moulded head rail. Fragments only of this survive in the rear wall. The roof is of queen-post type. A square trimmed hole astride the roof ridge has cut-outs suggesting a former smoke louvre, such as survives more completely at the nearby Chapel Inn.

As a vernacular form, queen-post roofs flourished in mid East Anglia as an alternative to more usual crown posts, being most common in north-east Suffolk and south Norfolk. This roof type derives from the 'raised aisle hall' concept, which is to be found in the same area, with outliers in Essex and Hertfordshire. The White Hart example is designed in a manner akin to a raised aisle hall, with square set purlins and octagonal posts with moulded capitals. Some of the detail is reminiscent of The Stables, Fressingfield.

The eastern 'truss' against the side of Cavendish House is decorative, rather than structural, appearing almost as a deliberate optical illusion to suggest a further bay. Very little of the front or rear walls survive, but there is short projecting timber at eaves level over the usual door position that must have supported a porch. A number of similar porches can be identified, but normally they projected from a cross-wing (e.g. The Swan, Maldon).

In the late 16th century, the appearance of the hall was completely altered: a floor and a brick chimney were inserted, and a jettied display gable was added to the front at first floor, a typical feature for this period in Coggeshall and elsewhere.

History

The building is on land held of the manor of Coggeshall Hall. Beaumont identified it with *Makynes*, a property which in 1526 passed to Thomas Paycock, son and heir of Robert Paycock, deceased, and formerly belonging to his cousin John.[1]

The White Hart was an inn by the 17th century. The landlord, Ambrose Armond, who died in 1675, was assessed for nine hearths in the 1671 Hearth Tax, more than any other inhabitant of the town.[2]

Photographs of 1911 and 1920 show Cavendish House to have been the premises of Joyce Family Butcher. Later it was Saunders butchers, and then Mowers grocers and provisions.

Discussion

The 15th-century house that comprised the White Hart and Cavendish House was of exceptional quality. The cross-wing was a plain structure, but made of timber of unusual size, jettied on both sides and on three storeys, the only building of its time in the town known to have been that high. The ground floor room was probably a shop. If there were a void or well in the second floor structure, then it presumably related to a commercial use of this wing. The handsome queen post roof of the hall, with its arched bracing, is a rare and very early example of this type of roof in Essex. It raises the possibility of the employment of a non-local carpenter, probably from Suffolk. It is curious that so special a house should be small in size, with only one wing. In this, however, it resembles other properties in Coggeshall which occupied plots which only allowed space on the frontage for a hall and a single wing. That it belonged to the Paycocks, the wealthiest family in the town, by the early 16th century, makes it tempting to speculate that it might have been built by them.

---

1   Beaumont 1890, 233.
2   Beaumont 1890, 221; Ferguson et al. 2012, 245.

7 West Street, the former Cricketers public house

David Stenning, Richard Shackle and David Andrews

Description

The Cricketers occupies a commanding position on the south side of the east end of West Street where the road narrows. The street frontage now has a brick façade which dates from a major refurbishment probably in the early 19th century, but within it is a substantial timber frame measuring about 6.7 x 7.1m (22ft x 23ft 4ins). The building was recorded after a fire in 2010.

The frame was most clearly visible at ground floor where there are timbers of massive scantling. A large axial beam 16 inches (0.41m) wide, reinforced originally by braces at each end, runs east-west between the storey posts in the flank walls of the building. The mouldings on the soffit of this beam have been removed. None of the other visible timbers have mouldings apart from chamfers. The joists on the north side of the axial beam were originally jettied to the street. These joists, 7 inches (0.18m) wide, are jointed to the axial beam with housed centre tenons with spurred soffits.

The walls had narrow studding, with studs 6-7 (0.15-0.18m) inches wide at 16 inch (0.41m) centres. The posts do not have jowls. At the south-east corner, part of a tension brace could be seen, together with the wattle and daub infill which was made with three vertical oak laths at centres of about 3 inches (0.075m) tied to three horizontal ones.

The west wall in its southern bay at ground floor had an unusually large window with nine large diamond mullions 4 inches (0.1m) square. A gap in the framing at the north end of this wall at first floor, together with a mortice for a door head in a stud, shows that there was a door here which must have been reached by an external stair. No evidence was found for an internal stair. In the southern bay of the west wall at this level, there was a shutter groove and three diamond mullions for a window.

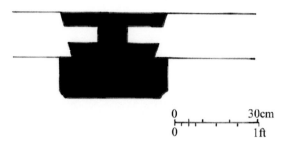

Typical floor joist joint

A large diamond mullion window like that of the west wall, existed in the south bay of the east wall at ground floor. There was a window, possibly of similar size, in the north bay as well. A mortice for one mullion was seen, but the mid rail here did not otherwise show clear evidence for studs or mullions, its soffit probably having been trimmed back. The east wall was fully framed at first floor with studwork, except at the north-east where there was a gap wide enough for a door, but more likely a window as there seemed to be a shutter groove in the top plate.

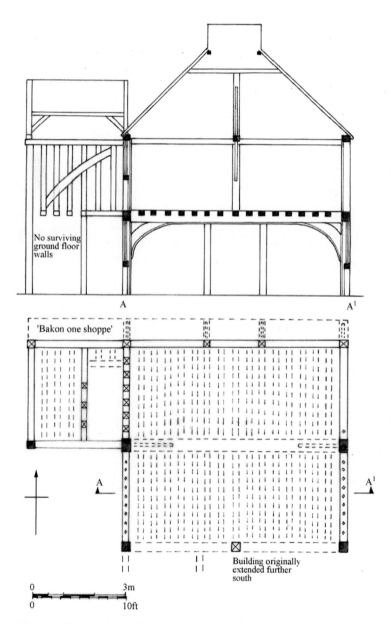

Plan and section of the Cricketers

The south wall is not easy to interpret, its fabric having been largely rebuilt. A mortice in the south face of the south-west corner post indicates that it extended further south, and it seems that the wall has been reconstructed after alterations took place on this side. The top plate has been replaced: neither the central north-south tie-beam, nor the rafters, seem to be properly jointed with dovetails or bird's mouths. The mid rail has no mortices in its soffit for studwork, showing that this side was open at the ground floor. Lamb's tongue chamfers on its inner arris are of a type normally dated to the later 16th century, indicating that this timber is also a replacement. The rail is in poor condition, its top surface cut back and eroded, but it seems to comprise two timbers, a narrower one at the top 6ins

(0.15m) deep forming a rebated edge over a larger one 13ins (0.33m) deep, as if for boarding or plaster placed against it. Below the level of the rebate, there are in the south face recesses and at least one mortice at regular one foot intervals. The wall above the mid rail included old studs with wattle and daub, but these timbers seemed reused or repositioned. These features have been seen as evidence for a pentice roof on this side of the building.

The central north-south tie-beam has three mortices in its face for a crown post and braces rising to it, all now missing. In the soffit of the tie-beam, at its ends, are large mortices for braces. An eroded mortice in the post at the south end of the tie-beam could have housed a brace descending from the tie-beam. The existing roof is pyramidal in form, rising to a short east-west ridge with gablets. The collar purlin of the crown post construction was fixed into mortices in the rafters in the east and west pitches. The attic space had been plastered, and painted on it at one point was a crude heart shaped cartouche enclosing the partially legible inscription 'These shambles repaired at the ……Nehemiah ….'. The reference is to Nehemiah Lyde, a Hackney merchant who bought the lordship of the manors of Little and Great Coggeshall in 1693. An inscription formerly recorded his restoration of the Long Bridge in 1705.[1]

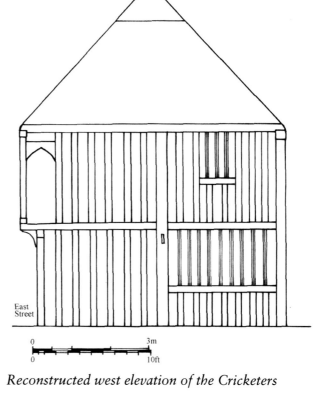

Reconstructed west elevation of the Cricketers

Painted inscription in the roof of the Cricketers recording its restoration by the lord of the manor

A structure 3.3m (10ft 10ins) long and corresponding in width to the front bay of the building was added to its north-west corner. It has substantial floor joists like the main building, with a trimmer for a stair trap. The mortice for this trimmer is set into the girt of the main building and cuts into one of the mortices for the studs (no longer existing) of the side wall, showing this structure was a later extension. On its south side, the joists were supported by a girt which was a reused timber (a former floor joist with mortices for relatively narrow joists with soffit tenons) and must have been a replacement for the original timbers at this point. None of its fabric survived at

1   Beaumont 1890, 110, 235.

the ground floor. The south wall at first floor was fully framed up, with a tension brace, but the west wall had a central post with openings, presumably windows, either side of it. The structure had a small crown post roof, indicating it was built before the end of the 16th century.

Discussion

The Cricketers was clearly not a domestic building. Its structure, combined with documentary evidence, shows that it was one of Coggeshall's most important buildings. Its location indicates it must have had a role in the marketplace, and its form suggests a use as a market house or court hall, or indeed both. It dominated the Market Street triangle, with the meat market on the west side and the fish market on the east. Documents reveal it to have been the Town House, where the manorial court for Great Coggeshall would have held its sessions. When the infamous Coggeshall murderer George Craven was arraigned in 1600, it would have been at this building, prior to his march along East Street to the gallows. In the 18th century it was called the Old Hall, or the Shambles, and its drainage problems were mentioned in the Manorial Court Rolls for 1775.[2] It is also identified as the shambles or meat market. It is unclear whether this function was original to it, and how it was combined with the court use. The butchers' stalls may have been in it or around it, and indeed their location and arrangement no doubt changed through the centuries. It is difficult to imagine the shambles actually being housed in it, but that is the implication of the 17th-century inscription in the roof.

The evidence indicates that the ground floor was put to market use, and the first floor served for the court. The north side on the street was apparently virtually open sided, or else may have had shop windows either side of a large central entrance. The very wide mullion windows in the end walls would have made this space light and airy. The building extended further on the south side, but there is insufficient evidence to reconstruct this part of it, the best suggestion probably being that there was a pentice or lean-to roof which could have formed a canopy over stalls. Beaumont records that the roof of the back part of the Shambles collapsed in 1686.[3] If the collapse indeed affected the rear of the building worst, then this may well have been the time when the southern part was dismantled. The painted inscription formerly inside the roof (and no longer extant after the fire) shows that the Shambles were restored by Nehemiah Lyde, the lord of the manor, sometime after 1693.

Like the ground floor, the first floor was a single undivided space, large enough to house court sessions. Access seems to have been via an external stair on the west side to an upstairs door. This changed with the construction of the small building with a stair trap at the north-west corner which provided new covered access. The large two-light window in the side of this would have effectively formed a balcony which could have been used for announcements relating to the proceedings of the court. The ground floor of this structure was apparently a shop, its dimensions corresponding with those of the property listed by the 1575 rental on the west side of the Town House, the entry for which reads 'Bakon one Shopp by Indenture 10 feet *fynoure*'.

Later history

In the late 18th or early 19th century, the building was refurbished. As well being given the brick front, it was slightly enlarged so that it became a rectangle measuring 10.6 x 9.0m (34ft 9ins x 29ft 6ins). A staircase

2   Beaumont 1890, 120.
3   Beaumont 1890, 233.

was provided in the extension on the south-east (if it did not already exist). A neo-classical shop window with Corinthian columns was inserted on the east side. Three brick chimneys were built, one with a corner fireplace. Arched entrances and passages typical of the provincial Regency style were formed inside. The windows are all small pane sliding sash with narrow glazing bars and no horns. These changes must have occurred about the time that it became a public house. It acquired a more commonplace appearance, with most people accepting it as a Georgian building and not being at all cognizant of its extreme age or its seminal role in the history and development of the town.

On its west and south side are modern extensions relating to the use of the building as a public house. The 1st edition OS map of 1875 shows a building on the west side of the Cricketers and a large one, probably stabling and outbuildings, to the south, both lost. In 2010, the public house was damaged by fire and closed, its roof being the part which suffered worst.

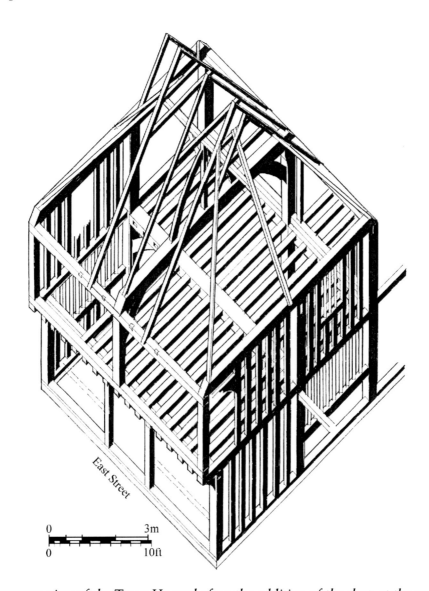

Axonometric reconstruction of the Town House before the addition of the shop at the corner

Reconstruction of the Town House with the shop added at its corner, providing stair access to the first floor where there was an open balcony

BIBLIOGRAPHY

Alston L. 1998 The hip bonnet or gablet hood in Suffolk, *Historic Buildings of Suffolk,* **1**, 59-71.

Alston, L. 2005 *Paycocke's, Coggeshall, Essex. An historical survey*, unpublished report for the National Trust.

Andrews, D.D. 1987 Coggeshall, Old Fire Station, *Essex Archaeology and History* **18**, 94-95.

Ayers, B. 1994 *English Heritage Book of Norwich*, London: Batsford.

Baillie, M.G.L. and Pilcher, J.R. 1973 A simple crossdating program for tree-ring research, *Tree Ring Bulletin* **33**, 7-14.

Beaumont, G.F. 1899 *A history of Coggeshall*, Coggeshall: Edwin Potter.

Blair, J. and Ramsay, N. eds 1991 *English medieval industries*, London: Hambledon.

R.H.*Britnell 1968* The *making of Witham, History Studies*, **1**, 13–21.

Britnell, R. 1986 *Growth and decline in Colchester, 1300-1525*, Cambridge: Cambridge UP.

Carus-Wilson, E.M. 1967 *Medieval merchant venturers*, London: Methuen.

Clark, D. 2000 The shop within? An analysis of the architectural evidence for medieval shops, *Architectural History* **43**, 58-87.

Clarke, C. P. 1988 Roman Coggeshall: excavations 1984-85, *Essex Archaeology and History* **19**, 47-90.

Dymond, D. and Betterton, A. 1989 *Lavenham industrial town*, Lavenham: Terence Dalton.

Edwards, A.C. and Newton, K.C. 1984 *The Walkers of Hanningfield: surveyors and mapmakers extraordinary*, London: Buckland Publications Ltd.

English Heritage 1998 *Dendrochronology: guidelines on producing and interpreting dendrochronological dates.*

Essex County Council 1994 *Revolving Funding. Historic buildings in Essex 1970-91. A record of the achievement of the Revolving Funding programme in saving buildings at risk*, Chelmsford: ECC.

Ferguson, C., Thornton, T., and Wareham, A. 2012 *Essex Hearth Tax Return 1670*, British Record Society Hearth Tax Series vol. VIII.

Flook, R. 1988 The old St. Peter's School site , Coggeshall; excavations 1987, *Essex Archaeology and History* **19**, 272-75.

French, H.R. and Hoyle, R.W. 2007 *The character of English society. Earls Colne, 1550-1750*, Manchester University Press.

Gervers, M. 1989 The textile industry in late 12th and 13th century Essex: a study based on occupational names in charter sources, *Essex Archaeology and History* **20**, 34-73.

Godbold, S. and Andrews, D.D. 1992 Observations at West Street, Coggeshall, *Essex Archaeology and History* **23**, 159-61.

Green, L.S. 1999 The *Essex Landscape. In search of its history*, Chelmsford: Essex County Council.

Harris, R. 1990 Jetties, *Vernacular Architecture* **21**, 33-36.

Hervey, F. 1902 *Suffolk in the XVIIth century. The breviary of Robert Reyce, 1618*, London: John Murray.

Hewett, C.A. 1980 *English historic carpentry*, London: Phillimore.

Hillman-Crouch, B. 2008 *Thaddeus (Thadews). Formerly Bucks - 21-23 East Street, Coggeshall, Essex* (unpublished report).

Heard, N. 1970 *Wool. East Anglia's golden fleece*, Lavenham: Terence Dalton.

Hoskins, W.G. 1955 *The making of the English landscape*, London: Hodder and Stoughton.

Isserlin, R.M.J. 1995 Roman Coggeshall II:excavations at 'The Lawns', *Essex Archaeology and History* **26**, 82-104.

Martin D. & B. 1997 Detached kitchens in Eastern Sussex. A re-assessment of the evidence, *Vernacular Architecture* **28**, 85-91.

McClenaghan, B. 1924 *The Springs of Lavenham*, Ipswich: W E Harrison.

Morant, P. 1768 *The history and antiquities of the county of Essex*, London (2 vols).

Pearson, S. 2001 The chronological distribution of tree-ring dates, 1980-2001: an update, *Vernacular Architecture* **32**, 68-69.

Pearson, S. 2009 Medieval houses in English towns: form and location, *Vernacular Architecture* **40**, 1-22.

Petchey, W. J. 1991 *A prospect of Maldon 1500-1689*, Chelmsford:Essex Record Office.

Power, E. 1941 *The wool trade in English medieval history*, Oxford.

Quin, W.F. 1981 *A history of Braintree and Bocking*, Lavenham: Lavenham Press.

Poos, L. 1991 *A rural society after the Black Death. Essex 1350-1525*, Cambridge University Press.

Riley, N. and Beckwith, A. 2000 *Carved in wood. Country practice, the business of Ernest Beckwith 1872-1952*, Braintree District Museum.

Royal Commission on Historical Monuments (England) 1916 *An inventory of the historical monuments in Essex. Vol. 1. North-west Essex*, London: HMSO.

Ryan, P. 2000 The buildings of rural Ingatestone, Essex, 1556-1601: 'Great Rebuilding' or 'Housing Revolution'?, *Vernacular Architecture* **31**, 11-25.

Schweingruber, F.H. 1988 *Tree rings*, Kluwer Academic Publications.

Shackle, R. 2001 Two late medieval buildings for housing animals, *Essex Archaeology and History* **32**, 267-71.

Smith, R. 2001 *Ancient House, Thetford*, unpublished analysis of the building

Smith, R. 2002 *The cellars beneath No. 19 White Hart Street, and the Ancient House Museum.*

Smith, J.T. 1992 *English houses 1200-1800. The Hertfordshire evidence*, London: HMSO.

Stenning, D. F. 1985 Timber-framed shops 1300-1600: comparative plans, *Vernacular Architecture* **16**, 35-39.

Stenning, D. 1988 Coggeshall, rear of 6/6A East Street, *Essex Archaeology and History 19*, 257-9.

Stenning, D.F. 2003 Small aisled halls in Essex, *Vernacular Architecture* **34**, 1-19.

Stenning, D. F. 2013 *Discovering Coggeshall. Timber-framed buildings in the town centre*, Coggeshall: John Lewis.

Stenning, D.F. and Wadhams, M.C. 1986 The cross wing with integral cross-passage and opening with 'speres', *Historic Building Studies no. 1* (ECC photocopied publication).

Stenning, D.F. and Andrews, D.D. 1998 *Regional variation in timber-framed building down to 1550*, Chelmsford: Essex County Council.

Thornton, C. 2011 *Paycocke's House, Coggeshall*. Historical report (unpublished report for the National Trust).

Twiss, T. ed. 1873 *The Black Book of the Admiralty, Vol. 2*, London: Longman.

Tyers, I. 2011 *The tree-ring analysis of 22 timber framed buildings in Coggeshall, Essex*, Dendrochronological Consultancy Ltd Report 39 (unpublished report).

Tyers, I. 2012 List 245: tree ring dates from Coggeshall, Essex, *Vernacular Architecture*, **43**, 94-97.

Walker, J. ed. 2011 *The English medieval roof. Crownpost to kingpost. Report of the Essex Historic Buildings Group Day School 2008*, Essex Historic Buildings Group.

Ward, J. C. 1983 *The medieval Essex community. The lay subsidy of 1327*, Chelmsford: ERO.

Watkin, B. 2004 1 Church Street, Coggeshall, *Essex Archaeology and History* **35**, 161-65.

Watkin, B. 2009 Coggeshall, 19 East Street, *Historic Buildings in Essex* **12**, 5-13.